Forty Years with Berenson

Nicky Mariano and B.B.

FORTY YEARS WITH BERENSON

by *Nicky Mariano*

With an Introduction by
Sir Kenneth Clark

New York:
~~RELEASE~~
Alfred A. Knopf
1966

CONTENTS

vii

ILLUSTRATIONS

ix

Illustrations

INTRODUCTION

by Sir Kenneth Clark

EVERYONE WHO HAS READ the books and articles about Bernard Berenson published since his death will remember the name of Nicky Mariano. For forty years she was his helper, companion and guardian, organizing his work, saving his energies, reassuring his friends, mollifying his enemies and shielding him, as far as possible, from the rough usage of ordinary life. No man ever had a greater piece of good fortune. The story of this perfect relationship has now been told by Miss Mariano herself with a candour and vividness which makes it far the most enlightening book that has been written, or is likely to be written, about Berenson and that curious microcosm of civilization that grew up around him at I Tatti. With delicate art Miss Mariano first of all sketches her own background, so that when she finds herself drawn into the world of I Tatti the process has the gradual, accidental, inevitable quality of life itself. She was captured, for complicated reasons, by Mrs. Berenson; and one of the many merits of Miss Mariano's book is the portrait she draws of that extraordinary woman. Recent writers on Berenson, including the author of a deplorable biography, never even knew her, yet on any English or American visitor to I Tatti before the war she left an impression almost as strong as that of her husband. She had a great influence on his life, and, at one time, on his studies; and since Berenson has become a historical figure, posterity will be glad to know what she was like. May one of Mrs. Berenson's later protégés assure them that Miss Mariano's picture is accurate? The initial bonhomie, the apparent good sense that often disguised

xi

obsessive impulses, the love for strong flavours, in life and food, the strange mixture of unthinking optimism and profound pessimism, all are there. So is the ultimate goodness of heart, which allowed Miss Mariano gradually to assume her position at I Tatti, without a word of jealousy or reproach. As illness and despondency engrossed her, this once splendid figure withdrew. But she retained her massive humanity, and her last letter to Miss Mariano, printed on p. 288, is surely one of the most generous and moving tributes ever written by one woman to another.

Even those who are not interested in the history and criticism of art will read this book for its vivid portraits, some sketched in a line, others—Geoffrey Scott, Robert Trevelyan —developed through the years. And there is one admirable "full length," which occupies a whole chapter, the portrait of Edith Wharton. This maddening and lovable woman was a Janus figure, a boundary goddess staring icily at those outside, smiling at those within; and Miss Mariano, like all who approached her in the wake of earlier friends, saw first the chilly stare. But one day she asked after Mrs. Wharton's maid, who had been ill; immediately the boundary goddess revolved, and recognizing Miss Mariano's sweetness and sympathy, became sympathetic in return. In consequence we are shown the Edith Wharton who so successfully concealed herself from the outside world, a rich, warmhearted, vulnerable human being, delighting in stories of human extravagance and an artist devoted to her craft. May I, once again, guarantee the authenticity of this picture, which can be of more value to future historians of American literature than many doctoral theses.

But inevitably, and progressively, the subject of the book is Mr. Berenson himself, and it is safe to say that no more sympathetic description of this complex being can ever be written. Miss Mariano does not disguise his faults. The rages, the flirtations, the atavistic suspicions are all there. But they are balanced by a tolerance and wisdom of which only a few of Mr. Berenson's friends can have been aware. I suppose it is true that the thundering anathemas and piled-up epithets of abuse with which he used to frighten pious visitors to I Tatti were due partly to a spirit of mischief, a desire to see how his audience would respond; and Miss Mariano tells us that if people stood up to him and answered back he was delighted. I never observed this myself; but like all his friends I did notice a great contrast between the brilliant, destructive performances at table and the wise, gentle and almost lyrical tone of his conversation when one was alone with him on a walk. An awestruck social group tempted him to abuse his brilliant gifts of improvisation; the spectacle of nature and the sympathy of a single friend brought him back to his true centre.

For this reason he was at his best when travelling and, fortunately for posterity, several chapters in this book describe his travels in Greece, Yugoslavia, Turkey, Syria, North Africa and, of course, in Italy. They bring out a characteristic that his social life in Florence or Paris obscured, his tireless concentration on the objects of his study. No man has ever been less of a dilettante. He could not know enough, or look enough, or look long enough. His companions would be stupefied with fatigue while he was still nipping up ladders or hopping over fallen masonry like a mountain goat. The objects of his nimble curiosity would often appear worthless to an untrained eye, but they might have added one grain to his immense store of knowledge. More surprising still was the way in which he would listen to the interminable outpourings of local archaeologists. I have seen him at the age of eighty-seven in the Sistine Chapel listening patiently to one of the specialists on Michelangelo and nodding gravely while his persecutor announced discoveries that Mr. Berenson himself had published over fifty years earlier. But as he frequently said, *ennui auguste* is often the prelude to enlightenment, and the self-satisfied bore in the Sistine might produce one particle of information. The same passion for knowledge enabled him, on his travels, to tolerate discomfort with a philosophy which those who saw him in the apparently luxurious setting of I Tatti would not have credited (and let me add in parenthesis that the "luxury" of I Tatti is a myth. No ordinary American middle-class housewife would have been satisfied with Mr. Berenson's bathroom). It is true that even in the most squalid North African inn there was Miss Mariano to bring him tea and read to him. But for a frail little man of over seventy it was hardship none the less and a remarkable proof of how his ideal of direct experience of a work of art, the ideal that had led him in his youth to visit every village church in the Upper Adiage, continued to rule his life.

Miss Mariano's book will supplement and to some extent correct Berenson's own *Sketch for a Self-Portrait*. Perhaps all confessions, from those of St. Augustine onwards, if they are too insistent, produce a disturbing effect; and Mr. Berenson's self-dredging, as he called it, may give Anglo-Saxon readers the feeling that they would not have been at ease in his company. But all readers of the following pages will wish that they had known him and enjoyed the range and sympathy of his intelligence. Although I saw a good deal of him for over thirty years, I close this book with the feeling that I never made the most of my opportunities, and that he had far more to give if only I had known better how to release his genius.

There remains one more portrait in the book, and that is the portrait of Miss Mariano herself. Except in the first chapter it is entirely unself-conscious; yet it appears on every page, in every perceptive comment and in the inflections of a style which is like the sound of a sweet-tempered voice. Although I do not think the attentive reader of this book will be in much doubt about Miss Mariano's character, he may like to have some notion of her physical presence. The first impression she made upon me (in contrast with the lamentable impression I made on her) was of the most perfectly lovable human being I had ever encountered. She was beautiful, with fair hair and blue eyes set at a slightly Slavonic angle; but one did not think of her as a beauty, because she did not think in that way herself. One thought of her warmth, her naturalness and above all of her gaiety. The atmosphere of I Tatti, as will be apparent even in the following pages, was often charged. A book had been lost, a guest had shown fascist sympathies, Mrs. Berenson had made some extravagant gift to her children, and we would stand round the book stacks like guilty courtiers, anticipating shafts of Princely lightning. Then Nicky would come in with her brisk nautical step, laughing and chatting. The sun shone again, the threatened storm was forgotten and by the time the Prince appeared we would all be at ease. If Nicky had left I Tatti it would have been like the departure of Freia from Valhalla: but of course that was unthinkable. She was as much part of that strange little kingdom as were the Berensons themselves. Her life, as the reader will see, was by no means easy, and she sometimes suffered from loss of confidence. She had none of Mrs. Berenson's blind optimism and foresaw trouble, as only those can do who have had the envelope of established life suddenly removed. Yet her resilience was extraordinary, and a few minutes after some catastrophe she would be laughing and singing, in a very pretty voice, airs from Mozart's operas. She suffered most from the endless stream of visitors, many of them quite meaningless, which poured through I Tatti, day in, day out. Both the Berensons seemed to feed on visitors, almost irrespective of their quality. Mrs. Berenson once said to me that nothing in English poetry meant more to her than the lines of Hood,

> Give me new faces, new faces,
> I've seen all the old ones a thousand times oe'r.

Even Mr. Berenson, whose physical digestion was so delicate, could swallow the toughest Anglo-Saxon bore. But Miss Mariano, who had to organize arrivals, hasten departures, and smooth ruffled feathers, did not feed on visitors. They fed on her. She gave and gave, more generously than anyone I have ever met; and at the end of the week she was exhausted. No wonder that, as time went on, her eye sometimes had a faraway look and she would seem to be a little deaf. One guessed that an American millionaire, a French countess, a German scholar and an Italian explorer all expected to be picked up in different parts of Florence at the same minute, and that even if this difficulty was overcome there was the prospect of a somewhat inharmonious luncheon.

After the war the atmosphere of I Tatti changed. Vituperation became very rare, explosions almost unknown. To some extent this was due to the influence of those years of isolation which gave Mr. Berenson the opportunity of regaining the contemplative life. But it was also due to the presence of Miss Mariano. Whereas Mrs. Berenson had shown a kind of genius for enraging her husband, Miss Mariano had developed that sixth sense by which sailors and horsemen can foretell squalls and panic boltings and marvelously avoid them. So gradually Mr. Berenson changed from a Hebrew prophet into a sage. Instead of picturing him at some great luncheon party in a Paris hotel, one thought of him in the Casa al Dono, that remarkably unluxurious house on the heights of Vallombrosa, where, in a northern landscape of birch and conifer, both he and Miss Mariano could recapture some part of their Baltic background. He would sit in a fir-cone hut, gazing down to the cities of the plain, a cross between some wise man of the woods in Nordic legend and a Chinese statesman in retirement. In spite of the stealthy advance of old age, so marvellously described in his diary, he was more truly himself than he had been at any time in this century. He had achieved this sense of peace and wholeness because, in Mrs. Berenson's favourite phrase, he had found his natural protector.

Forty Years with Berenson

CHAPTER I

Prelude [1913–19]

W HERE DID YOU MEET the Berensons? When were you first introduced to I Tatti? How did it all happen? Innumerable times I have been asked these questions. They were difficult to answer, not because I did not know exactly how it all came about but because it seemed a rather long and intricate story, longer than the questioners were perhaps inclined to listen to. Readers may have more patience.

No bridge, no natural link connected the world in which I grew up with the world of the Berensons.

My mother, Cecil Pilar von Pilchau, belonged to the Baltic aristocracy descended from the German knights who in the twelfth century undertook the christianization and colonization of the Baltic lands. In spite of Polish, Swedish, and Russian infiltrations they kept their language and their German cultural background through the centuries.

My father, Raffaele Mariano, was born and brought up in Capua. His father, a lawyer, insisted on his following him in his profession. My father obeyed and got his degree in law at the University of Naples, but thereafter broke loose from his provincial background, studied philosophy and church history, travelled a great deal, got deeply interested in the Old Catholic movement in Tübingen and followed the historian and theologian J. J. Doellinger's lectures. Then he returned to Italy and was teaching philosophy at the

University of Rome when my grandmother happened to spend the winter there with my mother and other members of her family. Together with the historian Ferdinand Gregorovius (whom he had accompanied on many of his southern Italian explorations) my father used to frequent the studio of the German painter Karl Lindemann-Frommel. Both Lindemann-Frommel and his wife were very hospitable to foreign visitors and my mother was taken there by friends of hers. Thus she and my father met and as her favourite subject of study was church history, discussions about the Church Fathers Tertullian and Origen may have attracted them to each other. It took them several years to get my grandmother's reluctant consent. From her point of view it was an utterly unsuitable alliance and she was stubbornly opposed to it. They were married in 1879 and went on living in Rome until in 1885 a chair for church history was created for my father at the University of Naples. It was there that I was born and spent my childhood interrupted by summer trips to my grandmother's house in what was then the *gouvernement* of Livonia. Consequently our social links were to German-Baltic, Italian, and German friends. It was only after my mother's death and our settling down in Florence in 1898 that I learnt to speak English and had occasion to meet English and American girls of my age.

Meanwhile my father was becoming more and more a misanthropist and gradually cut himself off from his former friends and colleagues. Not one of them seemed to him to have the right kind of Hegelian *Weltanschauung*, and yet, while unwilling to see them again, he was deeply grieved by his intellectual isolation. Most of his time was spent on completing and perfecting his studies on church history and particularly on radical reform of the Catholic Church; he published one book after another and very little notice was taken of them. My stepmother—my mother's younger sister whom my father had married in 1898, a Baltic old maid of

4

limited intelligence—divided her social activities between the German church, its pastor, other members of the German community, and relations and friends from the Baltic provinces who happened to visit Florence. Later on, when we moved to the Villa dei Pratellini or Frescobaldi in San Domenico[1] we began to meet our neighbours, a variety of American or English couples or spinsters. They were all friendly and hospitable and I liked going to their tea parties, but never did I hear the name of Berenson mentioned by any of them. That far more interesting groups of foreigners existed in Florence and its surroundings I knew vaguely but had no access to them. Sometimes when the Fiesole tram stopped in San Gervasio it was boarded by several manly looking women. One of them seemed to be the central figure. Her face in spite of its snout-like ugliness was fascinatingly witty and intelligent. Somebody told me that her name was Violet Paget and that she wrote books as "Vernon Lee." Through one of our girl friends, Mai Boyle (who later became the secretary and assistant of the paleontologist Abbé Breuil), we heard about a formidable woman, Mrs. Ross, who lived in a sort of crenellated castle on the Settignano road, but no mention was made of the Berensons, who were her neighbours and close friends.

A channel that might have led me to I Tatti went through Villa Gamberaia. I was sent to a small English school in Florence for one year and made friends there with several American girls. One of them was Olga Converse, the niece of Miss Florence Blood who lived at the Gamberaia with Princess Ghyka. More than once this girl took me to the Sunday afternoon receptions of her aunt, a dainty small woman in a long velvet dress with a magnificent blue-greyish Angora cat on her lap. She was very gracious and welcoming but never did I hear her speak of her neighbours at I Tatti.

---

[1] Now called Villa Sparta and belonging to the queen mother of Rumania.

In the autumn of 1909 a German friend of mine came to stay with us at the Villa dei Pratellini, and I found her one morning in the *loggia* with a reddish-brown volume in her hand. "What are you reading?" "A book which my aunt has insisted on my taking along. She said that one should not try to look at anything in Florence without reading it first." I looked at the title page. *The Florentine Painters of the Renaissance* by Bernhard Berenson. "For Helene," I thought, "this must be very useful, but surely I do not need to bother about it. I knew all that can be known about Florentine painting."

Three years later, 1912, my cousin and contemporary Leonie Keyserling (sister of the philosopher Hermann Keyserling) came to spend a few days with us and told me about the friendship she had struck up in London with Karin Costelloe and that she was looking forward to meeting Karin in her mother's, Mrs. Berenson's, villa near Settignano. Next day the Berenson car came to fetch her and brought her back full of glowing accounts of the lunch party and of how entertaining it had been, particularly the conversation between Mr. Berenson and his Italo-Spanish friend, Countess Hortense Serristori. Leonie did not offer to take me to I Tatti and I did not expect it. Both she and her brother Hermann were a bit like Proust's Monsieur Swann and liked to move in different circles without mixing the one with the other. She may also have considered me not particularly presentable with no special gifts or capacities and carrying a very commonplace southern Italian name. Before leaving she pressed a book on me lent to her by the Berensons and which I was to return to I Tatti. It was Edith Wharton's *House of Mirth*. It revealed a new world to me, almost loathsome in its hardness and cruelty.

That same year I made the acquaintance of a German art connoisseur and writer, Ludwig von Bürkel, who owned part of the Gronau villa on the Via delle Palazzine and went with other friends to have tea in his house. He had walked over to I Tatti the day before and talked about the works of art he had seen and about his conversation with Berenson. A sort of image of the Tatti world began to take shape in my mind.

In the autumn of 1912 the Villa dei Pratellini was sold and we moved to the Villa Rondinelli on the old road to Fiesole. It was there that my father died in December 1912. Early in 1913 I left for the Baltic provinces to stay with my sister Ada, who since 1909 had been married to Egbert von Anrep, the owner of Schloss Ringen near Dorpat (Tartu in Esthonian). On my return to Villa Rondinelli in the autumn I heard that Hermann Keyserling was staying at Villa I Tatti. That he never got in touch with me did not surprise me. There was not much love lost between him and my stepmother, and besides, I did not consider myself worthy of particular attention. I was at that time still suffering from a slight inferiority complex due to my not "belonging" anywhere in Italy. I knew too well what "belonging" meant, what a sense of security it gave me when I found myself among people who knew all about my mother, my grandmother, my ancestors, for whom I was like a cog in a wheel. My father, after emancipating himself from his *petit bourgeois* Capuan background, had travelled a lot, had made friends everywhere, in academic and political circles, had frequented elegant salons in Rome and elsewhere and had been admired and sought after. Part of these connections were kept up during the seventeen years of his marriage with my mother, but then most of them dropped away. Only later did I learn to appreciate fully my freedom from conventional ties and the joy of making friends entirely of my own choice.

In the same autumn of 1913 I went to stay with Byba Giuliani and her mother[2] in their villa above Scandicci. They

---

[2] Beatrice Giuliani, Byba's mother, was the daughter of Philip Schwarzenberg, from Brunswick, who when obliged to leave Germany because of his liberal way of thinking, settled down in

7

were my closest friends in Italy, and their house was like a second home for me. "I must take you over to the Villino Corbignano near I Tatti," Byba said one day. "It has been lent by the Berensons to a young English couple I have met at my singing teacher's in London. They are both charming and excellent musicians." We went and found Dolly and Thornley Gibson in a slightly furbished-up peasant house, pleasantly furnished, with a rustic *loggia*, surrounded by vines and olives. While we were having tea a tall thin man came in and was introduced as Geoffrey Scott. His lank black hair was brushed back from his forehead and he wore a pince-nez over very short-sighted eyes. It turned out that he was looking after the decoration and furniture of various new rooms at I Tatti and at the same time working on a book to be called *The Architecture of Humanism*. I asked him about Keyserling's visit and he described to me Mary Berenson's indignation over Hermann's bad manners and his arrogant assumption that everything should be done for his comfort. There was much laughter and an immediate link of sympathy between the newcomer and me. His voice, his laughter, his sense of fun, his whimsical expression, his choice of words, all appealed to me. Physically I found him rather unattractive and therefore considered him from the first moment not as a possible flirt but as somebody who might be-

---

Florence and bought the Augustinian convent on the Costa Scarpuccia, gave up politics and buried himself in scientific research. This led him to the discovery of the mercury mines on the slopes of the Monte Amiata. He rented them from the Italian government and called in foreign mining engineers to work them. Meanwhile his wife worked herself up into a romantic passion for the Italian *risorgimento* and opened her house to the sons of Italian patriots who had come to Florence for their studies. Many of them were from the south of Italy and it ended with three of her daughters marrying the sons of Calabrian *risorgimentisti*. Beatrice's marriage with Giuliani was not a happy one. Disgusted with the backwardness of life in Calabria she returned to Florence where she later inherited the old house on the Costa Scarpuccia.

come a real friend. Many encounters between the Gibsons, Goeffrey, Byba, and me followed. The Berensons had left for the United States and in their absence I was taken for the first time over the house and the grounds of I Tatti.

I was surprised to find the villa not a monumental one in the usual Florentine style with an imposing façade but an unassuming well-proportioned Tuscan house with a small enclosed lemon garden to the south and groups of old cypresses to both sides of it. Goeffrey's friend, the young English architect Cecil Pinsent, had used the underlying lemon house as a connecting link between the enclosed garden and the new formal one descending in terraces to an ilex wood. All this was in its infancy at the time of my first visit and looked out of proportion, the statues in the new formal garden ridiculously large as compared with the tiny box and cypress hedges. The long cypress avenue, the first addition made by the Berensons, was growing up well but looked puny against the majestic old cypresses near the house.

The interior of the villa I found very impressive, not so much for the size of the rooms as for the way in which they were furnished quietly, almost severely, with antique *credenze* and *cassoni,* comfortable chairs, Italian Renaissance paintings and sculpture mixed with Oriental sculpture and *objets d'art.* I had never seen anything like it before and it struck me as both fascinating and awe-inspiring. A long corridor lined with pictures had been added to the old house and led to the central library in Quattrocento style and through it to a small conventual library. A third long library with a terrace at its end, also a wing with guest rooms (later called by B.B. the 'Ritz suite') was under construction. On that first tour I met Cecil Pinsent, the architect himself, and saw him again repeatedly. I found him rather cold and impersonal and only in later years did he become a real friend. He may have been aware of Geoffrey's growing interest in me (perhaps Goeffrey talked about me a

9

good deal and Cecil got bored) and may have preferred to keep out of it.

Used as I was to Italian "beaux" and to a more direct and impetuous form of approach I was far from suspecting any special feeling of Geoffrey for me. I found him a most congenial friend and companion and when Byba teased me about his being in love with me I assured her that even during our occasional *tête-à-têtes* not one word had been said by him that could be interpreted as an even veiled declaration of love.

In the spring of 1914, a few days after the return of the Berensons from America, Geoffrey and Cecil gave a small party in their flat in an old palace in Via delle Terme and invited me to it. Both the Gibsons, but particularly Thornley, who had a lovely voice, were to perform for us. When I came in Thornley was seated on the piano stool and was talking to a woman of majestic proportions and with fine regular features who at once came forward to greet me with such a radiant smile, with such a glowing welcome that I felt almost embarrassed. A sort of world-embracing goodwill seemed to emanate from Mary Berenson—for it was she I met for the first time that day—and reminded me at once of another American woman I had seen a few years before in the house of Russian friends. Her name was Mabel Dodge and subsequently I was to read and hear a great deal about her. I doubt whether there was any fundamental likeness between them. It was just an aura of boundless optimism— perhaps a typically American one—that seemed to surround both of them.

It was decided then and there that I should have lunch at I Tatti on the following Sunday. Again I met with a warm welcome from Mary. Several guests had already assembled in the ground-floor sitting-room, two or three Americans on their way through Florence and a tall young woman with a fine figure and pugdog face who turned out to be a Swedish masseuse and a family friend, Naima Löfroth. Then B.B. himself appeared looking elegant and aloof and somehow very intimidating. I was alarmed at finding myself seated on his left and having to talk to him. My connection with the Keyserlings, brother and sister, served me well and he asked me to tell him all about their background and upbringing.

I never met B.B. again during that spring of 1914 but saw Mary repeatedly. She became almost importunate in her eagerness (as I understood later on) to bring Goeffrey and me together, made all sorts of proposals, wanted me to change my plans and to join her and Geoffrey on a trip to the Dolomites instead of leaving for the Baltic provinces. It was all a little bewildering and seemed to me to have no relation to the length of our acquaintance. How often in later years have I seen Mary taking such *engouements*! I hear B.B. saying with a sigh: "Now Mary is again ready to cut us all up particularly fine in order to favour her new friends." I do not know who was to be sacrificed for my sake in the spring of 1914 but I know that I did not let myself be roped into these to me utterly incomprehensible schemes and that I left late in June for the North. One of the last messages to reach me from the outer world before the iron curtain of that time dropped down was a copy of Geoffrey's *Architecture of Humanism*.

I was not to return to Florence till five years later in the spring of 1919. The intervening years I spent inside Russia, staying mostly with my sister and brother-in-law at Schloss Ringen but also with other relatives. In 1916 I spent several days with the two Keyserlings at Raykuell, Hermann's property in Esthonia. My fear of not being able to cope with these two super-clever cousins was groundless, for they talked so much and in such a stimulating way that all I had to do was to listen and enjoy myself. One evening Hermann spoke at length about B.B., about his immediate, almost sensual reaction to the quality of a work of art, about the help and advice

11

he had given Hermann before his trip to the Far East. He also mentioned Goeffrey with appreciation for his literary gifts but seemed to have little use for Mary, who, he said, wanted to marshal her guests, like a stationmaster his trains, her chief ambition being not to have a car return empty from Florence.

A message from I Tatti reached me that same year. It was a letter from Mary Berenson herself, urging me to leave Russia as soon as possible, to meet her in England and to return with her to Italy. I answered and explained why I did not feel like moving but she never got my letter.

We led a quiet and materially comfortable life during the first three years of the war, free from any kind of privation, but always under a cloud of anxiety as to when and how the unsteady legs of the giant Russia would give way and as to what the ensuing upheaval would be like. For that a terrible upheaval was brewing nobody could doubt. We lived mostly on rumours or on accounts of eyewitnesses returning either from the front or from the capital, and very rarely read the Russian papers—with the result that in March 1917 we learnt of the catastrophic events in Petrograd through my little nephew Cecil Anrep coming in for his usual play-hour after tea with a pointed red cap on his head. When we asked him what it meant, he said the housemaids had told him to put it on because the Czar had been sent away and the *Wabbarik* ("the republic" in Esthonian) had begun. Then followed the rest of the colossal landslide, the Kerensky era, the Bolshevik seizure of power, the terror, the persecutions, the arrests, the German occupation, the German break-up, the fear of the Bolshevik invasion, the flight from Dorpat with a minimum of luggage. All that would make a story by itself and has already been told by too many other people. The only thing worth recalling because it had a certain importance in my subsquent relation to B.B. was my getting acquainted through these years of seclusion with the Jewish communities all around us. I had not been aware of them before. For errands, for concerts, for meeting friends we went regularly to the small university town of Dorpat and lived there during the last year (1917 to 1918). Most of Dorpat's shopkeeping and artisan class as well as many high-class professionals, like doctors or lawyers, belonged to the Jewish community. Getting to know them better I learnt a great deal about their sense of charity, their profound respect for learning, their loyalty to each other, their principles of honesty in business. Our best friend among them was Dr. Jaffe, the head of the hospital, a first-rate surgeon and a wonderful human being. It was from him we learnt all the details of how in 1915, before the German advance, the order to chase out the Jewish population of Kurland was carried out by bands of Cossacks in the most inhuman way, leaving many to die along the highways and how a perfect service of help was organized in the course of twenty-four hours by the Jewish community of Riga. In the west of Europe very little, I believe, was ever heard of this tragedy.

When we finally reached Berlin on Christmas Eve of 1918 the Spartakist rising was in full swing and we expected things to take the same turn as in Russia. But the Prussian officials with their iron sense of duty kept the administrative machine in order and did not allow the complete breakdown of all civilized life to take place.

Letters from distant friends began to reach us and in the first from Byba Giuliani she mentioned among other news that *Gambe Lunghe* (Long Legs, her nickname for Geoffrey Scott) had married Lady Sybil Cutting. I had heard her name mentioned in connection with her having rented Villa Medici, just above my home, Villa Rondinelli, on the old road to Fiesole.

After many complications, delays and passport formalities, I finally reached Switzerland, while the three Anreps stayed on in southern Germany. It was an almost uncanny sensation to be all of a sudden in a country untouched by war. When I began to meet English or French or Belgian friends of Byba Giuliani's (with whom I was staying in Lausanne) I realized the enormous difference between our experience and theirs: a difference like that between a house destroyed by an earthquake and a house damaged by shelling, but still inhabitable and repairable. I heard some of them make accurate calculations of what they had lost and what was due to them as war damage repayment. Whoever had been through the great storm in eastern Europe knew that there was nothing to recover and nothing to expect.

While waiting in Lausanne for my passport to be sent back from Florence, I heard from Beatrice Giuliani, Byba's mother, that Mrs. Berenson had been calling on her to ask for news of me and to propose my taking the job of librarian at I Tatti. This unexpected offer seemed like an answer to prayer. My one preoccupation was how to earn a living. The income from our mother's portion was lost, the Anreps had only saved the cash they had been able to carry away with them and the income from the small capital left to us by my father was not enough to keep us all going. But could I confidently accept Mary Berenson's proposal? It made me only too conscious of my incompetence, of my lacking any university or even high school degree, of all the gaps in my unsystematic education. Had Byba Giuliani not been there to scold me for being so timid and unenterprising I would probably not have taken the first step which consisted in writing to Mary Berenson and in telling her that if she and her husband would agree to let me look around the library during the summer (for it appeared that they were not planning to return to I Tatti before the autumn) I would do my best to make myself acquainted with its contents and would begin working in it. Of course my thoughts turned at once to Geoffrey Scott as I felt sure that this extraordinary piece of good luck had come to me thanks to him.

In April I left for Florence and went to stay in the Giuliani house on the Costa Scarpuccia from where I called up Geoffrey at Villa Medici, and thanked him warmly for having recommended me to Mary Berenson. He made no response and only reluctantly promised to take me to the Tatti library for a first impression. When we met for the first time in Florence, it was Thursday in Holy Week and crowds of people were moving from one church to the other to admire the *Sepolcri*. Everything seemed delightfully unchanged and civilized and untouched by the war. Deeper down there was of course a great deal of change and bitterness and unrest. Geoffrey too seemed unchanged on the surface, witty and humorous, full of affectionate interest in all that had happened to us. Only strangely reticent on the subject of Mary Berenson and on the part he had taken in getting me employed by her.

The next step was Geoffrey's taking me to Villa Medici to have tea with his wife. I found the house exquisitely furnished, almost too much so for my apprehensive eyes. For I could not help hearing Bolshevism knocking at the door and felt as if people living in such refinement of luxury must be struck with blindness. Lady Sybil Scott I found stretched out by the open fire, with a lovely silken coverlet spread over her legs, looking incredibly fragile and elegant in a capricious and original way. I was fascinated by her delicate hands and the beautiful rings she wore with the stones turned inside towards the palm of the hand. She received me very cordially and said a great many probably pleasant things in a twittering voice but out of practice as I then was in listening to English I could not understand a single word. Besides speaking very rapidly she was unable to pronounce certain consonants, like R or L. The only other guest was a tall man with a pleasant dreamy expression and an agreeable voice called Percy Lubbock. I was relieved to find him easy to understand. Lady Sybil invited me for dinner a few days later and I remember asking Geoffrey why Iris Cutting, Sybil's daughter from her first marriage was having her meal with her governess and not with us. "Iris never appears at the dinner table because she has not yet come out," he said. With eastern Europe and its complete upheaval foremost in my mind this struck me as a rather comical and mysterious ritual.

At dinner I began to understand Lady Sybil a little better and enjoyed her quaint way of expressing herself. This was a type of Englishwoman I had never met before. She asked me whether any English books had reached us during those years inside Russia. I told her of a few novels and of one of H. G. Wells' "prophetic books." "Only one more serious book, lent to us by the Keyserlings, Bertrand Russell's *Justice in Wartime*, we found it very original and stimulating," I said. An embarrassed silence followed and then protests from all three. They said we had been taken in by an utterly worthless and dangerous book, to which nobody in England had paid the slightest attention. Were they right? Was I wrong? I have never read the book again and do not know how it would affect me now.

When Geoffrey took me over to I Tatti and I had my first look around the library, what struck me was the vast number of unopened parcels of books that had arrived ever since 1917. Geoffrey seemed rather casual and aloof, praised the library as a wonderful place for browsing, pointed to a comfortable chair in the small library as the best place for undisturbed reading. I felt doubtful about ever having the leisure to occupy it.

Meanwhile Mary Berenson's answer had come and my definite acceptance had been sent off.

Casignano Scandicci   April 5th 1919

My dear Mrs. Berenson,
    Thank you ever so much for your letter which reached

The new formal garden, I Tatti, 1908

Nicky Mariano, 1918

me this morning and filled my heart with joy for I somehow could not believe that Mr. Berenson would really and seriously think of me as a librarian. My confidence in my own capacities is very small indeed; if you will give me the chance I will try and do my best. As soon as I am back in Florence Geoffrey Scott will take me to I Tatti and explain to me what he has done so far.

I do hope that nothing will prevent your coming home in the autmn. Everything looks rather gloomy to me but it may be that I am over apprehensive after the bad experiences we have had up there.

Madame Giuliani sends her kind regards to you and to Mr. Berenson. *Mille amités* and many thanks.

Sometime in May, on a heavenly forenoon, Geoffrey took me to the upper garden of Villa Medici and there began to read some of his favourite poems to me. Deeply stirred by them he went on to talk about himself and in words that seemed almost incoherent poured out his bitter resentment against Mary Berenson. Thus I learnt that during the first years of my absence Mary and he had worked out and cherished plans for Geoffrey's and my future, of how at my return we were to get married and settle at the Villino, I as librarian and he as general adviser and secretary. When in 1917 Goeffrey had decided to marry Lady Sybil, Mary's disappointment, disapproval and even rage had been so great that she had written very offensive letters both to Goeffrey and to Lady Sybil. "And now," he said, "she wants to punish me by keeping to her end of our agreement and by employing you as librarian at I Tatti in my nearest neighbourhood, so that I should never stop regretting that I did not wait for your return."

Things became very difficult during the next days. Letters from Geoffrey brought by hand kept pouring into the Casa Giuliani and created alarm and criticism, for it looked as if I was encouraging him. Then he rang up to say that he had told his wife everything and that he was now ready to make an end of himself. I did not believe he would. Next day Lady Sybil persuaded him to leave for Switzerland and to try a cure for his highly neurotic condition. After thinking the whole thing over I decided to go up to Villa Medici and to ask for Lady Sybil. She received me at once and I told her my side of the story and that I felt in the words of the old French song *Comme un chien dans un jeu de quilles* (like a dog in a skittle alley). I assured her that I had not given him any encouragement, at any rate not willingly, and had no intention of giving him any in the future. She accepted my words in a very simple straightforward manner, and although in the following winter appearances were very much against me she never changed in her attitude to me and we remained very good friends. Behind her fragile exterior, her reputation of being a highly hysterical woman, there was hidden a strong almost manly character and whoever had had the chance of getting to know that side of her would never forget it.

Later on when I became intimate with Mary Berenson, she spoke very openly of her deep protective affection for Geoffrey and of how she had made plans for his future happiness in connection with me. It became clear to me that had it not been for Geoffrey's falling in love with me and for Mary's considering me at first sight the right sort of companion for her *protégé* I would never have been invited to work at I Tatti.

When many years later B.B. would speak about the caprices of destiny I liked to tease him by imagining what his reaction must have been when Mary decided to employ me. "Mary, what is this new craziness of yours? What do you know about this girl after seeing her only two or three times? Why do you feel so sure that she will be the right person for us?" But Mary pursued her course unmoved by any protests or warnings.

CHAPTER II

First Contacts
and Impressions [1919–20]

A LL THROUGH THE SUMMER of 1919 I worked in the library
at I Tatti, unpacking books and following the footsteps
of my predecessor, Lance Cherry (who had been killed at
the front in 1915), in putting them in order. I felt shy about
asking for a light lunch and walked over every day around
one o'clock after an early lunch at Villa Rondinelli to stay
till seven or eight. It was a very hot walk, but I did not mind
it and I found the handling of such a variety of books very
enjoyable, especially as there was nobody to disturb me. The
quietness of the house was interrupted only once when during
the political upheavals in August a troop of rioters appeared
at the gate and clamoured for wine. The butler who kept the
keys of the cellar was off duty and, enraged by the timid
refusals of the other servants, the rioters ended by forcing
the door of the cellar and carrying away most of its contents.

About the middle of September Mary Berenson arrived
on the crest of a wave of euphoria, kissed and hugged me,
told me to call her by her first name and urged me not to
work too much. She brought with her a young American
self-made man, who, she told me, was a real prodigy with a
natural eye for appreciating works of art and ready to dedicate
a large part of his fabulous earnings to the purchase of old

paintings. The young man's name was Carl Hamilton. I found him looking rather uncouth and speaking with such a strong American accent that I had great difficulty in understanding him. Unusual animation was brought into the quiet house. Mary kept rushing out in the car to take her young friend on sightseeing tours and her enthusiasm for his plans was visibly growing. "I must give him one of our smaller pictures as an encouragement," she said, and there and then selected a charming small Quattrocento panel representing the youthful John the Baptist in the desert. "It has no definite attribution," she explained, "and B.B. will not even notice its not being there any longer." [1]

From the first moment Mary Berenson made it clear that I was not to be an impersonal librarian but a member of the household taking part in everything. Again I felt a little bewildered by the suddenness, the impetuosity of all this. When she paid her first visit to her old friend and neighbour Janet Ross at Poggio Gherardo, she insisted on my coming along and there I met for the first time Lina Waterfield, Mrs. Ross' niece, and felt immediately drawn to her while Mary's beloved Aunt Janet seemed to me rather stern and difficult to talk to. Lina, who had been the correspondent of an English paper during the war, had a lot to say about the alarming political situation in Italy.

When Carl Hamilton's visit came to an end, Mary decided to accompany him as far as Padua and asked me to come along. We were driven by Parry, the Welsh chauffeur, who had been since 1912 in the service of the Berensons.

---

[1] Sam Behrman has told this story in a very different way in his book on Duveen, and when he sent us the typescript of the chapter about B.B., I called B.B.'s attention to this particular point. B.B. shrugged his shoulders. "If Sam thinks his version more amusing you must not spoil his fun. Who cares anyway?" Carl Hamilton was able to sell this little picture—later definitely attributed to Domenico Veneziano—to the National Gallery in Washington for, I believe, a considerable price.

Parry was a real character, independent, free from any servile attitude, laconic and forthright in his way of expressing himself. Mary once reproached him for being too slovenly in his appearance. "Nobody would take you for a gentleman's chauffeur," she said. "You look like a workman." "As a matter of fact, Madam," he said, "that is just what I am." Our sightseeing on this trip turned out to be a quick tour of what Mary called "sacred pictures" and watching Hamilton's reaction to them. It was indeed rather surprising to see him dashing towards the finest picture in a church or a gallery as if pulled towards it by a magnet. In the Vicenza gallery it was Cima's enchanting *Madonna under the Pergola*, in Santa Corona, Bellini's *Baptism*. From Padua we went as far as Castelfranco and when we stopped before the church Mary urged Parry to have a look at the famous altar-piece by Giorgione. "I do not expect to be any better after seeing it," was the answer. When Hamilton left for Paris, Mary announced that we were going to return to Florence by way of Adria Codigoro and Pomposa. "I must see Pomposa," she said. "B.B. has been raving about it." So to Pomposa we went on a glorious September day and while wandering about in the abbey—then still so unspoilt in its romantic solitude—Mary kept saying, "This is perfect." "Now he will have to stop boasting about it. I have been here too." During our drive over the Apennines she started talking about Geoffrey, very quietly and sensibly, yet I preferred not to reveal to her what had happened between him and me.

Geoffrey, to whom I had written about our travelling companion and my first impressions, answered from London:

> . . . I am amused by the contrast between your account of Carl Hamilton and Mrs. B.B.'s. She describes him as a mixture of Dionysius and Saint Francis, a mysterious awe-inspiring and love-compelling force and a kind of mystic genius. There are a lot of them in America! Your description sounds quite convincing. Such people make one realize the

full significance of the Atlantic. I find Mrs. B.B.'s admiration of them human and touching and yet I used sometimes to feel it rather a barrier between us . . .

No sooner had we returned to I Tatti than Mary's whole attention was taken up by the arrival of her grand-daughter Barbara Strachey and her cousin Ursula Strachey, both about six years old. For the first time I watched in amazement Mary's way of dealing with her grandchildren. Had Barbara said: "Gram, lie down, I want to trample on you," Mary would have obeyed without the slightest hesitation.

Finally the great day came early in October: B.B.'s return from Paris where he had been staying almost uninterruptedly since the United States joined the Allies in 1917. I was not in the house when he arrived but was told by Mary next morning that he had immediately noticed the disappearance of the small picture and on hearing that it had been given by her to Hamilton, had got, as Mary called it, "into an unreasonable and undignified rage."

Later that same morning while working at the end of the small library I heard a light step and saw B.B.'s slender elegant figure walking towards me. I was too flustered to say much, noticed his beautiful eyes and his charming smile, heard him utter a few words of appreciation of what I was trying to do and then he was gone. Already during the first lunch I was relieved to find him very different from what I had expected in his political attitude. On our way through Germany I had seen the hungry children with white transparent ears, the shop windows of bakers and pastry cooks filled with loaves of bread and cakes all made of cardboard. I knew about the exasperation of the common man over the insane policy of his government, and I felt very hotly about the folly of the Allies in not using that very moment for stretching out a helping hand and making a durable peace. I had armed myself against the cruel things I would have to listen to in the Berenson house. Instead of that I found

B.B.'s indignation over the policy of the Allies and the infliction of the blockade in absolute harmony with my convictions. When Carlo Placci, one of B.B.'s oldest Italian friends, came to lunch a few days later and boasted of how he and a group of his French friends had taken an excursion to the Rhineland and of how they had rejoiced in seeing it occupied by the Senegalese troops, B.B. only said: "Carlo, you have forgotten your Bible. Vengeance is mine saith the Lord." Without my being aware of it this created the beginning of a bond between us.

THE FIRST GUEST who came to stay in the house after B.B.'s return was one of his new friends from the Parisian world, a writer of Corsican origin and a fascinating monologist, Abel Bonnard.

When Geoffrey heard about his being expected, he wrote:

> . . . I thought Bonnard the most charming talker that I met in Paris, so much wit and subtlety and at the same time a sense of great balance and of a serious mind held in reserve. You will find I Tatti a strange meeting ground of the most diverse types of the world. . . .

Bonnard shared many of B.B.'s interests but not his views on the political situation. His narrow nationalism did not allow him to admit that B.B. might be right in accusing the Allies of preparing the next war instead of making a durable peace. "*On peut partager l'amitié,*" he would say, "*on ne peut pas partager la haine.*"

To my delight and surprise I was invited to join Mary, B.B. and Bonnard on a motor trip to Umbria. My first serious sightseeing expedition with B.B. and the fulfilment of the glamorous visions I had had when Mary's initial message reached me in Switzerland. Perugia, Assisi, Spello, Arezzo, B.B.'s delight in seeing again the landscapes and sights he loved so much, Bonnard's witty and poetical flowers of speech, Mary's comments and humorous attempts to throw cold water on B.B.'s raptures; it was all as I had vaguely imagined it. Solid nourishment to my curiosity combined with a carefree congenial human atmosphere. During that trip we saw a lot of a most engaging young superintendent of the fine arts, Umberto Gnoli, who remained a close friend for many years.

When Bonnard had left and B.B. was no longer monopolized by him, I began to know him better and discovered how familiar he was with German literature, how much he enjoyed being read to in German. "Do you know Platen's 'Busento Ballad'?" he asked me one day, and when I began reciting the first lines his delight was great and made me feel very close to him. At the same time I was awed by other aspects of his personality, by the vast layers of learning that seemed to rise up behind him, even if—thanks to my acquaintance with the life of the Jewish communities in eastern Europe—I was able to understand where it all sprang from. I felt intimidated by my ignorance of so many subjects discussed by him. On his return from Paris his studies were concentrated on mediaeval and Byzantine art and his hunger for information was insatiable. I dreaded not being able to find the books or the notes or the photographs he was incessantly asking for, often in a very vague way, remembering the contents of a book but not the author nor the title, or clamouring for the photo of a picture without mentioning its location.

Also in other respects that first winter was not easy. Geoffrey had returned to Villa Medici and was still in an alarmingly neurotic condition. Almost every morning I would find him wating for me at the gate of Villa Rondinelli to accompany me on my walk within a few steps of the gate of I Tatti. While I was thinking of my work, he dwelt on his sufferings in what seemed to me a hopelessly self-centered and depressing way. On the other hand, Mary—who had of course been told about these morning walks—was beginning to talk about Geoffrey's and my elopement. I had to beg her to stop it. It was all most embarrassing and I daresay partly through my own weakness in not being able to treat Geoffrey roughly. Early in 1920 I felt utterly exasperated and wondered whether I had not better give up the whole connection with I Tatti and look for work in another town. By good luck, just at that point Geoffrey was offered the job of press attaché at the British embassy in Rome. Lady Sybil asked me to come to Villa Medici, while Geoffrey had gone to Rome, to talk things over. I urged her to let him go. "Let him be perfectly free to come and go as he likes," I said. "It is your only chance of keeping him." She was deeply disturbed. "Marriage is a constructive thing," she said, "and no good can come from all these separations." But she had to give in, and out of this first separation grew the final one, although several years later.

With Geoffrey safely in Rome I felt at last free to give myself up entirely to my new life and its duties and pleasures. Of course I did go on seeing him during his brief and not very frequent visits to Villa Medici or when I happened to go to Rome. A very difficult relation for both of us until gradually things became easier.

Later on while working on his *Portrait of Zélide* Geoffrey wrote from Mark's Hall, Cogglesall, Essex, July 1922:

> . . . The thing which makes me stick in the mud with my book is that Madame de Charrière's relations to Benjamin Constant after his marriage to Madame de Staël, have an uncanny likeness to Mary's feelings and actions four years ago. I understand it almost too well to write about it in the detached and light manner which the tone of the book requires, and indeed I would much prefer not to write about it at all. Yet humanly it is the most interesting part of the life. The idea of Mary reading the Mss. and drawing the unavoidable parallels at each point embarrasses me a good deal in writing it. However it is easier to do it than

25

it would have been a year or two ago and I am going to finish it off as soon as I can. It is curious how intimately one gets to know the people one writes about. Madame de Charrière is as real to me as almost anyone in real life.

When the *Portrait of Zélide* appeared, we all read it and discussed it. If Mary felt hurt by it she did not show it. Probably she had by that time freed herself completely from her obsession.

DURING THE SPRING of 1920 I went on working hard in the library and still walked over every day from the Villa Rondinelli to return there in the late afternoon. Mary, B.B. and their guests I saw only at lunch and at tea-time. In the beginning a good deal of the general talk, especially if connected with the United States, had been above my head and only through listening carefully did I learn to follow it. For "shop talk" about pictures and attributions I was better prepared, for although lacking any systematic training in art history I had a natural inclination for it. What I enjoyed most was being asked over the weekend to I Tatti and if there happened to be no guests, to spend the evening reading aloud myself or listening to Mary's reading and to the talk that grew out of the books. Very early I learnt to appreciate B.B.'s quiet moods more than his so-called "brilliant" conversation and witticisms or paradoxes. I felt in him a spring of profound wisdom if only one knew how to tap it. His comments on books, his analysis of the people he had seen during the day, his humane understanding of their shortcomings or difficulties, his freedom from any kind of fixed *Weltanschauung,* his boyish sense of fun, all that appealed to the whole of my being. It would have been impossible not to be aware of Mary's personality, of her excellent mind and often very original approach to whatever was being discussed, of her generous impulses, of her irresistible high spirits. But somehow her light faded when B.B. appeared on the scene. Did I feel this only because of my being a woman and susceptible to his charm as a man? I do not think so, for again and again I have seen his men friends captivated by him likewise.

One of these men friends and perhaps the first of the Tatti circle that emerges for me with a clear outline from a confusion of new faces was "Trevy"—alias Robert Trevelyan, the older brother of the historian George Trevelyan. He arrived for a long stay in the early spring of 1920 and struck me at once as an unusual type of Englishman, unusual for me at least, with a foreigner's rather conventional idea of what an Englishman would look like. Tall, lean, uncouth, with dishevelled grey hair, a long inquisitive nose, corduroy trousers, heavy boots, very poor table manners. But listening to his agreeable voice, to his charming laughter one forgot all about his lack of polish and was completely won over by his spontaneity. Lady Sybil and Geoffrey told me that meeting him once on the Vincigliata road with a knapsack full of books on his back, they had stopped the car to talk to him and had asked him to come and lunch with them at Villa Medici. Trevy, scratching his head, had asked: "Whom have you got staying with you?" "Nobody at present." "Then I had rather come another time."

Trevy was the first of the Tatti friends to take an interest in me. He began to peer over my shoulder at what I was writing, to inquire what book I was ordering or cataloguing, to give me his advice on the classification of books. Then he invited me to take a walk with him and talked charmingly, chiefly about books but also about people. I told him how intimidated I was by B.B. and almost afraid of accompanying him on a walk for fear of having nothing to say that could interest him. "Nonsense," Trevy said. "Do not have the slightest hesitation in saying whatever comes into your mind. He will know what to make of it. Never worry about being or not being interesting."

27

Both B.B. and Mary were devoted to Trevy, loved to tease him and had endless discussions with him. They told me that his wife was a highly cultivated but rather heavy Dutch woman whom Trevy had married because she shared his ardently pro-Boer feelings during the South African War. During the 1914–18 war Trevy had got into serious difficulties through being a conscientious objector. Finally he had accepted employment by the Quakers and was looking after their library in Paris when B.B. arrived there in the autumn of 1917. B.B. introduced Trevy to a number of his friends, among them the fascinating Gladys Deacon (later married to the duke of Marlborough). She made a deep impression on Trevy and for the first time in his life he fell desperately in love. From then on he became a sort of Cherubino, always infatuated in a schoolboyish manner with some young woman, usually repulsed because of his uncouth manners and ever yearning for an ideal fulfilment.

On the Italian side of the Tatti scene I have already mentioned Carlo Placci. It was, I believe, Vernon Lee, to whom B.B. on his first visit to Florence had brought a letter of introduction from Harvard, who made them acquainted with each other. From then on he had played a great part in the life of both B.B. and Mary. They had adored each other, they had quarrelled, they had taken any number of trips together. During recent years in Paris their friendship had been somewhat shaken because of Placci's raging nationalism and consequent fury over B.B.'s sharp criticism of Italy's demands and appetites. I did not take to him at all at first, probably because he did not pay the slightest attention to me. In the course of time we became very good friends and I learnt to appreciate his wide culture, his wit and his uproarious sense of fun whenever he came to spend a few days with us. His way of giving himself up to being a guest was most engaging, taking part in what was going on as if he had no other preoccupations. When he appeared only as a lunch or dinner guest it was more of a gamble. He could be most entertaining but more often was tired out from having been too social and, querulous like a naughty child, he would insist on bringing up controversial subjects. Not unfrequently B.B. and he quarrelled at the lunch table, went off to have a nap, met again for a walk and came back in complete peace and harmony.

Another friend of many years belonging to the Italian scene was the Spanish-born Countess Hortense Serristori. I felt at one with B.B. in finding her a fascinating talker, subtly stimulating and witty. Mary did not really care for her. Perhaps she resented the attention of the countess being turned almost exclusively to B.B. or she may have been simply jealous, although her Quaker education did not allow her ever to think herself capable of jealousy. Or possibly during the years of B.B.'s and Mary's free union, when Mary did not accompany B.B. to St. Moritz or Paris, a sort of animosity against the women belonging to the elegant crowd frequented by B.B. in these places may have grown up in Mary. I say against the women because presumably the men belonging to that same world would have been free from any prejudice against Mary's irregular position and were therefore more likely to be accepted as friends by her. Such was the case with Placci, with Don Guido Cagnola—a member of the Lombard aristocracy and the owner of a fine collection—and with others. Cagnola was the first of her Italian friends mentioned by Mary on her return in 1919 and whom she hoped to see again as soon as possible.

As I was not yet living in the house, I did not see much of such close friends of B.B.'s and Mary's as Gaetano and Fernande Salvemini who frequently came to spend the week-end at I Tatti when I was not there. But the few times I was invited with them I enjoyed myself enormously listening to the discussions between B.B. and Gaetano. They did not see eye to eye in all political questions, certainly not in what touched the German problem that preoccupied B.B. so much and Gaetano much less, but temperamentally they were very close to each other, impetuous, passionate and at the same time wise and penetrating in their analysis of events and able to help each other in throwing new light on various historical questions while enjoying each other's sense of fun. Gaetano's laughter was irresistible and his whole personality intensely life-enhancing. There was a curious physical resemblance between his and B.B.'s heads, both brachycephalic (broad-headed), both bald with short beards, and it became more marked as they grew older. There was none between their bodies. B.B.'s so slender and delicate and Gaetano's stocky and vigorous with a heavy almost peasantlike gait. Fernande had none of her husband's charm but made a good partner in a serious conversation with her thorough French university training. She was very pedantic and I remember B.B.'s intense amusement when having borrowed Proust's *Du Côté de chez Swann* from him she brought it back fully annotated with her corrections of style and syntax.

In connection with Fernande the visit of a curious English trio comes into my mind—Vanessa Bell, Maynard Keynes and Duncan Grant. They appeared in the spring of 1920 eagerly expected by B.B. who was looking forward to having wonderful talks with them. He was disappointed. Mrs. Bell was almost invariably wrapped in sulky silence, Keynes was aloof and oracular and only Duncan Grant unconcerned and pleasant. One morning Trevy had strolled out to chat with Duncan while the latter was painting near the ponds in the formal garden. Feeling very hot Trevy decided to take a plunge in one of the ponds and then proceeded to dry himself by walking up and down naked. Meanwhile Fernande Salvemini had come in by the garden gate and finding herself a little in advance of time for lunch thought it would be pleasant to sit for a while in the lemon house and to climb up to it through the formal garden. When I met her a little later in the library she was *consternée* to have found *une espèce de sauvage tout nu qui se promène de long en large comme si c'était la chose la plus naturelle du monde.*

THE FIRST OF B.B.'s AMERICAN FRIENDS who came to stay at I Tatti in the spring of 1920 was Belle Green, the keeper of the Morgan Library. I had not yet heard about her nor about her expected visit. One evening, when I had been invited to dine with Mary and B.B., we settled down in the green leather armchairs near the fireplace in the libary and B.B. sent me to fetch a book. When I returned Mary was no longer there. "Where is Mary?" B.B. looking very gloomy answered, "Something very unfortunate has happened between us. I wish you would go and look for her and try to calm her." I searched and called everywhere upstairs, downstairs, in her bedroom, in the sitting room on the ground-floor, no answer. The doors leading into the garden were all locked. I went a second time to the sitting room and instead of calling switched on the light and found her curled up on one of the sofas. "Let me hear some music," she said. I put a Bach roll on the Welte-Mignon pianola and went back to the library to tell B.B. that she seemed better. Neither he nor she gave me any explanation, but when a few days later B.B. left for Rome and I heard Mary's scornful remarks on his having gone it became clear to me that the disagreement was connected with Miss Greene. Then Mary told me herself that the latter had played a dangerous part in B.B.'s life. When B.B. returned from Rome in Miss Greene's company I tried to understand what had attracted him to her. The first impression was not agreeable. Great vitality and plenty of intelligence, a provocatively exotic physical type and something unharmonious, almost crude, in speech and manner. In later years I got to know her better and was able to enjoy her wit and her zestful approach to her work. But I never got a sense of real harmony with her. A young Italian friend once said to me speaking of Mary Berenson: "She is not only a foreigner; there is the whole Atlantic Ocean between us." I could have more easily applied this to Belle Greene than to Mary.

The jealous affection of their Swedish masseuse, Naima Löfroth, accompanied Mary's and B.B.'s life like the barking of a faithful watchdog. She had been warmly recommended to them by another Swedish friend of theirs and they had found her fierce Nordic temper—worthy of the heroine of an Icelandic saga—somehow very entertaining. Thus she grew into being a family friend and *habituée* and in the course of time developed into a real problem. Full of honour-destroying gossip about Florentine society and the foreign colony, and suffering bitterly from not being treated as a social equal by most of her clients, Naima was at the same time a wonderful friend, especially in moments of crisis. B.B. used to say that she was made for pestilence and evil days, not for peaceful everyday life. I doubt whether Mary and B.B. did her a good service in beginning to ask her up for week-ends, for it led her to expect the same kind of hospitality from others. When Mary in the summer of 1919 wrote to me giving me various instructions, one of them was to call on Miss Löfroth. I went and was received with some caution but quite civilly. Belonging as she did to a good Swedish family of military traditions she knew a lot about the Baltic provinces and had even met some of my relations. This created a sort of bond and I generally managed to keep on friendly terms with her. At rare intervals there was between us what might be called an armed truce.

One of Mary's special pets, but very much appreciated by B.B. as well, was Edmund Houghton, who had played a considerable part in their early wanderings through Tuscany. Edmund had been a pioneer motorist and in his small car had taken them to many of their favorite sites, particularly in the region of Siena. The car could not climb up a steep hill with more than one person in it and frequently they had to get out and help to push it. Houghton was the most endearing type of English loafer, utterly disinterested, with good taste in decoration and furniture, taking up one hobby after the other. At one time it was photography which he developed into a real art. In the photographic archives at I Tatti there are still a number of photos of unusual quality done by Houghton for B.B. In the late twenties a wealthy California woman, Mrs. Crocker, appeared with a letter of introduction and asked Mary to recommend to her somebody who could take her round the Florentine art dealers and advise her. Mary asked Houghton to accompany Mrs. Crocker, and she was delighted with his guidance but distressed because he had refused to let himself be paid for the hours he had dedicated to her. Mary urged Houghton to say what kind of present he would like to receive from Mrs. Crocker. "My tobacco pouch is getting worn out," he said. "I would be glad if she gave me a new one." His wife, Mary Houghton, appeared rarely at I Tatti. She too was an original figure, just as indifferent as he to worldly advantages but with none of his charm. I remember her looking frumpish with untidy hair and as being abrupt and not very amiable. Both the Houghtons were intimate friends of Cecil Pinsent and after Mary Houghton's death Cecil—having given up his professional work in Florence—shared a house with Edmund in Bournemouth and looked after him till his death.

But during my first year at I Tatti Cecil was only beginning to be in demand as builder of country-houses, planner of gardens or modernizer of old houses. He was always a welcome guest at I Tatti and frequently had small additions or repairs to superintend there. B.B. and Mary both enjoyed his quiet impersonal manner, his excellent mind, the variety of his interests. Sometimes there were stormy *intermezzi* in their relations because of Cecil's being rather casual in his

33

estimated expense and B.B. being suddenly confronted with bills far exceeding his calculations. But these storms soon blew over as B.B. knew that Cecil had no intention of cheating him. He just lacked the capacity to keep his accounts in order.

The rest of the picture, the casual guests coming and going all through that first winter and spring, remains strangely nebulous in my memory and I shall not attempt to recall any names. Hard at work in the library and delegated only on exceptional occasions to take visitors round the house, I met some of them briefly and others not at all. My chief concern was to give the impression of being efficient as librarian, yet I was all the time fully aware of my lack of knowledge and experience.

CHAPTER III

Life in New York
and in the Villino [1920–21]

IN THE EARLY SUMMER of 1920 my three Anreps—Alda, Bertie and Cecil—were able to leave Germany and to return to Italy. B.B. and Mary gave them a warm welcome and proposed that we should all four settle down in the Villino. We did so in the autumn after selling most of the furniture of Villa Rondinelli. A few weeks later the Berensons left for the United States and put I Tatti at the disposal of Kingsley and Lucy Porter[1] for half a year. B.B. had met both the Porters during the summer of 1919 in Paris and the immediate mutual sympathy had grown into real friendship during a long motor-trip they took together visiting the finest mediaeval monuments of France. I too became very fond of them as I went on with my work in the library.

Lucy Porter was almost uncannily perceptive of our difficulties and of how she could come to our help. For difficulties we had and not only financial ones. My sister was suffering from a sharp reaction after living for two years as a refugee in Germany. To find herself suddenly surrounded by people whose life had gone on in a normal almost pre-war way did

---

1 Arthur Kingsley Porter (1883–1933), author of books on mediaeval architecture and sculpture, and poet; professor of arts at Harvard University from 1920 to 1933.

not make it any easier for her. On the other hand my brother-in-law was pursued by the fear of using up the small capital he had been able to save for daily living expenses before finding some sort of employment. Mary had put him in touch with her daughter Ray (Mrs. Oliver Strachey), who was interested in a new way of building cottages of dried mud and arranged for him to go to England so as to learn all about it. As usual when a new scheme appealed to her, Mary felt sure of wonderful developments and of pots of money to be made. My brother-in-law enjoyed the trip to England and we were all grateful to Mary for letting him have a complete change. But in the end his scepticism about the mud buildings was justified, for nothing came of the whole scheme.

Meanwhile Mary and B.B. were staying in Carl Hamilton's apartment on Park Avenue, surrounded by wonderful pictures. The small crucifixion by Piero della Francesca (now in the Frick museum) and Giovanni Bellini's *Feast of the Gods* (now in the National Gallery, Washington) were among them. Mary wrote to me about the kind of life they were leading, sometimes with engagements for thirty days ahead. It sounded to me like a monstrous and life-shortening programme. Even now, looking through B.B.'s small engagement book makes me feel giddy. He told me later that when asked whether he was enjoying himself his answer was: "I don't know, I just spin."

Mary to Nicky   New York   December 5th 1920
   . . . It is an utterly unimaginable world as you say. But we do not belong to it and we are dreadfully homesick. B.B. betrays his sense of misfit by fiendish brilliancy which leaves people uncomfortable and gasping and I betray mine by extreme and heavy amiability. We long for the quiet and sunshine of home and the congenial society of the few people there we feel at home with like you. You can't think what a difference it makes to us having you and also to have your sister and her family in the Villino. It has come to me

as heavenly healing after the crushing disappointment of Geoffrey's marriage and the break-up of the architect's partnership which used to interest me so much.

. . . Tell me all the little things that happen. Under the shadow of this doom[2] home with all its familiar details seems somehow doubly precious while all the parade and display and wealth and worldliness and hurry and ambition are horrible. Death changes the proportions of things and makes the simplest most natural satisfactions the most precious. Our books, the garden, our friends a little while we have them to enjoy, a touchingly brief space and then "our place will know us no more."

. . . Belle Greene is very much to the fore over here and most helpful about collections, etc. Poor Hamilton's apartment is nothing but a super-museum and of course very uncomfortable. His Japanese servants are rather awful too. Eliza has a difficult time with them. They serve us fairly well though and we can entertain as much as we like which we prefer to going out.

Nicky to Mary   I Tatti   December 6th 1920
. . . On Saturday night I dined here and had an American friend of the Kingsley Porters, an artist or art critic, sitting next to me. He knows Carl Hamilton quite well and gave me a description of the apartment you are inhabiting by this time. If it has not been changed for you, it must be rather a gloomy place in a skyscraper with no sun, he said, with thick curtains keeping out the daylight. An electric lamp over every picture and crimson coloured lampshades. This last detail does not seem to me in harmony with Hamilton's pious habits. At least I am told that crimson coloured shades help to make the atmosphere of a room very erotic.

. . . You cannot imagine how nice and friendly the Kingsley Porters are to me and if the so often ill-used adjective "good" can be applied in the nicest sense of the word

---

[2] Alys Russell, Mary Berenson's sister, seemed to be threatened by cancer.

to anybody I am sure it is Lucy Porter. He is a charming man but not at all stimulating. He always seems lost in a dream and I do not want to disturb him.

Tell B.B. that I am getting some rare books on early Christian and mediaeval art from Germany and feel as pleased as if I had written them myself.

Mary to Nicky   Boston   December 29th 1920

. . . What has happened this time which makes it different from our previous visits is the war (nobody here has any real feeling about it) and our experience that no matter how nice the people seem we are very unlikely to see them again. Of course there are exceptions—Walter Lippmann of the *New Republic* for instance and some already acquired friends who come over every summer. Otherwise it is as the poet says: "If she is not fair for me what care I how fair

Nicky to Mary   I Tatti   January 13th 1920

Dearest Mary,

Mrs. Ross has just sent me over a letter from you written from Boston and I have enjoyed it so much that I feel like thanking you for it. When you have no special commissions for me you must always address your letters to her and let me have them afterwards. It spares you time and she prefers being the first to get your letters.

Mary to Nicky   New York   January 17th 1921

Dearest Nicky,

Your letter of the 26th rejoiced our souls today—just the things that make our far away home seem real. If you discoursed on abstract subjects we should grind our teeth with rage. A Japanese female poet already in the tenth century enumerated among "six boring things" letters from your country place which tell you no news.

. . . Lucy's descriptions of New York cannot be too lurid for the reality. We go to see collections, we have luncheon parties here, we go to large parties every single day. We have streams of callers in the afternoon, we always go to dinner parties and sometimes from them to musicals.

... A horrid thing is the necessity we are under of sometimes chucking less important for more important people, like Rockefeller, etc., a thing I hate to do, it seems so snobbish. We attended a millionaire dinner party the other night. I am sure Kingsley and Lucy never sank so low. The table literally groaned under orchids, caviar, turtle soup and golden plate. Twenty-two gross old people sat around it guzzling champagne and all sorts of wine (in spite of prohibition), the women all over 50 all fat and all except myself nearly naked and hung with ropes of pearls and diamonds. After dinner opera singers came in and yelled horrible music. B.B. nearly fainted away. We came away "early" (at midnight!) and he actually said he was glad I did not look like other women.

Mary to Nicky   New York   February 8th 1921
... Every few days we get into a new set of people and some of these sets are interesting and delightful. There is the *New Republic* set (very congenial) the art set (horrible) the doctor set (absolutely enchanting) the musical set (not at all intellectual) the bankers set (interesting) the business pirates (fascinating and breathtaking) the collectors (rather dull) the old society hacks we have known for years (I do not care for them) and lots of others. One could live for years in New York and never come to the end of people and movements here.

... B.B. is awfully tired and so am I though much less so. When we are tired we tend to quarrel. Fatigue brings out the serious cleavage in our lives. Still on the whole we are getting more and more harmonious with the years.

Nicky to Mary   I Tatti   February 23rd 1921
Dearest Mary,
This letter and then one more *e poi basta* not with writing but with catching you over there in the unimaginable world. What I can imagine with great vividness is a

beautiful spring day and you two puffing up the road in a new car, then tea on the small terrace at the end of the library and a wonderful sensation as if you had never been away. The Kingsley Porters frighten me by saying that all the people you have been seeing and visiting will begin visiting you here. Will they really start doing it this spring?

Of course B.B. and Mary went also to other places in the United States besides New York and Boston where B.B.'s parents lived and where they saw Mrs. Gardner[3] for the last time. They stayed in Bryn Mawr with Mary's cousin, Carey Thomas, in Washington, in Baltimore, in Cambridge to meet a number of friends, particularly Paul Sachs and Edward Forbes, the creators of the Fogg Museum, and B.B.'s youngest sister Rachel, who married the professor of philosophy Ralph Perry.

At the end of his American season, B.B. was so worn out that he went to recover for several weeks in Edith Wharton's new home on the Riviera before returning to I Tatti.[4]

With the reappearance of the two principal characters the Tatti scene at once became animated in the usual way, guests coming and going incessantly. Towering above others, not in their physical but in their intellectual size, I remember two Englishmen of letters, Lowes Dickinson with his Chinese skull-cap, his wisdom worthy of a Mandarin, his exquisite sense of humour, and Lytton Strachey whose *Queen Victoria* had just appeared. B.B. urged him to take up Pius IX as his next subject and I remember that he was tempted by it. I was by that time familiar enough with the intricacies of the English language to catch and appreciate the witty squeaks that

[3] Isabella Stewart Gardner (1840–1924) was one of B.B.'s earliest friends and sponsors. With his help she built up the collection which is now the Gardner Museum in Boston.

[4] Both B.B. and Mary had from the very beginning mentioned Edith Wharton as one of their closest friends, but I did not meet her until two years later.

interrupted Lytton Strachey's silences. One evening we had him to dinner at the Villino and there in a small circle and feeling perhaps no necessity to be on his guard he talked freely and charmingly. His inquiries about our experiences at the end of the war were so full of delicate understanding that I wondered whether he had not more heart than his usual manner would have led one to suppose. Lowes Dickinson, accompanied by Trevy with whom he shared a house at Corbignano, came to see us more than once and he too was deeply interested in all we could tell him about the beginning of the great storm in Russia.

Less inspiring was Elsie de Wolfe's visit. This famous Parisian hostess and interior decorator (later married to Sir Charles Mendl) appeared in a huge car with a *cavaliere servente* whose name I have forgotten, and was visibly disappointed with the style in which I Tatti was furnished and appointed. She gave plenty of advice on how to gay up the rooms, contributed an eighteenth-century looking-glass to this purpose and disappeared. To me she seemed not made of human flesh and blood but of wire and metal and although I met her again and again in Paris and admired her enchanting house I never got over this first impression of her.

The next visitor I remember and to whom my reactions were anything but negative was Don Guido Cagnola. All that Mary had told me about the charm, the exquisite manners, the cosmopolitan outlook of this great Lombard nobleman was confirmed by his actual presence. He corresponded to what B.B. years later got into the habit of calling "a living work of art." There was a special bond between him and Mary through the interest they both took in Buddhism. B.B. and Cagnola were drawn to each other by their long association in art studies and publications. Later, as they both became staunch anti-Fascists, they found a lot of solace in each other's company and in being able to give vent freely to their indignation. Don Guido looked so English and spoke

English so perfectly that he was regularly sent to the English passport side when the division between black and white sheep took place on the Channel boats.

Another foreground figure on the Berenson scene, whom I met for the first time in the spring of 1921, was Princess Mary von Thurn und Taxis, born Hohenlohe, the friend of Rilke, of Kassner, of Keyserling, a remarkable type of *maîtresse-femme,* a product of the old Italo-Austrian aristocracy, comfortably at home in four cultural worlds, a commanding presence in spite of her homely features and inelegant bulky figure. She was too vital, too free from self-consciousness to feel any petty vanity and her huge strangely rotating behind did not seem to make her the least bit uncomfortable or embarrassed.

A commanding presence of a different type, more self-centred and more subtly feminine was Eugenie Strong, born Sellars, who also came to stay at I Tatti that same spring. B.B. and Mary called her the Gorgon because of her classical features and her large expressive eyes. They had many sagas to tell of their rather stormy friendship with her. B.B. called her an "enemy-friend," but always enjoyed his meetings and his disputes with her.

In the early summer of 1921 two young American women appeared in Florence, Alice De Lamar, wealthy, cultivated and of a rather original turn of mind, and Evangeline Johnson (later married to Stokowski, the great conductor, and now Princess Salten-Zalesky), deliciously feminine and full of charm and high spirits. B.B. and Mary, who had seen a lot of both of them in New York, took them on various excursions and finally proposed a longer motor-trip to Urbino and the Marche to them. I was invited to come along and we started in two cars, the three of us driven by Parry and the two girls with Cecil Pinsent in Alice De Lamar's car. Soon the girls had enough of B.B.'s slow method of sight-seeing and Pinsent took them off on a quicker trip. We remained alone and for the first time I felt at my ease with B.B. discussing with him and Mary what we were looking at freely and saying stupid things without any self-consciousness. Weather, temperature and light, all were perfect, and B.B. was in one of his happiest and most carefree moods. He suddenly changed our itinerary, taking the road from Camerino along the tumultuous Nera down to Terni and from there by way of Orte and Viterbo to Tuscania (then still called Toscanella) to gaze at those two honey-coloured Romanesque façades in the light of a late summer afternoon. Then on to Orvieto, skirting the lake of Bolsena through oakwoods all golden with yellow broom. I was in the seventh heaven of joy yet not aware of how much my responsiveness to everything we were looking at was due to B.B.'s presence. Did he realize it? I daresay he did but showed no sign of it. Perhaps in his relations to women, whether serious or superficial, he always preferred to let them take the first step. Like the guests of *Schlaraffenland* he liked to have the roast pigeons fly into his mouth.

IN THE SUMMER while Mary and B.B. were at the Saltino near Vallombrosa I went with my three Anreps to stay with Byba Giuliani's brother and sister-in-law in Calabria near Paola. On my return to the Villino I found I Tatti still empty. Mary had left for England while B.B. was taking a motor trip with Baroness Gabrielle La Caze, another of his Parisian friends. Mary, I knew, did not approve of this friendship, and I found out later through B.B. himself that there was good reason for it. During B.B.'s long residence in Paris the baroness had tried hard to persuade B.B. to cut himself free from all his ties in Europe in order to join her and her friend, the Russian archaeologist Victor Goloubev, in Indo-China. And there B.B. was to devote himself exclusively to Far Eastern art. B.B. said that it had not been easy for him to resist this temptation. When they both arrived at I Tatti, the baroness struck me as one of the freest spirits I had ever met, a great traveller, highly cultivated and full of fun. Later on in Paris I saw her repeatedly surrounded by a group of unusual men, like the mediaevalist Joseph Bédier, the geographer Jean Brunhes, the sinologists Sylvain Lévi and Paul Pelliot.

During Mary's absence I had to function as hostess at I Tatti and one of my first tasks was to assist B.B. through one of Sir Joseph Duveen's visits. Of course I had already heard a lot about this famous art-dealer with whom B.B. had made a business agreement around 1907 to advise him what Italian Renaissance pictures to buy or not to buy. I was also aware of Mary's being much keener about keeping on good terms with him than B.B., who rather dreaded personal contacts with him because of Sir Joseph's restlessness and capricious demands on B.B.'s time and energy. On the other hand, B.B. could not but enjoy Sir Joseph's intense vitality and irresistible sense of fun. For me he was a new and rather fascinating variety of *homo sapiens.*

One morning B.B. told me that three English guests were coming to lunch, Lady Colefax and Mr. and Mrs. Robert Greg. They arrived before B.B. had come down from his study and I had to receive them without being able to make out who was who. So I concluded that the stiffer and more reserved of the two women must be the "Lady" and the more easy-going one the "Mrs." It was just the other way round. The woman with whom it was easy to talk on any subject was Sibyl Colefax, who later on became a real friend. B.B. talked mostly to the Gregs about Egypt, where he and Mary planned to go in November and where the Gregs had their home near Gizeh, Robert Greg being in a semi-diplomatic position connected with the administration of the Suez Canal. Listening to them it never occurred to me that I might be included in the trip and nothing was said about it when Mary and B.B. left for Naples to sail on the *Esperia* for Alexandria. But already from Naples Mary wrote urging me to follow them with the next boat. She said that they could not bear my not sharing this new experience with them. I had work I wanted to finish in the library and was besides anxious to spend Christmas with my people, especially with my small nephew, who, after all we had been through together, I felt to be like a child of my own.

In the week after Christmas I left for Brindisi and caught the boat by a miracle. It was the period of the great railway strikes and the sleeping-car I was in was left standing for hours in one of the smaller Adriatic railway stations.

During the voyage I kept asking myself whether I was not taking too great a risk by "letting myself go" to the growing affection between B.B. and me.

In the late afternoon of the third day, against an apple-green sky streaked with orange, a low stretch of land became visible, then a few palm trees, then some low houses. As we came in sight of the great port, a small boat appeared and in it sat a bearded man in a long cassock and a green turban, a symbol of oriental romance. I suddenly felt that to see all this was too marvellous a chance and that it was nonsense to spoil the fun by being too apprehensive. I thought of B.B.'s smile, of his voice, of Mary's warmth of affection and understanding and all my doubts were dispelled.

CHAPTER IV

The Two First Journeys [1922]

O F MY ARRIVAL in Cairo and of my first days there, a very confused picture remains in my mind. Marvellous light and temperature in daytime, penetratingly cold blasts after sunset, tall palm trees in the garden of Shepheard's Hotel, the air filled with the piercing cries of small hawks in swift flight, Nubian servants in long white cassocks and red belts gliding about the corridors, but above all—the struggle to follow B.B. in his new pursuits, to get acquainted with the treasures of the Egyptian museum, with mediaeval Cairo and its fascinating Fatimid and Ayubid buildings. It was amazing how in a relatively short time B.B. had mastered all this and could meet the various connoisseurs on their own ground, and discuss dates and dynasties and reconstructions with them. Among the new friends he and Mary had acquired the most prominent were E. Quibell and his wife at the Museum of Egyptian Antiquities and Cecil M. Firth, the superintendent of excavations at Sakkara, Achille Patricolo, the superintendent of Arab monuments, and Archie Creswell, who was then already working on his magnum opus on Arab architecture. I remember particularly Patricolo as congenial, expansive and uninhibited as only an Italian can be, gifted with a delicate sense of quality combined with an enormous amount of technical knowledge. To wander about with him in the old city or outside its gates, among the

Mameluk tombs or on the Mokattam hill was sheer delight. Creswell's erudition was, I daresay, deeper than Patricolo's, but his being more pedantic and dogmatic made him less enjoyable as a guide and mentor.

On my arrival I found Mary and B.B. handicapped by the absence of their English maid Eliza, who had been in their service for many years. She had been taken to the hospital with typhoid fever around Christmas and there was little hope of her being able to accompany us to Upper Egypt. She was one of those rare English old birds, crotchety and impenetrable, oracular in her utterances, plucky and self-sacrificing beyond words, trained like a perfect valet, knowing an astonishing amount about every kind of domestic occupation, yet obstinately almost crazily ignorant about things she had not been brought up with. Thus she would not admit the existence of moths and refused to take any precaution against them. Although much less attractive as a woman, she belonged in her courage and self-discipline to the same breed as Lady Sybil Scott's maid Luty. Of her Geoffrey told me that when after a ride of many hours on camel back through the North African desert he had asked her whether she was not very tired, her reply had been: "Sir, we are here to enjoy ourselves."

We did manage to be ready with all our complicated packing for the start on the Nile boat and Eliza was allowed to join us although unable to be in attendance for some time. I was enchanted with the comfort and neatness of the Nile boat. We had an apartment with a cosy, small sitting-room where we were able to spend our evenings reading together Breasted's *Egypt,* Kremer's *History of the Arabs,* Herodotus' description of Egypt and Mrs. Quibell's invaluable guide to the Egyptian monuments. Of the other members of the tour we saw very little, for the dragoman Abudi became aware at once of B.B.'s requiring special attention and arranged for him whenever possible to see the sights at his own slow pace. It was as if an aura surrounded B.B. which filled people in every walk of life with respect for him, at first sight.

I wish I had the capacity to recreate the enchantment of those days beginning with the sound of the rhythmic songs of the sailors washing the decks and ending with the reflection of the glorious sunsets in the river and the procession along the banks of peasant families with their animals returning to their villages after a day's work in the fields. Sometimes a single woman would appear, wrapped in a blue cloak, her baby in her arms and her husband leading the donkey—a perfect flight into Egypt.

Mentioning a donkey makes me think of our modes of conveyance. On leaving Cairo Mary had declared that she was too stiff and rheumatic ever to ride again on either horse or donkey. So at the first stop, the one for Sakkara, she and B.B. let themselves be dragged along in a so-called "sand-cart," while I found myself perched on the back of a lively donkey, and as I had not mounted one since my childhood the tempo terrified me. But I hung on for dear life and had no fall. Whenever the donkey showed signs of slowing up the boy running after it would twist its tail to speed it on. Meanwhile Mary and B.B. had a very uncomfortable journey and swore that they would never use a sand-cart again.

At the second stop, for the Middle Empire temple of Beni Hassan, B.B. tried riding a donkey and loved it. Mary got into a sort of palanquin carried by four men and expected us to ride close to her and to exchange impressions with her. But the four carriers in order to keep in step never stopped singing lustily and she found herself separated from us by a wall of sound. Once more she was disgusted and said she would never again let herself be carried in such a barbarous way. Several stops followed where no conveyance was necessary, the sights being at easy walking distance from the Nile.

At Aswan where we stayed for several days the dragoman proposed an excursion to the granite quarries where an

Carlo Placci

Robert Trevelyan

Belle da Costa Greene

unfinished obelisk can be seen. Suddenly Mary ordered a donkey for herself and although only a very small one was available she mounted it with astonishing ease. Her massive figure looked very incongruous on it, and the amount of old-fashioned complicated underwear that appeared as a consequence of the pulling up of her skirt horrified B.B. "Mary, you are too shocking a sight for a Muslim population." "Nonsense, Bernard, the unveiled face of a woman is so shocking for these people that they do not pay any attention to the rest." During the excursion to Wadi Halfa and the second cataract again no donkeys were used, but when we returned to Luxor for a long stay one of my first duties was to order a riding skirt for Mary, buttoned all the way in front and back like the one I wore. The dragoman took me to the Bazaar where I chose the material and then to an Indian tailor to whom he transmitted my order. Early in the afternoon I was writing in my room while Mary and B.B. were resting when one of the Nubian boys ushered in the Indian tailor. He started talking earnestly and softly fixing his beautiful liquid eyes into mine, then realized that I was unable to understand him and began making incomprehensible gestures, clutching first his sleeve and then pulling at the fly-buttons of his trousers. Suddenly I understood what he wanted. Were the buttons on Mary's skirt to be visible or invisible? The skirt was a great success and Mary, who had been an excellent horsewoman in her youth, enjoyed our daily rides thoroughly.

Often we would spend the whole day on the other side of the Nile visiting temples, tombs and excavations, generally in the company of one or other of the leading archaeologists. B.B. has told the story of his first encounter with H. E. Winlock, the head of the Metropolitan Museum excavations at Dher-el-bahari, in his *Sketch for a Self-Portrait*. Among the people we met were also Howard Carter and Lord Carnarvon, the latter looking like one of Dickens' villainous grand-seigneur characters. Their spectacular discovery of the Tut-ankh-amen tomb was made half a year later. Two young French archaeologists who were digging near the Valley of the Kings allowed us to climb into the tomb of a nobleman a few minutes after it had been uncovered. A rather frightening experience: the ladder was very shaky and the centuries old dust asphyxiating. Norman de Garis Davies, the famous English archaeologist, went around with us more than once, and I remember his amazement over B.B.'s being fascinated by the freshness and intensity of colour on the hieroglyphs. He was unable to answer B.B.'s questions about the colour technique of these ancient artisans and had evidently never noticed this particular feature himself. Our picnic lunches among the ruins could have been most enjoyable but for the swarms of flies. To fight them off, one had to keep a hand free to wave a fly-whisk.

Toward the end of our stay in Luxor, we were joined by a young woman about whom B.B. had already told me a great deal. Her name was Philomène de Lévis-Mirepoix. B.B. had met her in Edith Wharton's house at Hyères on his return from America. Her grace, her gift for expressing herself, her poetical imagination, her exquisite sense of humour made her into an incomparable travelling companion for the three of us and for each of us separately. Her career had been an unusual one for a woman of her class. From her first appearance in Parisian society she had been courted and admired for her looks, her charm, her gifts. Her first book—published under the *nom de plume* Claude Sylve—describing a retreat in a convent had an immediate success. Then she went into a sort of retreat herself as the consequence of a passionate love affair with a married man and of her having the courage to give birth to a child out of wedlock. Edith Wharton, who had been an admirer of Philomène's from the beginning, persuaded her to settle down in Hyères. There they went on seeing a great deal of each other and several of Edith's closer friends, like B.B. and the English painter Robert Norton, became devoted friends of Philomène.

Our return to Cairo did not go off as smoothly as the upstream voyage. The level of the river had already sunk so much that we were stuck again and again and finally near Assiut for so long that both Mary and Philomène insisted on getting off and returning to Cairo by train. B.B., who happened to be in a dreamy, contemplative and nostalgic mood, would have preferred to stay on the boat to watch the life on the river with plenty of leisure for reading and wait for the natural development of things, but both Mary and Philomène were longing for news of their offspring.

The rest of our stay we spent half at the Mena House Hotel near the pyramids and half in Cairo itself. B.B.'s appetite for revisiting Sakkara and the Cairo museum after the experience of upper Egypt was insatiable. At the end of a journey he was apt to get into a fever of anxiety over not having seen, absorbed and understood enough. His energy was concentrated on making the art treasures and the landscape all his own and only occasionally would he allow himself to waste time on purely folkloristic and picturesque spectacles. The only ones I remember him watching and enjoying were the performance of a snake charmer in Luxor and the dancing dervishes in Cairo. When a young English official proposed taking us to see Arab night life in a quarter out of bounds for English troops, B.B. refused to come along and only Philomène and I walked with our guide through the dark narrow alleys lined with small ramshackle houses. Some doors were shut. Before each of the open ones a prostitute was seated placidly waiting for a customer without the slightest effort to attract him, spread out like merchandise. Lustrous eyes, painted cheeks, voluptuous attitudes were the prerogatives of graceful young boys, languidly sprawling on a divan under an arch. Mary would have enjoyed this expedition hugely, but she was ill most of the time during our second stay in Cairo, having caught some mysterious infection. Bonté Elgood, a friend of Mary's family, married to an English government official and herself a doctor, came to our help and insisted on Mary's being taken to a hospital. Bonté Elgood's account of her work in the English health service I remember as deeply interesting and revealing of what the English were doing for the Egyptian population in a quiet, unobtrusive, unboastful way.

Mary got well enough to join us on the boat that took us back to Venice, but was unable to see the sights of Alexandria with us. She did not really recover entirely until several months later when B.B. took her to a sanatorium in Kissingen.

Between our return to I Tatti and Mary's and B.B.'s leaving by car for Germany, there was the usual bustle of guests. As an amusing interlude I remember Ronald Storrs —the Governor of Jerusalem whom B.B. and Mary had met in Cairo before I joined them—with Lady Irene Curzon (later Baroness Ravensdale), whom he was violently courting at that time, and an older woman, Mrs. Leggett, who was supposed to act as chaperon to Lady Irene. Suddenly Mrs. Leggett, fed up with Storrs' insistence and Lady Irene's indecision, left for England. Storrs and Lady Irene were both keen on hearing Toscanini conduct *Die Meistersinger* at the Scala and persuaded my sister to accompany them as *guarde d'honneur*. Alda's descriptions of Storrs' unsuccessful attempts to storm the fortress were very entertaining.

When I left the Villino to join Mary and B.B. in Kissingen, my sister and brother-in-law also left for Munich and to settle down there. Life was much cheaper in Germany and both had vague hopes of getting work.

In Kissingen Eliza started instructing me in all the little things needed on a trip to keep B.B. in good shape. He was a curious mixture of fragility and toughness, had to be very careful about his food and his regular rests, but was on the other hand almost undauntable when it came to standing about for hours in museums and churches or taking long walks and climbs. Of the utmost importance to him was to have his books and papers, his clock, his writing paper, his pens and pencils and paper-cutters neatly arranged and in a way to make him feel at home in the simplest hotel room. I remember how once Lucy Porter came into his bedroom in a more than primitive inn in Patras to talk over plans and was amazed to find him so comfortably settled in. "Why, B.B.," she said, "I did not know you went on living as if you were at home." Almost absurdly meticulous and exacting where he suspected laziness or slovenliness, B.B. was perfectly ready to rough it when he felt sure that under the circumstances he was getting the best that could be obtained.

When Mary and Eliza left for England, I undertook to valet B.B. with many misgivings. It was lucky for me that I did not have to be ready with everything at a set hour since we were travelling by car. We took a trip through northern and central Germany with a dip into the south where B.B. had to meet Sir Joseph Duveen in Munich and I had the joy of seeing my three Anreps again and of meeting several Baltic relations and friends among the refugees.

GERMANY WAS STILL in a very vulnerable condition and repeatedly we met with rather rough treatment from guides, museum custodians or sacristans, who hated the sight of a foreign car and considered all foreigners as base exploiters of the relative cheapness of living in Germany. But almost invariably they became aware of B.B.'s real and serious interest in the monuments and art treasures and ended by being friendly and helpful. The old librarian at Aschaffenburg refused to put his foot into our car when we sent it for him to his house and appeared under his umbrella muttering imprecations against *die Alliierten*. But as he watched

B.B. looking at the illuminated manuscripts with his magnifying glass, turning over the leaves with his delicate hands, asking questions that showed how much he knew about mediaeval script and illustration, the old man thawed out completely and B.B. and he took leave of one another like life-long friends.

Only in the library of Wolfenbüttel the librarian—the caricature of a rigid snarling Prussian official—refused point blank to accept the letters of introduction B.B. had brought as valid and we had to leave.

Most of the hotels in the smaller towns were run down yet the general progress seemed astonishing after what I had seen in the winter of 1918–19.

It was in Magdeburg on our way to Berlin that the news of Dedo Serristori's death—Countess Hortense's only son—reached us. B.B. was crushed by it, knowing what a tragedy it meant for his friend, who had gone through agonies of fear when her boy had insisted on enlisting and on being sent to the front before being called up. As in the Persian tale death kept its rendezvous with him not at the front but in the high Alps. His passion for mountain climbing induced him to take a very hazardous expedition without a proper guide. Caught by a snowstorm, he was frozen to death. Dedo was an unusually promising boy, mature for his age and an utterly free spirit.

On our arrival in Berlin we were told at the Hotel Bristol that we had to go personally with our passports to the police station. After a long discussion I was allowed to spare B.B. this extra fatigue and to go there with his and my passports. Parry also came along and when it was his turn to be interrogated and they asked him for the date of his Italian wife's birth he said he did not know. All the clerks in the room stopped writing and looked at each other and then at Parry as if he had come from Zululand. *Er weiss nicht wann seine Frau ihren Geburtstag hat*—he does not know his wife's birthday. I tried to explain that in Italy the saint's day was really more important than the birthday. "Besides," I said, "it might be considered very chivalrous of a man never to ask for his wife's age." But they shook their heads over such a frivolous interpretation and looked at Parry with undiminished disapproval.

Later on that same day the chief assistant to Sir Joseph Duveen appeared with an urgent request and while I was arranging B.B.'s things in his bathroom I could not help overhearing the discussion that went on between the two men. Duveen wanted B.B. to endorse the attributions of several pictures sold by him during the war and shipped to America without waiting for B.B.'s opinion and over which he was now having some trouble. B.B. refused categorically in spite of the financial advantage that his acquiescence would have brought him. The chief assistant was a man whom B.B. admired for his seriousness and integrity, and I got the impression that he was not displeased over B.B.'s refusal of Sir Joseph's unreasonable demand. In the evening we went with him to a perfect performance of Offenbach's *Orpheus in the Underworld* set up by Max Reinhardt. The high standard of both light and serious opera at that moment in Berlin was astonishing. We saw several excellent shows and were even taken to a Russian cabaret, the Golden Cock, by Rolf Ungern Sternberg, an ex-Russian diplomat and distant relation of mine whom B.B. had met in Paris.

In the museum world B.B. saw a great deal of Friedländer, of Sarre, of Kühnel, of Valentiner. The last arranged a meeting between B.B. and his old enemy Wilhelm von Bode. It was not a success. More than once we went out to the home of the Sarres in Babelsberg and enjoyed its congenial atmosphere. Frau Sarre was a woman of unusual charm and distinction. As daughter of the German archaeologist Humann, she spent her early life in Constantinople, and it was there that Sarre on one of his expeditions to the

Near East had met her. To go round the various collections, looking at pictures, sculptures, art objects in the company of the men dedicated to their study was one of the special treats in travelling with B.B. I will not say that it was invariably a treat. Sometimes we would fall into the clutches of a boringly learned and pedantic man, and it would be what B.B. called *un ennui auguste*. In Berlin I remember only the man who looked after the Far Eastern collections belonging to that category. He gave B.B. no credit for knowing as much as he did on the subject and was insufferably pompous and arrogant. Delightful were the hours spent with Miss Fechheimer in the Egyptian section, so rich in things that linked up with our recent visit to the Egyptian sites. The marvellous frescoes from the caves of Turfan[1] we were shown by le Coq himself, the man who had discovered them and brought them to Berlin. A courteous old gentleman who talked about his experiences in Central Asia with charming modesty and simplicity.

Then Mary joined us and while she and B.B. left by car via Frankfort and Basel for Italy, I went by train to Munich to see my people and from there to Meran where my stepmother had settled down. The train I had to change to in Bozen was stormed by a group of Fascists from Trent, wild looking fellows with huge tassels hanging down over their foreheads from their black caps and armed with clubs. It was my first sight of this new variety of Italian patriots and reminded me most unpleasantly of what I had seen of the Bolsheviks. These heroes behaved like real barbarians in Meran, tore down the Tyrolese coat of arms from the houses, mutilated the monument of the Empress Elisabeth, and defiled tombs with German names on them. Up to that time the southern Tyrol had been governed quietly and correctly by the Italian army and the Italian police. It was the Fascists

[1] Destroyed in 1944 during the Russian advance.

56

who started the trouble which has gradually taken on such alarming proportions.

Meanwhile Mary and B.B. had stopped over in Frankfort where Georg Swarzenski, then the head of the Städel Museum, arranged for them to see various collections. They also drove out to Darmstadt to meet Keyserling in his new rôle of founder and head of the "School of Wisdom." Unfortunately they found him in one of his most arrogant and boastful moods, totally different from how B.B. had known him before the war, and B.B.'s disgust at what seemed to him a vulgar form of self-advertisement was so great that he wrote him off there and then from his list of friends and never saw him again. It was a pity, for Hermann had very different sides to him, and they might have gone on giving a great deal to each other. But where B.B. had felt real affection and admiration he was unable to make compromises and tended "to throw out the baby with the bath water."

B.B. to Nicky   Karlsruhe   September 28th 1922
Dear Nicky,
      The Keyserlings lunched with us today. He looked little older than nine or more years ago but the Mongol aspect of his face has got more accentuated. She fascinated the pedigree student in me. Her profile although so girlish had in the projecting eyes and in the short but decided nose something distinctly Bismarckian[2] about it. She was quiet simple and a lady. She never took her eyes off her husband and listened to him with *Andacht*. Of politics and events he talked sensibly enough although with a strong and perhaps unconscious resentment against England. When he got away from events to abstract matters he became blasphemously, sacrilegiously autolatrous. It was to me repellent and painful and made me uncomfortable and unhappy.
      I returned to the Museum where I discovered a cache

[2] Countess Gödela Keyserling, daughter of Herbert Bismarck and granddaughter of the famous statesman.

of Byzantine early Christian and Romanesque ivories, also enamels that I enjoyed hugely. Among the pictures was the loveliest Lochner in the world, like a fairy world where roses have taken human shape and all but acquired souls. There was a huge triptych, all silver and gold more gorgeous and flat than any Japanese screen. There was a fine Venus and Adonis by Paolo Veronese.

Swarzenski took us to Wiesbaden, to the Henckells. We passed Moroccan troops, very goodlooking and some Senegalese. The Henckell house in the best Long Island style. The men in full tennis uniform, the lady of the house very distinguished, magnificent tea, fine pictures Italian and German. Returned to Frankfurt, to von Hirsch,[3] a young man in a beautiful house, full of splendid books, carpets, tapestries and *objets d'art*. Among the pictures a darling little diptych of early 13th century, all but Byzantine.

Mary to Nicky   Lucerne   October 2nd 1922
. . . We fell upon a local *Festa* here with everything closed, church bells ringing and people dressed in their Sunday best. It is some local saint's day. Very secretly (for work is strictly forbidden) the Steinmeyers opend a door of their shop and showed us a lot of Italian pictures, some extraordinary good ones, including a Bellini of the finest type which they have sold to a man in Detroit.[4] And they had some very beautiful enamels and bronzes—really quite a remarkable collection. B.B. could not resist a small Ercole Roberti which he bought while I had gone to take half an hour's rest!

We met again in Milan and from there Mary went straight home while B.B. and I made a little detour by way of Bergamo, Brescia, Cremona and Bologna, All except Bologna were new for me while for B.B. it was like finding

---

3 Robert von Hirsch later on transferred his remarkable collection to Basel, where he still lives. He and his wife have been welcome guests at I Tatti more than once.
4 Now in the National Gallery of Washington.

old cherished friends again after years of separation. Looking back now I realize how good, how generous he was in allowing me to share everything with him, in not minding my stupid questions and chasms of ignorance. In Bologna his interest in Byzantine art induced him to have a look at the famous *Madonna of San Luca* in the monumental pilgrimage church on a hill outside the city. A paved path under arcades leads up to it so that worshippers need not fear either rain or snow or the scorching sun in summer. The legend says that after the fall of Constantinople a monk carrying a panel on his back turned up in Bologna and declared it to be one of the Madonnas painted by Saint Luke which he had miraculously saved from Turkish vandalism. B.B.'s request to have the Madonna unveiled was granted by a very intelligent-looking priest who proceeded to have the sacred shrine opened. This attracted a number of worshippers and with the greatest naturalness the priest performed the two offices, now turning to the worshippers, reciting prayers for them and giving them the image of the Madonna to kiss, now talking to B.B. and giving him all the information he had about the opinions of other students regarding the possible date and origin of the panel.

We took this short trip between the 8th and the 12th of October. It must have been a very tense moment politically, just preceding the Fascist march on Rome. Yet I did not notice anything at the time. Looking after B.B., packing and unpacking and above all trying to read the clockface —as B.B. used to say—of the things we were looking at absorbed all my energy.

On our arrival at I Tatti I found a charming apartment ready for me on the second floor, bedroom and sitting-room, very cosily furnished with a lovely view over the garden. It continued to be mine for over thirty-seven years and when I now think of it I feel as if my *Doppelgänger* must be still living in it.

CHAPTER V

The Two Berensons
and Their Family Backgrounds

WHAT TURNED OUT to be the most absorbing feature of my life at I Tatti was not the library nor my work in it nor the coming and going of guests nor the journeys in Italy or abroad but the character and temperament of Bernard[1] and Mary Berenson, as different from each other as the art of a jeweller is from that of a stonecutter. Already physically they presented a surprising contrast. He very slender and lithe, quick in his movements and step, his features more Slav than definitely Semitic. She taller than he, of ample proportions, awkward in her gait and moving rather heavily, with a northern long head, noble features and thin lips. Both had very agreeable voices, his rather low and soft, hers very melodious with a silvery note in her laugh. He loved to walk and to climb, she got easily tired out and preferred to drive. He considered good health as an exceptional condition among various bodily ailments that had to be accepted philosophically. She regarded perfect health as her right and looked upon any upset—frequently the consequence of her own intemperance or imprudence

---

[1] What reason B.B. had for dropping the "h" in his first name I do not know. Perhaps during the First World War Mary found the earlier spelling too Germanic.

—as a personal offence to be fought off immediately and energetically. For B.B. with his very delicate digestive organs, eating was often a painful duty. "If I for once enjoy my food," he would say, "it is sure to disagree with me." Mary had a splendid appetite and loved not only good but heavy food and plenty of it. When something she liked particularly happened to be in season, like asparagus or strawberries, she would insist on having it for every meal until she was thoroughly disgusted with it. This was not unlike her attitude to those human beings with whom she happened to fall in love. Mary tended to be slovenly and careless about her personal appearance and found everything connected with fashion and elegance a deadly bore. B.B. was always meticulously neat in his dress and personal habits, wanted everything of the best quality, noticed the slightest stain or tear or defect not only on his own person but anywhere in the house and tended to get into one of his "unreasonable rages" over any negligence.

When B.B. made plans for a trip or a journey, he frequently ended by being bored with them and enjoyed giving them up. Mary clung steadfastly to a plan once it had appealed to her imagination. It seemed to have been engraved in granite in her mind and nothing would keep her from carrying it out. This happened when she had set her mind on getting Geoffrey and me married to each other and established at the Villino. Sometimes when discussing the possibility of a journey with me, B.B. would say: "Let us not tell Mary anything about it yet, or she will pin us down to it." B.B. would occasionally compare Mary to a mighty "dreadnought" triumphantly sailing along, to which one had either to hang on or be drowned.

B.B. never fussed about his sleep or an occasional sleepless or partly sleepless night. Mary carried a large bag of medicines and particularly sleeping pills with her, took the greatest precautions about having a dark and quiet room and was outraged if anything disturbed her in her night's rest. B.B. used to tell her that she ought to pray for a good night as mediaeval Christians prayed for a good death.

Mary's belief in special diets, drugs, cures, surgical operations was as strong as B.B.'s scepticism towards all of them. If I praised the good effect of a medicine he had been taking his answer was invariably, "Who can say how I would have been if I had not taken it?" During a severe attack of lumbago he was once given an injection that acted strongly on the kidneys and made him produce bright blue water. His comment: "For the first time I have had to admit that an injection does affect the human organism."

Another marked contrast I noticed in B.B.'s and Mary's attitude towards money. Mary had an almost childish love of money, of the pleasure of handling it, of squandering it, of giving it away, one might say of throwing it out of the window. Everything seemed to her calculable in terms of money, every act of kindness or courtesy could be in her opinion repaid with a cheque. That in many cases one can only *payer de sa personne* was outside her range of vision. B.B. was certainly not indifferent to money, to its value, to the advantages of owning it, but he regarded it more as a means than as an end in itself. He was fully aware of what could be achieved with the help of money and averse to any form of splurginess and extravagance, to what he called "conspicuous waste." He would have liked to calculate income and expense not in a meticulous but in an orderly way, and Mary's wild outbursts of generosity or lavish expenditure made this almost impossible. Undoubtedly in his younger years he must have enjoyed the act of power that spending represents, especially during the growth and expansion of I Tatti. By the time I joined the household, the library and travel were the only expenses he took an interest in. Very few works of art were bought in my time,

foremost among them the small Crucifixion by Ercole
Roberti. In growing older B.B. became more and more
averse to the material handling of money and was grateful
if others did it for him. I remember Edith Wharton's indignation when having gone together for a walk they failed to
meet Parry where they expected him to wait for them and
she proposed telephoning for a taxi in a nearby village, only
to discover that B.B. did not have a penny in his pocket to
pay for it. In his last years he said to me more than once:
"The one thing that money can really buy for us is leisure
of mind and the liberty to indulge in wholly disinterested
pursuits."

Mary's generous, almost heroic temperament seemed to
come out of the Northern Sagas or the *Niebelungen* song.
Geoffrey Scott used to say that it was like a climate. She
could be bracing and invigorating like mountain air when
in good temper and depressing like a heavy sirocco when
out of sorts. Whatever went against established rules appealed to her: a passionate love affair, culminating in an
elopement; utterly unruly children; lunatics and asylums
for lunatics; the steepest roads with hairpin turns on which
no other car would venture. She told me once that the
essence of Quaker ethics was a revolt against the conventions
accepted by other communities. I began to look at her
behaviour from that point of view and wondered whether
it did not have its roots in the principles of her Quaker
forebears.

New inventions had an intoxicating effect on Mary. I
remember how she became excited over "contact lenses"
and the hope that her grand-daughter Barbara would adopt
them for her short-sighted eyes. Just at that time she had
to go for various examinations to a nursing home kept by
nuns. The nun who helped her to undress wore glasses.
"If you got yourself contact lenses you would not have to

wear those glasses any longer." "Oh, Madam, I am quite happy wearing spectacles." Mary was indignant. "Not a spark of enterprise in these poor benighted nuns."

Her ardent wish to have something that had appealed to her imagination robbed her of the most elementary sense of fact. One day she discovered in the *Illustrated London News* a double-page picture representing a field and sportsmen with their guns and their dogs walking or rather jumping across it. Small balloons attached to their shoulders allowed them to proceed by enormous jumps. Mary immediately wrote to the editors of the paper for further information on where to order one of these balloons. "I shall have no more trouble about walking uphill with B.B.," she said, "and I could hop over to see Aunt Janet in two or three jumps." No answer came. Mary, undaunted, asked Parry, the chauffeur, to construct such a useful walking help for her. Parry explained very carefully how difficult, even impossible, it would be to charge the balloon with the exact amount of gas needed and that she might easily be carried up higher than she wanted and be landed on a tree. Mary was deeply disappointed and said that Parry too was a hopeless stick-in-the-mud. For that was what she accused B.B. and me of being.

Mary was very kind to the servants but did not share B.B.'s interest in their characters or in the motives of their actions. She had a sort of rationalized contempt for "uneducated people" and was unable to put herself into their shoes or to understand their reactions. Having read the advertisement of a group excursion to French gardens and châteaux she decided that it would be wonderful for the head gardener to join it and told him to take the necessary steps. He appeared in my study looking very gloomy and begged me to help him. "I know the *Signora* means well and I do not want to offend her but believe me, *Signorina*, already the idea of that long journey frightens me. When I have to go to Pistoia to buy plants the journey seems endless. Imagine if I had to cross the frontier and to see what? Am I not in a garden all day long?" When I told Mary she was disgusted with such a lack of enterprising spirit.

B.B. was always polite and gentle to the servants and the smallest order from him was treated by them as if it came from God Almighty. Only Parry, after so many years of service, enjoyed the privilege of answering back if an order did not meet with his approval.

While B.B. found the contact with different worlds amusing and stimulating, Mary found it tiring if not outright boring. During one of her cures and in answer to the description I had sent her of one of the usual salads of guests at I Tatti she wrote:

> It is no use trying to combine different worlds. How nice it was in the old days in Fiesole and San Domenico when we had only one world and a tiny one at that, where the same discussion lasted in varying forms for weeks, even for months, the topic being *was ist die Kunst überhaupt* ["What is art, anyway?"]. However it was narrow.

From his early days in Lithuania B.B. had kept up a curious ritual—that of seeing the new moon under the most favourable circumstances. It became a habit to detect the slender silvery shape as early as possible but not on a Friday and not through glass. I see ourselves peering at the sunset sky in the most different countries and climates, on the banks of the Nile as in Manchester Square. B.B. laughed at himself for holding on to this superstition yet could not help feeling slightly depressed if persistently cloudy skies had prevented him from getting a sight of the young moon. Mary had no use for what in her eyes was pure folly and childishness. B.B. retorted by saying that she had no sense of the numinous, of the mystery all around us, of our always walking on the edge of a precipice. And she would laugh at his never saying, "I am well" or "I am fine" but finding some other cautious formula like, "I exist" or "I could be worse" as if being too sure of one's good health might arouse the anger of the gods above.

But it was not only in his comical superstitions that Mary was unable to follow B.B. They were miles apart in their attitude to religious belief. After a first rapturous honeymoon with Catholicism Mary had turned not only anti-Catholic but almost anti-Christian. The crudity of her jeering remarks on other people's beliefs was sometimes really painful. Buddhism alone meant something to her. B.B. likewise had given up being a practising Catholic but had kept a great tenderness for the Bible, for the ritual of the Synagogue and of its daughter the Catholic Church. He told me that when he first came to Italy and began following services in the Catholic Church he had felt at home in them and as if at last he had rediscovered what he had been yearning for since his early childhood in Lithuania. When the Berensons settled down in New England B.B.'s father—a stern free-thinker—had cut his children off from the Synagogue. Later B.B. out of his own free will had joined the Episcopal Church but it did not give him what he was looking for. Out of his first ecstatic experience on reaching Italy in 1888 grew his conversion to Catholicism. For a few years he remained a practising Catholic and from then on regarded himself—as he described it in the *Sketch for a Self-Portrait* —as a graduate of Christianity. His temperament was a religious one in the strictest sense of the word. He felt himself bound up, *legato,* with the Beyond and his approach to art, to poetry, to nature was a mystical one. Therefore he understood the religious needs of other people and sympathized with them. Only haughty dogmatism and theological casuistry could drive him wild whether it came from the Christian, the Jewish, the Muslim, or the Brahman side.

66

MARY PRACTICED A RELIGION of her own, the cult of her family. To think of Mary not in connection with her family would be difficult, so tightly was she knitted up with all of them, sister, brother, daughters, grandchildren. Their plans, their movements, their problems seemed always to be foremost in her mind and memory. B.B. on the other hand had little family feeling and this was unusual for a man of his race and ancestry. He could speak very tenderly of his mother and could be very sweet and affectionate to his sisters but was yet rather indifferent as to seeing or not seeing them. Once he had done what he considered his duty towards his own people by establishing a family trust, he no longer had them on his mind and was grateful to them for their great delicacy in never asking him for anything. Ties of his own choosing were definitely more important to him than blood ties. All the more incomprehensible was to him Mary's attitude and her constant preoccupation with her daughters and their financial problems. In a good mood he would tease her about never having cut off the umbilical cord between herself and her offspring.

My first impression of Mary's family I got through reading Ray Strachey's book *A Quaker Grandmother*. When I wrote to Geoffrey Scott about it his answer was:

> I quite agree about the Quaker grandmother. She was a great original and full of character and her family—especially Mrs. B.B.—keeps up a regular ancestor worship of more than Chinese intensity. Personally I found her an odious old woman, cocksure and overbearing to a degree, entirely uneducated and ready to fight like a tiger for any of her descendants in whatever cause. The last characteristic was rather dramatic and amusing but I could not feel it to be particularly noble as it was completely undiscriminating and savage. She brought up those two grandchildren monstrously, making them each in their way completely anti-social and egoistic. The doctrine that the world existed

to make them happy and that nothing ought to stand in the way of it was perpetually reiterated in their presence with the natural consequences. On the whole it has made them happy so far, but more because of the splendid vitality which runs in the family than because of their philosophy.

After Barabara, Mary's small grand-daughter in 1919, it was her brother Logan Pearsall Smith whom I next met. Tall and bulky like Mary with well-cut features, rather carelessly dressed, he struck me on his first visit in the spring of 1920 as being concentrated on English literature to the exclusion of everything else. As I was not yet staying in the house and had no chance of making friends with him I only listened at lunch time to his continual references to books and authors unknown to me or to witty and malicious gossip also mostly about people I had never met. During the following years I saw him again and again and became fully aware of his charming aspects, particularly of his quiet serious moods and the variety of his cultural interests. They were not all limited to the Anglo-Saxon world of letters as I had too hastily concluded at first. French literature turned out to be one of his pet subjects, particularly Proust and the new world created by his *A La Recherche du temps perdu.*

The rest of Mary's family, her sister Alys Russell, her daughters Ray Strachey and Karin Stephen, all came to stay at different times between 1920 and 1922. Mary had told me of Bertrand Russell's cruelty in leaving her sister, who worshipped him, so suddenly, and I was almost disappointed to find her looking so placid and cheerful and not at all like a woman with a great tragedy behind her. She too was big and handsome with fine regular features. There was nothing of Mary's wilfulness in her and even less of Logan's mischievousness. She seemed to have made almost a profession of being good and helpful on a definitely pedagogical basis. Mary told me that when they were both young Alys had said to her: "Mariechen, thee can get on relying on thy charm but I have got to be good." Both Mary and B.B. loved to tease her about her habit of taking care in a social gathering of anyone who seemed too shy or too dull to get on with the rest of the party. They assured her that this was by now well known and that as soon as she moved with an encouraging smile towards one of the guests, the person smiled at would get scared and wonder: "Am I really as dull as that?" Alys accepted their poking fun at her in a very good-natured way.

Mary to Nicky   I Tatti   July 21st 1921

Alys sits in the library in the morning and often sees B.B. come in "looking for trouble." But she will not afford me any sympathy for she says she would give her soul to have her ex-husband come in and find fault with her, expecting her to be completely occupied with his work. She says when he began to buy his own stamps and to write his own letters it broke her heart. She has come to the conclusion that B.B. by keeping me always on the hop, never knowing what is going to happen next prevents me from getting bored and this she thinks is a great method for keeping affection alive. Perhaps your dear mother felt the same. Children cannot put up with it but wives can as it is their own life.

Mary's elder daughter, the almost monosyllabic, placidly self-sufficient Ray (wife of Oliver Strachey) formed a strange contrast to her younger sister, the agitated problematic Karin (wife of Adrien Stephen). I got on well with both of them but felt more at home with Karin, a human being so full of doubts and problems and changing moods. It seemed cruel that craving as she did for easy communication with others she should be cut off from it by her growing deafness. Both sisters were remarkably gifted, although in very different fields, Ray all given up to political and social work, Karin to philosophical and psychological studies. Mary was passionately devoted to Ray and to all her pursuits and interests, less so to Karin towards whom she had therefore a sense of duty amounting almost to a sense of guilt. Having no direct human sympathy with her she tried to follow her in her studies and became deeply interested in Karin's chief pursuit, psychoanalysis. The rest of us heard so much talk about this that to this day I am allergic to the whole subject.

Of B.B.'s family I met first the eldest of his three sisters, Senda, and her husband Professor Herbert Abbot from Smith College, Northampton. I rather expected to find B.B.'s sister socially inferior to him, a contrast so frequent between a highly gifted self-made man and his nearest relations. I found her on the contrary not only very goodlooking and well-dressed but very much a lady, lively and easy to talk to, nowhere near B.B. intellectually and much more American-ized than he ever was, but well informed and with a spon-taneously gay temperament. The only difficulty in the spring of 1920 during the Abbot visit arose from Senda and Herbert's being passionately pro-French and anti-German and from Logan's intense enjoyment in getting them involved into violent discussions with B.B. for whom at that moment the French political rôle was the most damnable.

When a year later B.B.'s youngest sister Rachel and her husband Professor Ralph Barton Perry arrived for a long stay I was sent down to the station to meet them and I remember how I recognized Rachel at once as B.B.'s sister by her small graceful figure and her wonderfully expressive eyes. B.B. enjoyed his youngest sister's vitality and sense of fun, her *Pfiffigkeit* as he used to call it, but preferred her husband to her. Ralph Perry was indeed a delightful man, thoughtful, thorough, sometimes a little pedantic but never insistently so, and gifted with a most exquisite dry sense of humour. As a devoted pupil of William James he belonged to the kind of American world to which B.B. was ever nostal-gically harking back. They had a great deal in common and their intimacy and pleasure in each other's company kept growing with the years and lasted till late into their lives.

B.B.'s unmarried sister Bessie I met last of all. She too was small and delicate with marvellous eyes, fine features and lovely silver white hair. Cultivated, well read, subtle in her appreciation of literature and art, gifted as a sculptor, in artistic sensibility she was nearest to B.B.

B.B. to Nicky   December 31st 1922
> . . . My sister is turning out a totally different person from what she used to be. She is alive, zestful, intelligent, and perceptive. She owes it all to her sculpture and I bless it for giving point and direction to her life.

Mary was filled with good intentions towards B.B.'s family and conscientiously carried out her duty of writing regularly to B.B.'s mother. But her heart was not in it. The backgrounds were too different: Mary's of absolute security, affluence and optimism, the other of insecurity, financial and perhaps also social struggles. Mary was too rough-hewn for these quiveringly sensitive women whose feelings were easily hurt, for whom small attentions and proofs of affection—considered by Mary beneath contempt—were vitally important. In their turn they were perhaps not able to appreciate fully the big generous make-up of Mary's nature.

I never heard any other relations of B.B.'s mentioned until on his return from America in 1921 he spoke repeatedly of his regard for a young second cousin and promising lawyer, Lawrence Berenson. During all the following years Lawrence alone or accompanied by his family came regularly to stay in Florence and it was to him that B.B. entrusted all his financial assets and whom he designated as chief executor of his will.

By people who knew him only slightly B.B. has been repeatedly accused of feeling uncomfortable about being a Jew. In all the years I spent close to him I was never aware of this. Already the fact that he did not hesitate to choose a cousin who was definitely a member of the Jewish community as his general agent and adviser speaks against it. Had he had any snobbish wish not to be taken for a Jew, he would have certainly tried to find a Christian *homme de confiance* and he would have fought shy of his Jewish relations. In later years, particularly after the Second World War, a number of them came to I Tatti and were hospitably received by him. B.B. liked to speak of his early years in a closed community and was proud to be carrying on its traditions of great learning. In a diary I kept off and on during my first years at I Tatti among other sayings of B.B.'s I wrote down the following: "In the community to which I belonged as a child one of the things that left a deep impression on my mind was the profound respect for learning. No separation between one social class and the other existed in these Jewish communities, only the separation between the learned and the unlearned man. I never noticed considerations of money or worldly values, but became aware of an almost ferocious idealism."

What exasperated B.B. was the tendency of "goys" to speak of Jews as if one was like the other while in his eyes they were just as differentiated as any other human society. He may have felt uncomfortable over being measured with the same yardstick as certain *nouveaux-riches* Jews with whom he felt as little connection as he would have with any such Christians.

WHEN I STARTED being in daily contact with both Berensons, it did not take me long to understand that B.B. was not easy to manage or to serve and that Mary tended to brush him the wrong way. Through my father I knew the workings of a Mediterranean temperament only too well and such was B.B.'s through and through, in spite of the coat of paint left on him by his Bostonian education. The strong current of Jewish puritanism was not unlike the austerity so common among southern Italian people and my father had a lot of it in his nature. Both my father and B.B. had the weakness of many self-made men, the lack of a *Kinderstube,* of a good nursery with inbred rules of how to control one's temper. Being the eldest son of very young parents and mostly looked after by his grandparents, B.B. must have been egregiously spoilt by them. Besides, his family was one of the most important if not the first in his native village, Butrimanz in Lithuania, and probably everybody allowed him to indulge in his slightest whim and helped him to develop a good conceit of himself, all the more so as he was far ahead of his contemporaries in his studies. What he must have suffered in reaching New England and in not finding this atmosphere of worship any longer around him is hard to imagine. It explains—at least to me—why he was afterwards so keen on recapturing what from his childhood he must have felt was due to him, a first place in society.

It was trying to see him get into uncontrolled rages over the small mishaps and annoyances in the daily routine of work. Yet it was as easy to get him out of such moods as getting a child out of its tantrums with the help of a new toy. Mary never adjusted herself to his outbursts of temper and called the days when they occurred "black serpent days." One of the causes for them was the correspondence with the Duveens. Sometimes when the post brought a letter from them all would be smooth and easy. One look from B.B. at the photograph of the picture in question would be enough for him to write the required answer advising for or against its purchase. But on other days it was a rather nerve-racking business. B.B. would ask for a number of photographs for comparison, Mary would start looking for them frantically, then call for my help only to find me utterly inadequate, for during the first years the photos were still under her management and I only helped her occasionally to put new photos away. Then B.B. would appear in the library and relieve his feelings by being savage to both of us. Later when we knew each other better I was able to tease him and to make him laugh by telling him that he was no good at making a scene. "Your voice does not carry. When my father made a scene the whole house resounded from the power of his voice."

"Black serpent days" could also grow out of Mary's passionate concern for her daughters and their offspring, particularly for their financial problems. Having left her two little girls to the care of their grandmother when she began to follow B.B. all over the continent, she felt guilty towards them and as if nothing she did for them was ever enough. B.B. on the other hand felt that the allowance they were getting from him was generous enough. Whenever Mary, after a sleepless night, decided to ask B.B. for more money, she would sail into his room in the early morning, at the worst possible hour for him since he tended to wake up in an anxious and nervous state of mind. At another time of the day she might have had better results but could not admit that some adaptation to his moods might be helpful for achieving what she wanted. Already in the first years, although I was far from feeling at my ease with B.B., I started acting as go-between on such occasions, sometimes with success, more often with none.

Another sore point between Mary and B.B. was B.B.'s writing. Almost invariably Mary—imbued with Logan's rules of what good writing should be—found fault with it. And generally she expressed her fault-finding in a disagreeable contemptuous tone which drove B.B. into stubborn defence of his own careless way of writing. Even I, a foreigner, frequently detected errors of syntax or grammar in his first drafts and could see how justified Mary's criticism was. Whenever Trevy undertook to go over one of B.B.'s manuscripts, he proposed alterations and corrections gently and quietly and B.B. accepted them gratefully.

Mary to Nicky   Saltino/Vallombrosa   August 1921
      . . . B.B. has written a long article for the *Dedalo* on two Greek pictures of about 1200 which are in the Kahn and Hamilton collections in New York. He has been enjoying himself hugely over it and there has not been a single thing for which you are responsible that has gone wrong. His way of writing has not changed a bit. He scribbles down whatever he has in his head, in long ponderous awkward sentences, almost unpunctuated and then turns it over to me to put into shape. Then I groan and toil and that is where I am now. The next step is when we fight like devils over my changes. . . .

Mary's criticism of B.B.'s style of writing did not however diminish her appreciation of the contents. When during one of her cures she started re-reading B.B.'s early letters she wrote to me:

      . . . Those old letters written in B.B.'s cramped handwriting are not easy to read. I have not yet got through the autumn of 1890. But these are probably the most valuable letters, for B.B. at 25 was already exactly what he now is, mystical, ecstatic and scientific as regards pictures, interested in origins and development and influences, anti-democratic, anti-philanthropic, believing in culture above all else. It is all most interesting to me, but very slow work.

But I remember also very harmonious and happy days when Mary, after a good night, was in her best *lebensbejahende*—saying yes to life—mood and B.B. reacted to it joyfully. They could tease each other most charmingly and laugh and reminisce, and discuss books and pictures and people. There was much they had in common, apart from the interest in their work, love of the same kind of poetry, affection for their closest friends, intense enjoyment of landscape and sightseeing, memories of their past life. Sometimes they seemed to me like two musical instruments with a few of the highest and lowest notes out of tune. If one managed to play them without touching these unfortunate notes all was well.

Mary's note out of tune was her tiger-like love for her cubs and all that grew out of it, while B.B.'s was his suspiciousness. I could not help connecting this with generations of ancestors living in small secluded communities, always on the look-out for trouble, for persecutions, for clashes with Russian police or officials. When we drew nearer to each other we talked about this quite openly and he did not deny it. Many of the disagreeable things in his early career, clashes with dealers, quarrels with colleagues, must have been made much worse by this unfortunate tendency, by his being so ready to jump to conclusions, to interpret the behaviour of others as more inimical than it really was. No doubt his astonishing career and his so swiftly growing fame must have aroused strong feelings of envy and many malicious comments as to his being or not being scrupulous in business transactions. But his passionate reaction to all this cannot have improved things.

Perhaps the best thing I was able to do for B.B., far more important than my very amateurish secretarial assistance and so-called collaboration in his work, was to inspire him with complete confidence. He could at times get thoroughly annoyed with me but he never doubted that if I had made a mistake it had been with the best intentions in the world. Almost instinctively I learned to play a very delicate instrument and hardly ever to strike the notes that were out of tune.

CHAPTER VI

Spring in Greece [1923]

E ARLY IN 1923 our thoughts began to turn towards Greece.
B.B. was against reading intensely about the country
one was going to visit and believed more in doing so while
one was there or afterwards. He told me of how he had once
made the mistake of reading so voraciously about Egypt that
he finally gave up the idea of going there because he found
himself saturated and bored with the whole subject. So my
preparations for Greece consisted in selecting books to take
along and in collecting practical information. Happily in
those days it was not yet necessary to have a fixed schedule
months in advance and plans could be adjusted to the advice
of friends on the spot.

The trip was entirely to Mary's taste without the faintest
odour of smartness about it. Logan was to meet us in Brindisi
and the Kingsley Porters in Athens. Parry was to come along
with the car but not the long-nosed Eliza, who had asked
for a holiday. She was still there to help us with the packing
and when I said to her that I found it difficult to imagine
what one might need on the trip she answered: "It is not
the question of what you might need, Miss, but what you
might do without." In her place we took with us a young
Irish woman, Elizabeth Percival, whom Naima Löfroth had
had the good luck to pick up in Florence. She turned out
a real treasure and was to remain with us for over seventeen

years. She was pretty and graceful, full of fun and laughter
and proverbs and droll sayings. The only serious consequence
of so much concentrated Irish charm was that Parry fell
desperately in love with her. No wonder, considering how
much they were thrown into each other's company in a foreign land.

While Parry preceded us with the car and most of the
luggage, we went by train to Brindisi and as we had time to
spare got out at Bari to have a look at the Cathedral and at
San Nicola. As we were wandering through the old town we
met the great Good Friday procession very much in the
style of the famous Spanish displays although probably more
rustic. The huge elaborately carved Passion scenes were
preceded and followed by young men wearing crowns of
thorns and having their faces painted with red blotches,
symbolizing drops of blood. Between the groups small children were walking, incredibly serious and dignified, dressed
as Roman Centurions or as Holy Women or Apostles or
saints. All very solemn and at the same time delightfully
intimate.

Next morning in Brindisi we met Logan on the Lloyd
Triestino boat in the best of dispositions as he liked nothing
better than being on the sea. Arriving in Greece we were
met at Piraeus by the loquacious Milanese chauffeur of the
Porters and when we called out to him *"Come va, Anfossi?"*
he shouted back, *"Male, perchè sa, qui si parla il greco"*—
badly because here, you must know, they speak Greek. In
the Hotel Grande Bretagne the Porters had put their rooms
at Mary's and B.B.'s disposal and were camping in a miserable
one, where Kingsley could only develop his photos by shut-
ting himself up in a narrow cupboard. Nevertheless when
Lucy complained of such lack of comfort he said: "Lucy,
you should be grateful to B.B. and Mary for giving you the
chance to learn how to enjoy Greece in spite of these uncomfortable quarters." The reason for the hotel being so crowded

and unable to give us the rooms promised to us was the sudden influx of fugitives from Asia Minor after the defeat of the Greek army. All around the Theseum they were living in tents and even a number of churches had been turned over to them for temporary living quarters. It is from then on, I believe, that Athens lost its aspect of a well-proportioned smallish town with low classical buildings, such as we still saw and enjoyed there.

My first impression as we were driving from Piraeus to Athens was of a raging north wind, of clouds of dust through which I perceived what seemed a ridiculously small group of classical ruins on top of a hill. When I looked at it again next morning in dazzling sunlight I did get the thrill I had been expecting and got it again and again climbing up the steps to the Propylaea or looking at the Acropolis from the Pnyx at sunset time. Unfortunately both Mary and Logan suffered from the icy *tramontana* of the first days and we had to take several excursions without them in the Porter's car. One of these was to Chalkis where an utterly ridiculous thing happened to us. We arrived in the afternoon and managed first of all to see, housed in a sort of shed, one of the most beautiful and tender groups of archaic sculpture.[1] To look at it was B.B.'s only reason for taking the trip. Next morning we took a drive inland to visit the ruins of Eritrea and some Byzantine remains that Kingsley was hankering after. On our return we told Anfossi to collect our bags at once so that right after lunch we could start on our way back to Athens. He left the car at the door of the inn facing the sea front where no parapet separated the sidewalk from the water. We had hardly started ordering our lunch when a waiter rushed in waving his napkin wildly and shouting something about the *Aftomobil*. We ran out—the car was gone. Kingsley started running towards the sea front and I

---

[1] Now, I am told, transferred to one of the museums in Athens.

after him. There was the car gently basking on the water, wavelets caressing the cushions of the seat. Weeks later we met a woman in the train on our way to Olympia who recognized us and told us how from the terrace of the Chalkis inn she had watched some small boys approaching the car and pushing forward the brakes. The car had started rolling, had hesitated a second on the brink of the water, then had plunged in. To return to our plight, all we could do was to watch how Anfossi, without knowing a word of Greek, just by shouting and gesticulating managed to get the car pulled out of the water in a relatively short time. Meanwhile news of this extraordinary event had spread all over the island and for hours after the car had been salvaged crowds of people came just to peer into the water at the spot where it all happened.

ON OUR RETURN to Athens we found Mary much better but Logan no longer his own self, suffering acutely from an infection and only occasionally enjoying sights and excursions. He loved to sit on the steps of the Parthenon and to peruse Baedeker or to have it read out to him. "What a precious book," he would say. "What a unique quality! One can read it again and again and always as if it was for the first time."

The people we met in Athens belonged almost exclusively to the archaeological world. There was Della Seta, the head of the Italian School, Wilhelm Doerpfeld, formerly the assistant of Schliemann, from the German School, Charles Picard, the head of the French School, A. J. B. Wace, the head of the British School, and his American colleagues Bert Hodge Hill and Charles W. Blegen. It was at Della Seta's that we met Doro Levi [2] for the first time, as fellow of the

---

[2] Since 1946 head of the Italian School of Archaeology in Athens.

Italian School. Later on he became a close friend of B.B.'s.

Our next long excursion was to Olympia, by train as there was then no road by which one could reach it. We were to spend the night in Patras and had no sooner entered the inn than Mary began clamouring for bottles of mineral water. The innkeeper said he had never heard of it. I was sent to get it at a chemist's. Same answer. When I returned to the hotel B.B. and Logan had turned to what the inexhaustible Baedeker had to say about Patras and had found his first words to be in praise of its pure and refreshing water.

In Olympia B.B. had a bad attack of lumbago and while I was attending to him the other four paid their first visit to the museum without us. They came back visibly disappointed with the famous sculptures. Indignation chiefly, I believe, helped B.B. to get over his complaint and the next morning he drove us all back to the museum and managed to kindle us with the fire of his enthusiasm, all except Kingsley, who cared for classical art only in its most archaic forms. B.B. raged at him continually for concentrating his interests too narrowly on Byzantine art.

Not that B.B. was himself indifferent to the Byzantine monuments in Greece. They fascinated him but never to the exclusion of everything else. We went again and again to the small churches inside Athens, to other chapels outside of the town, to Kaisariani, to Daphne. One morning, not realizing that it was the Orthodox Easter Monday and a great religious holy day we set out for the National Museum and finding it shut decided to have another look at the mosaics in Daphne. We found the church crowded with country people and a group of women in one corner busy undressing their babies while men and boys were bustling about helping the *Papas* to mix cold and hot water in a small bathtub, getting towels ready, lighting candles. The *Papas* while measuring the temperature of the water with his elbow like an old Nanny kept scolding the women for their slowness

81

in getting the babies undressed. Before we realized it we found ourselves received into the circle with burning tapers in our hands, close to the bathtub and watching the total immersion of each baby, as required by the Orthodox baptism ritual, and its furious yells of protest greeted with shouts of laughter by the bystanders. We both loved the spontaneity and good cheer of it all and forgot the real object of our visit.

Our excursion to the Peloponnese began with Corinth and the ascension of the Acrocorinth and ended with Andritsina and the temple of Bassae. To avoid some of the long drives Mary and Logan took the boat to Nauplia and joined us there. For the second part down to Sparta and Mistra and from there to Arcadia a truck carrying field-beds and a cook followed us, for the inns and beds were more than doubtful and every morning the dragoman would appear at Mary's door with the question: *"Madame, avez-vous eu des animaux?"* When we left Sparta a car coming in the opposite direction made frantic signs and when we stopped two men got out of it and had a long conversation with our dragoman. They wanted to borrow our cook for the benefit of young King George and his bride, who were on their way to Sparta. We explained that it was exactly for our trip into Arcadia that we needed the cook most urgently. A little later we met the car of the royal couple but never heard how the question of their food was settled.

Our last excursion with the Porters took us to Distomo, following a river-bed rather than a road, and from there on horseback to the convent of Hosios Lucas, where a huge bearded *hegumenos* and a thin bearded *diakon* received us hospitably, having given up their own rooms to us while they camped in the garden. In the morning we could see them washing themselves at the fountain and rolling up their hair with feminine gestures into a bun, then pushing it under their tall caps. The *hegumenos'* sonorous eloquence went on steadily and unrelentingly. Having learnt enough modern Greek in Athens to muddle through, I had to sustain the conversation with him helped by B.B.'s knowledge of ancient Greek. He presided at the head of the table and served us and when a whole lamb was put before him he skilfully cut out both its eyes and placed one on B.B.'s and one on my plate. Gradually he became a little too friendly and made me feel uneasy. On the second morning while we were all gathered in the church studying the mosaics, I had to return to our rooms to fetch some medicine for B.B. Stealthily the *hegumenos* followed me into my room, caught my waist in his huge hands like in an iron prong and wanted to kiss me. I yelled in protest and must have looked so frightened that he retired with a look of offended dignity. At the two following meals he never lifted his eyes from his plate and only the next morning when I was already mounted on my horse he appeared and offered me a rose. I daresay he was used to dealing with more accommodating tourist ladies.

Riding along the slopes of the Parnassus accompanied by the gentle ringing of the flock-leaders' bells down in the valley, we reached Arachova, where Mary and Logan were waiting for us with both cars. In Delphi B.B. was already full of nostalgia at having to leave Greece. I see him in the mind's eye wandering about in the temple area wearing the same topee he had used in Egypt to protect him from the strong sun of early June. He made us all laugh by assuring us that Delphi as a going concern must have looked like the famous cemetery in Genoa, filled with hideous little sanctuaries one on top of the other. He loved to startle one with such debunking statements, as when he described the Acropolis covered with statues, each carrying a small umbrella to protect it from birds' droppings. Once when he and I were climbing about in the theatre of Dionysius and I tried piously to imagine how wonderful the performances must have been in antiquity, he said: "But do not forget that they were all munching garlic while watching the show." B.B. had been once before in Greece, in the autumn of 1888. It seemed to him all-important to have his feet firmly planted on classical ground before attempting to get acquainted with the various layers of art and culture in Italy. So on entering Italy for the first time he went from Milan straight to Brindisi and took ship for the Piraeus.

His early impressions and raptures were awakened by our visit in 1923 and he spoke again and again of how relatively unchanged they were in essentials. Of course many treasures, like part of the archaic statuary in the Acropolis museum, were not yet on display in 1888 nor perhaps the golden cups from Mycenae. Excursions to Sparta and Mistra, to Bassae or Hosios Lucas he was unable to take during his first visit and Bassae in particular represented the fulfilment of a long-cherished dream. Again I see him before me galloping away fearlessly and unmindful of the narrow path along a precipitous ravine, while I being a hopeless coward had already climbed down from my horse and was following on foot.

We spent a day in Corfu on our way back to Italy and saw in a small museum the archaic Gorgon, grinning, powerful and life-enhancing. As we were steaming along the Dalmatian coast the captain told us that we were due to reach Venice in the early morning of the next day. We decided to get up and watch our entrance into port. The sun had not yet risen when we climbed to the upper deck. We were already inside the lagoon and Venice lay stretched out before us like a fata morgana, not a soul moving in it, San Giorgio and its trembling reflection in the water on our left, the Doge's palace on our right, the opening of the Canal Grande and the Salute before us. It would have seemed natural to see it all disappear before our eyes like a vision or a dream.

During our short stay in Venice we happened to meet several of B.B.'s smart friends, among others Mrs. Lanier and Mrs. Ralph Curtis. The latter asked us all three to dinner at the Palazzo Barbaro. I remember huge and rather sugary portraits by Sargent but not who else had been invited. What I recall vividly is the talk which turned unfortunately towards politics and the blind hatred of Germany, the rejoicing over the occupation of the Ruhr, appalling manifestations of fanatical ignorance. When we were able to leave I cheered up Mary and B.B. by telling them what one of my Baltic uncles used to say on particularly difficult occasions: "We should have run out into the street and called for help."

It was the same Palazzo Barbaro which Isabella Gardner used to rent from Ralph Curtis for the summer months. B.B. told me of how he was once asked by her to spend a couple of weeks there with her and how on arrival he told her that he was looking forward to meeting a woman friend of his expected in Venice at that time. To his surprise and disappointment no message from her reached him. On his last day he mentioned this to Mrs. Gardner. She laughed and said: "Of course there was a message from her, but it never reached you because I tore it up."

BACK AT I TATTI, when Mary had already left for England and B.B.'s sister Bessie was staying with us, I had an unexpected impression of Mary's family background through the visit of her cousin Carey Thomas accompanied by her brother Dr. Thomas from Baltimore and his wife. The Thomas couple were very civilized and gentle people while Carey seemed to me a real termagant of a woman, arrogant, crude and childishly ignorant. And yet she has been—I am told—a real driving power in the field of higher education in the United States. It must have been my fault that I was never able—for I met her again and again—to appreciate her positive qualities. Her dictatorial self-assurance put me off too much. Compared to this formidable cousin, Mary—who certainly had a crude side to her—was like a well-seasoned wine.

Then we all dispersed, B.B. to meet Mary in Gastein, I to meet my three Anreps in Venice, Bessie to return to Paris and to her sculpture.

It was sad for me to see B.B. go off on his own. I knew already that a separation from him, even a short one, meant cutting the golden thread of continuity which he knew how to spin in an almost magical way. Later on when my people settled down in Florence and I generally spent the weekends with them, I became aware of a slight, an ever so slight difference on my return on Monday morning. It was as if there was something to reconquer, to make entirely my own again. B.B. often used the image of love being like a delicate plant that had to be cared for day by day, that one could never afford to leave unattended. Living near him and for him I learnt the full truth of this.

CHAPTER VII

London and Paris [1923]

A<small>T THE END OF</small> A<small>UGUST</small> I left Venice to join Mary and B.B. in Switzerland and from there we set out for Paris— partly to inspect the apartment we were to occupy during October, partly because Duveen had entreated B.B. to come to his help in a controversial question of attribution. A replica of Leonardo's *Belle Ferronière* had been offered to Duveen and he had declared it to be a copy done much later than the original. This was considered by the owner as damage to her property and she had brought a lawsuit against Duveen. We went to Duveen's office on our first morning in Paris and found Sir Joseph in great excitement over the whole question and also indignant over an article in the daily paper containing a full description of his establishment, the organization of his business, his employment of well-known experts, etc. "Who could have written such an article?" he kept repeating. "Anybody who has been listening to your talk, Sir Joseph, could have written it," said his chief assistant very quietly. There was something of Sancho Panza in his way of treating his boss and the boss, having a good sense of humour, enjoyed it thoroughly. In the afternoon B.B. had to appear before the American consul general to let himself be interrogated by the legal adviser of the picture's owner. Having various errands to do I arrived a little late and the session had already started. I sat down near Mary and asked her in a whisper: "How is it going?" Mary whispered back: "Bernard has already made a fool of himself." What she referred to I never found out. The answers I heard him give seemed very simple and convincing. Nevertheless I seem to remember that Duveen had to pay a good deal of money in the end. What happened to the picture? Nobody ever spoke of it again. I daresay some day it will turn up once more and create agitation in the world of art critics and attributors.

Between sessions at the consulate and errands I managed to have an intoxicating first impression of Paris on a warm September day with the foliage of the trees beginning to turn and the sun setting in a rose-coloured sky.

Then we left for London and I had my first taste of a channel crossing. It happened to be one of the worst, a real glimpse of hell worthy to be described by Dante. B.B. and Mary had retired to a cabin and were spared the ghastly spectacle which brought me very near to collapsing myself. But soon the friendly atmosphere on the English shore and even more the peaceful beauty of the Kentish countryside made me forget the discomforts of the channel boat.

The beginning of our life in London was not exactly peaceful. Thinking only of the financial advantage of her beloved Ray, Mary had persuaded B.B. to rent the Strachey apartment in Gordon Square and no sooner had we settled down in it than the rows began. B.B. found it slovenly, ill-kept, badly appointed, worthy of what he called the "intellectual cave-dwellers." He never stopped cursing and grumbling as long as we were in it. It was in a way his own fault, for he should have known better than to accept such a doubtful proposal. I often teased him over his way of nursing a grievance, like a dog who hides a bone and digs it out again and again just to worry it. Added to this, Alys Russell had hired a car for us with a lady driver whose knowledge of the streets and of the traffic regulations of

London was more than sketchy. Of course B.B. came to the conclusion that this was just one of Alys' female protégés who had to be kept afloat at his expense. Mary's and Alys' perseverance in making arrangements that were sure to go against B.B.'s grain was amazing. Everything was explained by B.B.'s being "unreasonable."

The amount of things I tried to absorb in such a short time, the number of new people I met, seems to me now almost unbelievable. I marvel at B.B.'s and Mary's energy and at my own digestive power. Besides almost daily visits to museums and art collections, we spent weekends in Oxford and Cambridge, and went repeatedly to Windsor and Hampton Court. A weekend at Buckhurst staying with Robert Benson and his family was my first and only experience of being in a big English country-house kept in the old style, with housemaids and under-housemaids and iron rules about their duties and privileges. When I asked Elizabeth to call me in the morning she told me that it was out of the question, as only the under-housemaid had the right to call me.

Mary and B.B. made a point of taking me along wherever they went and I found this a little embarrassing and would have preferred to let things develop more slowly and casually. Except for Lady Colefax, Trevy and the Kitsons I had few links of my own in England. General and Lady Kitson with their daughter Monica (later married to a naval officer, John Knox) we had met in Egypt and taken various excursions with them in Luxor and from the Mena House Hotel. It was the beginning of a lifelong friendship. Trevy's place near Dorking I went to see and found the wooded countryside all around it enchanting, but his wife rather forbidding and the appointments of the house decidedly on the Spartan side.

In Alys' and Logan's dear old house, Big Chilling, near Southampton, we met Salvemini, who with premonitions of future exile in his mind was spending a few months in an English parsonage learning English. He told us that he had reached the point of understanding perfectly what he himself was trying to say but not a word of what others said to him.

B.B. never seemed to me as happy in London as I later saw him in Paris. Partly no doubt because of the unfortunate dwelling and driving arrangements made by Mary and Alys but partly because his whole relation to England was in the nature of an unrequited love. He admired England more than any other country in every aspect of its political and social life, but never felt completely at ease with its inhabitants, excepting of course some very special friends. He himself felt sure that there was something foreign and a bit uncanny about him which did not allow English people to feel really at home with him. Being a foreigner myself it is difficult for me to say how far he was right in having this ineradicable suspicion. As an instance of how offensive his vehemence and impetuosity could be, I remember a very stormy luncheon party in the Gordon Square house. Trevy had brought two young English *avant-garde* men of letters, Raymond Mortimer and Francis Birrell, whom B.B. was particularly anxious to meet. Instead of getting them to talk, he began shooting the darts of his irony against the poetry of Rupert Brooke, who was at that moment the idol of the younger generation. Both Birrell and Mortimer rose up in his defence and Birrell particularly was almost beside himself with indignation. Trevy's endeavours to smooth him out were not very successful. I do not remember B.B.'s ever meeting Francis Birrell again before his premature death. Mortimer asked B.B. out to dinner and B.B. came back delighted and seemed to have enjoyed himself enormously. But it was only much later, after World War II, that Raymond became a great friend of B.B.'s and one that B.B. never got tired of seeing.

EARLY IN OCTOBER Mary persuaded us to try the new way of reaching Paris by aeroplane. Not only was I very much frightened and dazed by the noise, but I hated to see the landscape like children's toys and the sea like a quilted bedspread. It has taken me almost forty years to overcome my reluctance against this type of transportation and I still regard it as a convenience in case of an emergency but not as a pleasure.

In Paris the apartment in a small hotel near the Etoile turned out to be most satisfactory. It had no restaurant but an excellent kitchen and every morning a treasure of an old waiter would turn up to take our orders for the meals to be served in our sitting room.

In France B.B. was in his element perhaps even more than in Italy. His tendency to express himself paradoxically was readily understood and appreciated, his vehement manner was not taken seriously and that was just what he wanted. Never have I seen him so bubbling over with mirth and with happy repartees as in the company of men like the Abbé Mugnier or Vignier, with women like Gabrielle Lacaze or Philomène de Lévis or Natalie Barney. Natalie, although American born, is essentially a flower of the Parisian earth.

Of course there was no lack of female worshippers all around B.B. in Paris, foremost among them the classically beautiful Linda Cole-Porter, one of the brightest stars on the American-Parisian sky, reminding one of the archaic *Korae* in the Acropolis museum. At that time B.B. still went himself to the telephone and we could see him hurrying in his dressing-gown and with flapping green morocco slippers to answer the call of one of these fair ladies. I do not remember what Mary's mood was like during our stay in Paris. Many of B.B.'s friends did certainly not meet with her approval while others meant a lot to her, like for instance Salomon Reinach who, ever since Mary's and B.B.'s early days in Paris, had remained very close to them. She saw

Edith Wharton frequently, and when Carey Thomas and Ray appeared in Paris she was able to devote herself to them wholeheartedly. Other favorites of both Berensons were the literary critic Charles Du Bos and his wife, Zezette, and Placci's nephew Lucien Henraux, married to the Florentine Elisabetta de Piccolellis.

A disappointment for me was meeting the famous Walter Berry,[1] Edith Wharton's adored friend, whose charm and gifts B.B. had described to me. He asked us all three to lunch in his apartment in the Rue de Varenne, full of lovely things and precious books. There were several other people all belonging to the "chic" set. At the table the conversation became fixed on the depreciation of the German mark and again like that evening in Venice in the Curtis house the gleeful and blind satisfaction over the total ruin of Germany was frightening. I should have expected greater perspicacity from a man of Walter Berry's education and intelligence, but he was the slave of a smart clique and just played up to its whims and fashions. Years later I had fortunately the chance to see what he could be like when cut off from what he called "notre bande."

Among B.B.'s old friends the one I felt most at home with was his contemporary, Charlotte de Cossé, a wonderful type of French aristocrat, highly cultivated and much travelled and yet close to earth in the fruitiness and frankness of her language. She was always at home in the late afternoon and we would find her and her old friend the Byzantinist Gustave Schlumberger seated opposite each other by the open fire, ready for serious talk as well as for the most uproarious and salacious gossip.

Now and then B.B. would take me with him to call on old Froehner, who had still been assistant keeper of the antiquities at the Louvre during the last years of Napoleon

---

[1] 1859–1927, American international lawyer, resident in Paris.

III's empire. A man of vast learning and rather gruff manners, he liked to see B.B. and to discuss archaeological discoveries and problems with him. Seated in a small study lined with books, a fur cap on his head and a candle as the only illumination, he looked like a portrait by Van Eyck.

Besides our frequent visits to the Louvre and to other museums, B.B. went with me a number of times to the Bibliothèque Nationale in connection with his interest in Byzantine late antique and mediaeval art. The struggle we had to see what was *à la réserve* is almost unbelievable. When Monsieur Omont, the keeper of the manuscript section, stomped in and found us already waiting for him he would have liked to throw us out like the librarian at Wolfenbüttel. Here was an astonishing difference from the easy access to the most famous manuscripts we had experienced in the British Museum and were to experience a year later in the Vatican Library.

EARLY IN NOVEMBER we returned to I Tatti where it was not easy for me to settle down and get into harness after such a whirlwind of new impressions. B.B. had an uncanny way of starting on a new project immediately and of expecting everything he needed to be at his disposal. In Walter Berry's library he had seen a codex with illuminations by a Sienese artist and had promised to publish it in the *Gazette des Beaux-Arts*. Mary was not interested in the subject and for the first time I had to collect all the material for study and comparison on my own.

A friendship that was to last for the rest of B.B.'s life had its origin in that same late autumn. The crown prince of Sweden came to spend a few weeks in Florence with his newly married second wife, Princess Louise of Battenberg, and Carlo Loeser brought them up one afternoon. Taking them round the house B.B. was at once struck by the intelligent interest the crown prince showed and by his thorough appreciation, particularly of the Far Eastern objects. Several visits followed the first meeting and each time B.B. became increasingly aware of the crown prince's personality, not only as a passionate archaeologist and lover of beautiful things but as a "work of art" in himself, to use one of B.B.'s favourite terms.

The year 1923 ended with my having the great joy of spending Christmas at the Villino with my three Anreps. The years spent together in Russia had tied us together very firmly and to be able to do something for them that might alleviate their difficult refugee existence gave me immense joy. Mary and B.B. understood this so well that they offered me the chance to look after my nephew's education, which meant taking at least one burden from them.

CHAPTER VIII

Daily Life at I Tatti

LOOKING BACK on many other journeys during the following years they appear to me like a sequence of sculptured scenes in high relief against an *estompé* background of daily life at I Tatti. And yet it is exactly that daily life with its rhythm of work and play, of walks and talks and readings that I should like to recreate. Why do I find it difficult, at any rate much more difficult than describing our journeys? Perhaps because at home I never experienced the delicious sense of leisure that would come over me when we started out for a trip, even a short one, to Siena or Pisa or Lucca or Ravenna. Being by nature averse to hurry and afraid of having too much on my hands, my crowded days at I Tatti have left in my memory an image without any clear outline. I see myself rushing about, trying to cope with too many things at the same time, always a bit anxious over my lack of experience, over my not having been educated systematically. As Mary was getting increasingly tired of the household, the receiving of guests, the kitchen, the planning of meals, I began to step in to give orders in her name, to discuss plans and dates with her, to entertain visitors and to take them round the art collection. During our sight-seeing expeditions I was not only able to listen to B.B. without having so many other things on my mind but could enjoy B.B.'s conversations with Mary instead of being afraid of their quarrelling, which at home was an everyday occurrence. Reasons for it seemed to lurk behind every corner. If it was not over Mary's extravagant expenditure for children and grandchildren, it would be over Mary's tendency to "work people off" regardless of their being or not being suited to each other, while B.B. wanted to consider invitations carefully and get people together who might stimulate each other. Or Mary would consider a piece of writing of his as unworthy of him in style and construction, or B.B. would reproach her for having ordered food that was too rich and indigestible for him.

B.B.'s DAILY ROUTINE was a very regular one. After a short morning walk in the garden he would settle down to his work in his study. If he ever appeared in the library it was a storm signal: something had gone wrong and he wanted the right book or photo at a moment's notice. If one was lucky and got them quickly and perhaps some additional material with them, he expressed his delight and gratitude very readily. Just as he could look at a work of art, at a landscape as if he were seeing them for the first time, so no service rendered him, even by a humble person, was ever taken for granted. That made working for him, in spite of the difficulties and harassing aspects of it, very rewarding and certainly never boring. Another thing I appreciated greatly was that our personal relation, our deep affection for each other, seemed non-existent when we were at work. He could get into a rage and storm and scold but never accept my blunders with an indulgent smile because it was I who had committed them.

Both B.B. and Mary were intensely letter-conscious and indignant over any delay in bringing the mail up to their rooms. As a rule they got masses of it, far too much for my taste. B.B. was relieved if none of the letters contained any unpleasant or sad news. Mary, once her hunger for family news had been satisfied, was full of pleasant anticipations. "There is no telling whether a letter might not contain a cheque," she would say. This was part of her curious and sometimes rather disconcerting attitude towards money. She seemed to regard it as a miraculous spring that might bubble up anywhere, anyhow, and as a panacea to cure most evils.

If things went smoothly with B.B.'s work I would not see him again till lunch-time. Our matutinal work on the "lists" began several years later. Guests staying in the house or guests from Florence or from the neighbourhood would gather in the small eighteenth-century *salotto* (which later became the French library) and generally we had to wait for B.B. He was, as Mary used to say, a "just-muster." Meals at I Tatti were always a very informal affair. B.B. has been, I know, accused of being a snob, perhaps because he enjoyed well-bred people and elegant women just as other men care for sports or cards as a relaxation from their work. It never interfered with his serious pursuits and he certainly never narrowed down his universe by conforming to the conventions or rules of a given clique or group. It amused him to play their game for a time but he kept completely free socially and saw people from every walk in life, utterly indifferent to their being or not being able to reciprocate his hospitality. I never saw him or Mary bother about "even numbers" and if anybody invited to a meal at I Tatti called off at the last minute, all they would say was: "Tell them to take away a seat from the table." What B.B. cared for was to get in touch with intellectually stimulating people or to have a gay time with agreeable and cultivated members of good society. Mary approved of the first category wholeheartedly but very rarely of the second and both she and Logan were rich in jeering remarks about society people and particularly society women favoured and admired by B.B. They chuckled over the way B.B. had been taken in by smart women and had read wonderful mental capacities into them. Once, they told me, Mrs. Baldwin and her daughter Gladys Deacon had joined them in Siena and B.B., having taken Mrs. Baldwin to the picture gallery, had returned full of admiration for her intelligent remarks and her ready response to all he had shown her, saying: "It is impossible to foresee how much taste and natural feeling for beautiful things such an apparently superficial woman may have." Mary had later heard from Gladys Deacon that her mother on coming back from the picture gallery had flung herself on her bed, utterly exhausted and had exclaimed: "What a delightful man he could be if only he would stop caring for those old *croûtes!*"

Particularly pleasant and carefree was the after-lunch gathering for coffee and liqueurs, whenever possible in the lemon-house where, sheltered from the wind, even in January it could be warm enough in the sun. The ilex grove at the end of the formal garden was still in its youth and the view over the Arno valley to the hills opposite was not yet hidden by it nor spoilt by the ugly buildings that have shot up since then between the city and Rovezzano. In bad or doubtful weather coffee was served in the large library and there also we met again for tea.

Between luncheon and tea there was generally a drive combined with a walk. Each walk had its established name, like the *Weisen* of the *Meistersinger*. The Morgan walk— because it skirted the property of an Englishman called Morgan—the crest walk, the quarry walk, the tree walk, the cross-country walk, the riviera walk, and many others. Parry knew exactly where to stop and where to meet us at the other end. Whatever B.B.'s mood might have been in the house, nervous, impatient, fault-finding, in the open air he was as happy as a lark, waved his stick at the view, walked briskly except when the conversation took up his whole attention or when light and colour were particularly beautiful. He used to regard himself as a born nomad and felt like a prisoner when obliged to stay in because of foul weather or a cold.

Almost invariably B.B. dedicated the last hour before dinner to the perusal of second-hand booksellers' catalogues and to picking out what he thought might be missing in one or the other of the library's sections. Very rarely he marked books that we had already. Information about new publications he got chiefly from reading regularly a number of literary, art-historical, archaeological and generally learned magazines. Great was his eagerness to see the new arrivals, to get an impression of their general condition—in the case of second-hand books—to put aside those he wanted to read at once. We had many bitter arguments over his tendency to hoard away in his rooms books that had not yet been catalogued. It made duplicated orders unavoidable. "Don't try to play the professional librarian," he would say. "I can't stand it." The experience of having to cope with Lance Cherry, the only professional librarian he had ever employed, had been enough for him. He preferred putting up with a certain incompetence provided it was coupled with devotion to the job and readiness to follow his instructions blindly. More than once I have heard him say that he had missed his real profession by not becoming a second-hand bookseller. I doubt whether he could have been successful on the business side. He would have thrown out clients he did not like and would have asked the lowest price from those considered by him worthy of a rare book.

In one of his diaries I have found the following entry:

March 11th 1952

My library may be the product of a curious habit. It is of conning catalogues of booksellers of books chiefly old but also new. At the end of the day, exhausted by walking, tired out by talking, it rests me to look through book catalogues.

99

I mark the books I have heard of but am not sure of having. The librarian then orders those necessary and in that way the library keeps growing. Were it not restful as an occupation it could be regarded as a waste of money and—worse— a waste of shelf-room. For once a book has reached me I have not the heart to get rid of it. Most wasteful are the French catalogues. I seldom get one out of ten ordered and those are generally either the least interesting or in the worst state. The most satisfactory are the English provincial booksellers, for unexpected rarities.

Only exceptionally was there a real dinner-party and even more exceptional was it to dine out or to go to the theatre. The rule when we were alone or with intimate guests like Logan or Trevy was to spend the evening reading aloud. It was lucky for me that my father had brought me up to read to him in several languages from my childhood on. I must have been about eight when he first tried me out and found me adequate to his needs, namely to spare his overtired eyes. At Ringen in the Anrep household we had also been very fond of reading together but there it was mostly my brother-in-law who read to us. At I Tatti my reading aloud gradually developed into various sections. More serious books in the morning between B.B.'s breakfast and his getting up. Lighter ones after dinner and sometimes also before dinner. Lightest of all at night when B.B. was already in bed and did not want to miss anything important through dropping off to sleep. Mary read aloud beautifully herself and liked to do it after dinner but frequently got too sleepy to go on.

If ever I tried to protest against a boring book B.B. refused sternly to give it up. "Now that we have got so far we must go on and give it a full chance." As if it was a capital already invested and that should bring its dividends in due time. When I found Disraeli's *Coningsby* insufferably tedious B.B. said: "Oh, but you must go on! Remember that you may be the only woman on the continent who has read it."

He was omnivorous in his appetite for books and always had piles of them waiting in his study, in his dressing-room, in his bedroom, on tables, chests and chairs. As a rule I did not read books on questions of art history or criticism or archaeological discoveries to him. He preferred reading these by himself. What he liked to listen to were literary classics (in different languages), history, memoirs, letters, accounts of travel, good stories. Manzoni's *I Promessi Sposi* he heard for the first time read by me and having expected to be bored by it was bowled over by the flow of the narrative and the masterly presentation of the characters. Also Dumas' cycle of historical novels he had never read before and he found them almost too exciting. Robert Norton introduced us to Trollope's political novels and through them we all three became devout Trollopians.

Everything regarding Russia had a special place in B.B.'s heart, from its earliest historians to writers on recent events, from accounts of the first colonizers of Siberia to the diaries of the Dekabrists, from the great classics of the nineteenth century to novels reflecting life in Soviet Russia. Having discovered some of Nicolai Leskov's stories translated into English, we got a complete edition of his works in German translation and never got tired of this incomparable story-teller. Aksakov's *Russian Childhood* and *Russian Gentleman* were already among Mary's and B.B.'s favourites when I started working at I Tatti and I must have read both more than once to them during the following years.

The love of Russian things included also translations from Yiddish, like Pauline Wengeroff's *Memoiren einer jüdischen Grossmutter,* a book I had found in my brother-in-law's library in Ringen and which I was able to procure for B.B. It fascinated him and awoke many memories of his childhood in Lithuania, of the rabbi who had been his first teacher and whose beard he loved to pull, of the Sabbath atmosphere in the house and the succulent Sabbath food his mother used to prepare, of the Russian soldiers marching and of his running after them intoxicated by the rhythm of their songs. Later on we both enjoyed Shmaria Levin's *Childhood in Exile* and *Youth in Revolt* as well as Sholem Asch's great trilogy about the war and the revolution.

Both Mary and B.B. were interested in translations from Oriental languages, particularly from the Chinese, and Arthur Waley's translations of Chinese poetry were among their favourites. When the *Tale of Genji* appeared I read the whole of it twice to B.B. and some of the characters became for us like people we had known and loved.

With only a smattering knowledge of Latin and just able to read Greek letters, I could not share B.B.'s intense enjoyment of the Greek and Latin classics in the original text. But reading translations of Pausanias and Herodotus or Plato's dialogues in Kassner's magnificent rendering or Theocritus in Trevy's charming translation was better than nothing.

I have already said that the love of German literature created a bond between B.B. and me quite early in our life together. It grew and accompanied us to the very end. The *Oxford Book of German Poetry* was never missing in B.B.'s travelling library and one of his earliest letters to me contained only the short poem in Middle High German *Dû bist mîn, ich bin dîn*. His knowledge of German classical literature was amazing and his way of expressing himself in German betrayed it, for he used expressions that reminded one more of Goethe, Jung-Stilling and Jean-Paul than of contemporary German. The Romantics were his favourites but I read also a great deal of history and historical memoirs to him. As a special treat I remember reading Voigt's *Wiedererweckung des klassischen Altertums* to him, more for my benefit than his for he had known it since his youth. Had I but been like Eckermann and written down B.B.'s reflections about what we had been reading!

And then there was the world of English poetry which he opened up for me. When I learnt some of his favorite poems by heart he was even willing to let me recite them to him in spite of my defective pronunciation. Mary used to tease him about his flirtations with women always going through a phase of reading poetry together and of course I came in for my share of it.

What we would always return to when we wanted to have a really good time was the *Thousand and One Nights,* generally in the Mardrus translation. Sometimes we would compare our favourite stories with a more serious literal translation, like Payne's, and detect Mardrus' interpolations and embellishments. Any good tale would delight the unspoilt child in B.B. Grimm's and Andersen's fairy-tales, the Northern sagas, Boccaccio, Cervantes, Croce's edition of the Neapolitan *Pentamerone,* Persian, Tibetan and Indian tales. Many of them became part of his mental reservoir and he would quote them as illustrations of what he wanted to say, like for instance Grimm's *Meister Pfriem* or Andersen's *The Emperor's New Clothes* or the Turkestani *Tale of Archiborchi* or the Indian *Tale of Kamrup.* Modern novels, particularly American ones, B.B. generally read by himself, as they were full of slang and difficult for me to read. When we had all three read Faulkner's *Sanctuary* Mary declared that it was impossible to understand what really happened between Popeye and Temple. I explained it to her and half an hour afterwards I heard how, while discussing the book with a guest, she said: "Only people with an utterly depraved imagination can understand what it is all about."

Also Proust's *A La Recherche du temps perdu* was read by each of us separately as the volumes appeared and then endlessly discussed, particularly by Logan Pearsall Smith.

THE CONCLUSION of a normal I Tatti day was not exciting. A tray with cups and a large teapot full of camomile tea was brought in and some of our guests were rather scared by this to them unknown beverage. Lady Sybil told me how her father, Lord Desart, on driving away after dinner from I Tatti had said to her: "I took some of that stuff and hope it will not do me any harm." Eleven o'clock was generally the hour for "turning in," as Mary called it, but guests were never prevented from going out or from returning late. There was a night watchman who would let them in. In an article written about B.B. after his death by Elizabeth Hardwick she speaks of the struggle guests at I Tatti had to escape into more breathable air and to get back into the house at night. Incidentally neither she nor her husband ever stayed at I Tatti, although they came repeatedly to see B.B. and were great favourites of his.

CHAPTER IX

The Tatti Bus

ALL THE YEAR ROUND but particularly at the height of the tourist season, in spring, the coming and going of guests was a standing feature of daily life. We used to compare I Tatti to a big rumbling bus. Some passengers got in to descend at the next stop, others occupied it for longer trips. A number of unknown Americans armed with letters of introduction would be invited for a meal, would go through a bit of "third degree" by B.B. about their work, their interests and beliefs, would be taken over the house and only in exceptional cases would be seen again. Others were brought to I Tatti for some definite reason that aroused B.B.'s interest and curiosity. Both B.B. and Mary loved new faces and new contacts, but Mary tended to be bored very quickly. B.B. used to compare her with the rich young man of Baghdad in one of the tales of the *Thousand and One Nights* who stood every evening on the great bridge watching the caravans come in and invited the first traveller whose face attracted him to come and spend the night at his house. There he offered him a succulent meal and made him tell his life's story. On the following morning he would speed him on his way saying: "Allah protect you and let me never see your face again." For B.B. a new friendship, a new flirtation and perhaps a new love could flower out of the most casual encounter. First of all he was eager to find out what newcomers were after in coming to see him, whether they had any pretentious high-brow programme or whether they were ready to talk about what interested them most, above all whether they would let themselves be teased by him. Shyness or awkwardness did not put him off if he felt real gifts hidden behind them. Sometimes his inquisitiveness led him to ask tactless questions and even to say offensive things. More than once serious misunderstandings were the result and what might have been the beginning of a real friendship was changed into coldness and animosity. B.B. did not want to be taken too seriously and could easily be laughed out of his over-pedagogical, not to say priggish, moods. When visitors approached him with a certain fear and even—as in his last years—with awe, he resented it and reacted by saying sharp and unkind things. And they probably carried away a totally false impression of what he was really like.

Sometimes when I think of B.B. he appears to me as the centre of a huge cobweb with threads spun in every direction. The number of links he managed to keep up and his capacity and elasticity for adding new ones was amazing. He was loyal to his old friends and more indulgent than Mary in summing them up or discussing their weaknesses. I remember for instance a long stay of Hutchins and Neith Hapgood at the Villino in the winter of 1922–23, friends to whom Mary and B.B. had been devoted for years. Hutch —as they called him—dropped in frequently and loved to discuss all his heart-searching problems with B.B. Neith showed signs of former beauty in spite of her slovenly appearance but was difficult to approach, because of her almost complete silence.

Mary to Nicky   December 23rd 1922
   . . . The Hapgoods came to dinner and suddenly I felt a perfect horror of their way of living and the friends they make and the horrid tales they tell of their goings-on, as if

they were not things that decent people loathe, getting drunk and kissing each other all over the place and chewing strange plants and going temporarily crazy. At their age they should know better. I am afraid I even think the *Story of a Lover* is a rather disgusting piece of exhibitionism. I liked it at first, but that is the impression it has left on me, that and a devout gratitude to my Guardian Angel that deterred me from letting Hutch make love to me or I would have been in that hysterical book. Literary men are certainly unsafe. . . .

B.B. to Nicky   December 24th 1922
    . . . here everything *al solito*. Night before last the Hapgoods dined and Mary quite obviously hated them. She refuses to see anything in Hutch except self-indulgence and dissipation. His deep need of ecstasy, his yearning for the impossible—silly but madly sincere—escapes her or rather sickens her.

An old friend for whom Mary's affection never wavered was "Aunt Janet," Mrs. Henry Ross, our nearest neighbour at Poggio Gherardo. B.B. had been very fond of her late husband and was loyal and always kind to her but found her gruff and authoritative manner a little oppressive and her complete lack of subtlety rather trying. When Mary went off to take a cure or to see her children she would delegate me to call on Aunt Janet if possible every day. It was not an easy task. With few exceptions—as in the case of Mary— Mrs. Ross had little use for women. I tried hard to amuse her with very tepid results. One day I tried to make her talk about her early days in Florence. She looked at me fiercely from under her bushy eyebrows and only said: "If you had read any of my books you would not ask such foolish questions."

Close to I Tatti, just under the picturesque hamlet of Corbignano, the so-called Casa di Boccaccio was inhabited for several years by the Austrian painter Victor Hammer and his family. They had been recommended to the Berensons by one of B.B.'s old Austrian friends, the collector Count Lanczkoronski. Hammer seemed to belong to another century in combining art and artisanship most happily. He was a superb draughtsman, an accomplished painter, a printer of fine books with characters designed by him, a constructor of musical instruments. His discussions with B.B. were sometimes so profound and involved that ordinary mortals would not follow them.

On the Settignano side there was Leo Stein, who used the library a great deal but rarely joined the tea-drinking circle in it because of his increasing deafness. It was dangerous to offer any help to him in finding the books he wanted, for that would start him talking, generally about his psychoanalytical experiments on himself. This meant being cut off from the rest of the world as on an island, since he was totally unaware of anybody calling or the telephone ringing or other visitors expecting me to attend to them.

Also at Settignano in D'Annunzio's Villa Capponcina lived Aunt Janet's great friend, the traveller and explorer Filippo de Filippi. Through his contacts with English scholars and colonial officials, also through his American wife, he had acquired English habits of hospitality and everything at his dinner-parties—which he loved to give—was as in an English house except for himself with his dark southern type of features and a voice so powerful that it seemed to add height to his small compact figure. At his own table he would deafen all his guests when one of his roaring rages got the better of him. I remember a dinner at which B.B. and Lina Waterfield were discussing the Greco-Turkish situation. Suddenly De Filippi started attacking them violently. Why did they have to take an interest in what went on in another country? Of course this was a veiled way of telling them that they should stop taking an interest in Italian affairs, which as foreigners they had no business to do. De

Filippi was not partial to the Fascist régime but as a nationalist he could not but approve of its foreign policy. Later, at the time of the sanctions, he insisted on giving up his English knighthood and never stopped feeling the bitterest resentment against Great Britain. He could be very agreeable and *gemütlich*, especially at tea-time when there was no danger of his drinking too much and of getting into one of his *vin mauvais* moods.

Another learned neighbour on the Maiano side, Tammaro De Marinis, was completely detached from political or nationalistic interests although as an intimate friend of Benedetto Croce surely not in favour of Fascism. All his energy was concentrated—and still is—on his library, his studies and publications, his discoveries of rare manuscripts. B.B. found him very congenial and entertaining, admired his vast learning and never failed to get interesting information out of him. Both Tammaro and his wife Clelia were delightfully hospitable in their magnificent villa at Montalto as well as in their country place near Pistoia.

Close to Montalto on the Maiano side we had as neighbour the famous columnist and art critic Ugo Ojetti, who later on became the director of the *Corriere della Sera*. B.B. had greatly enjoyed his company at the Hotel Acquabella-Saltino in the summer of 1917 and again in the summer of 1921. The result was that almost all of B.B.'s essays written between 1921 and 1932 appeared first in Italian translation in the art review *Dedalo*, created and edited by Ojetti. Consequently Ojetti was a frequent guest at the luncheon table of I Tatti, either to discuss his translations of B.B.'s articles or to try out his own *cose viste* articles on B.B.'s ears, before writing them down. Mary, who thoroughly disliked monologists, particularly if their medium was either Italian or French or German, took a dim view of these occasions. For the rest of us they were often as good as a play.

A little farther on the way to San Gervasio there was the

Villa del Palmerino and in it lived Miss Paget, better known under her writer's name, Vernon Lee. For years there had been a cold war between her and the Berensons and only in 1922 did a reconciliation take place. It was undoubtedly furthered by the complete agreement over political events. It created mutual sympathy and an inexhaustible subject of conversation. Vernon was by that time already too deaf to talk to B.B. directly. His voice was very low and did not carry at all. Through the experience with her own daughter Mary knew exactly how to adjust her voice to people hard of hearing. Vernon was supposed to use a large horn as hearing aid but had the curious habit of using it while she herself was talking and of dropping it the moment she was expected to listen.

In connection with her deafness I remember how one day Leo Stein appeared in the library wearing one of the first electric hearing aids, sent to him from the United States, and actually hearing much better. Mary, who had Vernon's deafness very much on her mind, entreated him to let her arrange a meeting between him and Vernon, during which this miraculous hearing aid could be tried by her. A few days later, both parties appeared at the appointed time, Stein took off his contraption, and we tried to fix it on Vernon's head, which was extremely difficult as she kept pushing it about with nervous, jerky movements. At last it was fixed on, but instead of listening she started talking, would not let herself be interrupted, and turned her attention exclusively towards Stein, who, deprived of his instrument, could not hear a word of what she said to him.

I had already met Miss Paget during the Kingsley Porter winter at I Tatti.

Nicky to Mary   January 13th 1921
I have been to a very amusing lunch party at I Tatti with Miss Paget. She tried to convince Kingsley and Offner

that a formal and undiscussable system could be made for art connoisseurship, just as there is one for mixing chemicals together. She seemed to be disappointed that B.B. had not been able to fix the iron laws of this system. The Porters like her and see her often in spite of Mrs. Ross's lugubre warnings. She has told Lucy that friendship with Miss Paget implicated the most horrible danger to Mrs. Porter's young niece, to her reputation and actually to her virtue . . .

Not among the bus-clients were two neighbours at Fiesole, for it was almost invariably B.B. who called on them. One was Lady Sybil Scott (later Lady Sybil Lubbock) who perhaps avoided I Tatti because of her former disagreements with Mary. B.B. kept up his friendship with her, loved to discuss books and political events with her and enjoyed his contacts with her nimble mind as well as the exquisite appointments of Villa Medici.

The other Fiesole neighbour was the American philosopher Charles Augustus Strong for whom Cecil Pinsent had built the Villa delle Balze, an attractive long, low house just opposite Villa Medici. More than once I accompanied B.B. on his visits to Strong and listened to the slow and rather laborious conversation between him and this very courteous, profoundly learned and rather inhibited man. It was not easy for Strong to communicate with other human beings. He was devoted to George Santayana, who frequently came to stay at Le Balze. I do not remember his ever coming to I Tatti although I know he used to come for even longer stays before my time.

B.B. told me that Strong on one of his return voyages from the States had been bitten by a passenger suddenly gone mad and that when he, B.B., had driven over to Le Balze to ask for news and to express his sympathy Strong's answer had been: "No, you must not pity me. It was a sensation of life."

AMONG THE FLORENTINE RESIDENTS who came to I Tatti during the first years I remember several of B.B.'s colleagues: Giacomo de Nicola, one of the best connoisseurs of Sienese art, Carlo Loeser, the American collector and amateur, Carlo Gamba, a fine connoisseur especially of Venetian painting, Pietro Toesca for whose thorough scholarship B.B. had the greatest regard, Georg Gronau, director of the museum in Cassel and owner of the charming Villa le Palazzine at San Domenico.

For several years the most frequent guest in the library and at the lunch table was Richard Offner, whom B.B. considered a student of art history of great promise and whom he was anxious to help. But his way of treating younger colleagues was not always the most fortunate. Whenever their pursuits seemed to him unpromising or over-pedantic he would pour cold water on them and forget how many wrong paths he had surely taken himself in his youth. I had many arguments with him on that subject. If consequently there were years of coldness between him and Offner it was partly due to this unwillingness of B.B.'s to give his young friends too much rope and partly to the fact that Mary did not care for Offner and made a greater fuss than was necessary over what Offner was reported to have said against B.B.

Other *habitués* of the library and also frequent guests at meals and at tea-time during their stays in Florence were Harold Edgell (later the director of the Boston Fine Arts Museum), Arthur McComb (a gifted and cultivated Harvard graduate), Tim Clapp (a delightful combination of poet and art critic, later the director of the Frick Museum), Walter Cook (who specialized in studies on Spanish art and later was for years head of the Fine Arts Institute at New York University) and Yukio Yashiro, the Japanese scholar, then already working on his *Botticelli*, having received the first impulse towards it through B.B.'s comparisons between Western and Far Eastern art.

B.B. and Mary, 1929

B.B. with (left to right)
Lucius Wilmerding,
Nicky Mariano, Carlo
Placci, and Walter
Lippmann, Poggio allo
Spino, 1937

Geoffrey Scott

Count Hermann Keyserling

THROUGH RALPH AND RACHEL PERRY we met the Spelmans, an American couple established in a pleasant villa on the Via San Leonardo. Leolyn Spelman came from Cleveland, where the extravagances of her wealthy mother are still remembered. I daresay Florentine society will remember the extravagances of Leolyn Spelman—but also her generosity, especially in her contributions to the musical life of the town —for a long time to come. Timothy Spelman was a friendly easy-going man, gifted as a composer, but a bit comical in his abject submission to his turbulent wife, ever ready to obey her slightest whim. They lived hospitably and lavishly, surrounded by dogs, believed in eating a lot, set up one of the first private swimming pools in Florence, cared beautifully for their garden and built up a first-rate library. It was for this genuine love of books that B.B. respected Leolyn and was willing to put up with her aggressive manner and emphatic utterances, also with her provincial fussiness over invitations and their punctual acceptance. My sister looked after their library for several years before taking over my job at I Tatti, and the Spelmans were invariably kind and hospitable to the three Anreps. Like many American residents in Italy they favoured Fascism and in their presence we had to avoid the subject carefully. A few years before World War II they had a disagreeable experience with the local Fascio and thereupon changed their minds. During the war they lived in America and became victims of the war psychosis which made them declare on their return to Florence that B.B. by staying on in Italy had betrayed his country. This brought our friendship of a good many years to an end.

THROUGH PLACCI'S INTERVENTION new friends were added to the Florentine group. When the former Austrian ambassador in Rome, Count Henry Luetzow, and his wife settled down in Florence, taking at once a prominent place in Florentine society, Placci brought them to I Tatti. From their point of view Mary and B.B. must have counted as interesting freaks whom it was amusing to see from time to time. It was generally the Luetzows who came to I Tatti, not the other way round. The old count was a cantankerous and difficult man, but elegantly cultivated, sharp-witted and well-informed and B.B. always got a great deal out of his talks with him. Both his daughters began to frequent I Tatti during their visits to Villa Bartolucci, their parents' home at Arcetri. The older one was married to another ex-Austrian diplomat, Count Adolph Dubsky, while the younger, divorced from an Hungarian magnate, was on the point of marrying her *cavaliere servente,* Count Carl Khuen-Belasi. She was a lovely woman, with the features of a Romanesque angel, sensitive, quick-witted, sparklingly gay. B.B. found her adorable and she became very fond of him. Also her future husband was a very endearing person, a typically Austrian grand-seigneur country squire, simple, unaffected, yet with cultural aspirations and interests, a great reader and devoted friend of the art historian Johannes Wilde.

Among visitors from the United States the most outstanding personality was Walter Lippmann. B.B. had met him first in Paris during the peace conference and again in New York during the winter of 1920–21. In 1924 he came for the first time to stay at I Tatti, bringing with him his wife Faye (divorced from him in 1937), a very attractive and gay young woman, keen on having a good time and therefore a rather incongruous companion for so serious an intellectual as Walter. The endless discussions between Walter and B.B. about Al Smith's chances in the presidential campaign cannot have been very exhilarating for her. I remember Walter being very sanguine in his hopes for Al Smith's success and B.B. very sceptical, chiefly because of Smith's being a Catholic. Many other visits followed through the years. B.B. was devoted to Walter and took a fatherly interest in his career.

I doubt that Walter went on feeling as close to B.B. as he had during their first encounters, but he never failed to look B.B. up when he happened to be in Italy.

Then there was Daisy Chanler, Edith Wharton's friend, a half-sister of the novelist Marion Crawford. Brought up in Rome and having kept many ties with Roman society, she represented the happiest combination of American freshness of outlook and lively curiosity with a firm European cultural grounding. A fervent Catholic yet never fanatical nor proselytizing. On her first visit to I Tatti after the war she was accompanied by her youngest daughter Bibo and by her son, the musician Teddy Chanler, and was on her way to visit Padre Pio at Monte Rotondo. There was at that moment much talk about his miracle-working presence, the stigmata in the palms of his hands and the sweet odour that seemed to surround him. In the following years Daisy Chanler came again and again and joined us for part of our trip to Palestine and Syria in 1929.

Hester, her daughter, married to Edward Pickman, became very dear to all three of us during a long stay of the whole family in a neighbouring villa. She had inherited her mother's ease of manner and intellectual aspirations and curiosities and was a perfect companion for her historian-philosopher husband. Among American visitors, I remember as very congenial Mary's cousins, Helen Thomas—sister of the formidable Carey, but very different from her—and her husband, the eminent physician and scientist Simon Flexner. Their son, Jim Flexner, a gifted and promising young writer, stayed for a long time in Florence around 1928 and was a frequent guest at I Tatti. B.B. enjoyed his company and discussed with him the various books that Jimmy was planning to write.

There was also the banker Tom Lamont and his wife, who came to stay and introduced the English poet laureate John Masefield—a close friend of theirs—to the Berensons.

He seemed terribly aloof and silent, and when I found myself seated next to him at dinner I was at a loss what to say
to him. But when he discovered that I was reading one of
Trollope's political novels to B.B., everything changed and
he became charmingly communicative on the subject of an
author greatly admired by him.

The composer Sam Barlow and his beautiful wife, Er-
nesta, were lent the Villino for a time, and their daily visits
brought us much fun and animation. Another friend from
the Berensons' last long stay in New York was the famous
monologist Ruth Draper, who, whenever she came to stay at
I Tatti, never failed to perform for us in the library, creating
the strange illusion that she had not acted alone but with
other people, and sometimes with a whole crowd of them.

A young man who was to become a life-long friend came
for the first time in the spring of 1924, brought up to dinner
by Byba Giuliani. His name was Charles Henry Coster,
descended from one of the old Dutch families of New York.
B.B. liked him at first sight while to the rest of us he seemed
a bit stiff and not very communicative. The friendship
between him and Byba flourished and when two years later
they were married in Florence, B.B. and Mary put I Tatti
at their disposal while we were taking a trip to Sicily. Thus
Harry—as we called him—became an habitué of the house
and, through his studious turn of mind, of the library as
well. B.B. understood his character and background, his
reserve and apparent ceremoniousness and appreciated his
unusually fine mind and delicate sense of humour. When
later on Harry decided to leave the diplomatic service and
to devote himself exclusively to his historical studies, B.B.
was delighted and gave him a great deal of encouragement.
To the end of his life B.B. continued to take an interest in
Harry's work and to enjoy talking to him or receiving one
of his masterly letters.

Mary, just like her brother Logan, tended to have an

anti-American bias. Left to herself she would have confined
her world not only to an English-speaking but to a British
one. When Belle Greene sent up Billy Ivins, the keeper of
the print room at the Metropolitan Museum and an ardent
admirer of hers, and he started shooting out the virulent
picturesque slang with which he liked to shock his inter-
locutors, Mary was horrified and B.B. intensely amused and
stimulated. He invited Ivins to come again and even to stay
at I Tatti and Ivins became one of B.B.'s most faithful
correspondents. The fact of B.B. and Ivins having been both
very much in love with Belle must have created a special
bond between them. But above all B.B. was fascinated by
this original type of Yankee, highly gifted, of penetrating
intelligence and quickness. Through his sharp, even veno-
mous tongue he made many enemies for himself and died
a very solitary man.

ALL OF OUR TRIPS ABROAD or in Italy, but particularly in
Italy, brought new links with the art world, the directors
of museums and their staffs, the members of the Italian
Fine Arts Service. Through being received *con tutti gli onori*
wherever he went B.B. created a lot of obligations for himself. When any of these old or new acquaintances turned up
in Florence he regarded it as his duty to receive them at
luncheon or at tea-time and to allow them to work in his
library. Not all of them were congenial to him and some he
regarded as his "enemy-friends" but in the hope of getting
solid information or at least amusing gossip out of them
he was always willing to dedicate some of his time to them.
Thus in the daily round of visitors these colleagues of various
nationalities took an important place.

It would be impossible and very tedious to make a list
of all the bus passengers. All I want is to throw some light
on those that made a lasting impression on me. And perhaps

also to give an idea of the curious vibration that all this coming and going gave to life at I Tatti. It was as if something unusual and exciting might happen at any moment.

B.B. to Nicky   I Tatti   May 8th 1930
. . . What a contrast between De Lorey and Sarre. The German recounts so impersonally. What had happened by the way did not matter or was forgotten as long as he saw what he went out to see. To the Frenchman it was a question of what happened to him in the meanwhile, what he ate, how he slept, what comfort or discomfort came to his lot, what kind of reception he encountered, in brief what mattered was his personal reaction. Sarre spoke with enthusiasm and highly recommended a voyage from Mardin to Bagdad on floats as described by Xenophon. He praised the silence, the solitude, the ease and repose, the towns and ruins you could so comfortably see on the way and at your leisure. De Lorey said it was all true, provided you were not devoured by every species of insect and potted at by natives as your float carried you through the narrows of the Tigris. He assured us that our experience at Antioch was exceptional. He had never been able to do anything there because of the terrible winds. . . .

From one of my holidays I wrote to Mary:

I had two letters from both my old birds[1] to-day, telling me all about L's visit which I regret to have missed. But there is no getting out of the Tatti diligence without missing many amusing stations and travellers. From your letters I get an impression of the *Lanterna Magica* of I Tatti as I never do while being in it myself.

---

[1] As Mary used to refer to herself and B.B.

CHAPTER X

"Flat Old Rome"
and Political Tension [1924–25]

IN THE SUMMER of 1924, during my holiday with the Anreps at the Lido, Mary wrote that to her great disappointment B.B. had decided not to go as she had hoped to some faraway land but to spend the autumn in what she called "flat old Rome" so as to get thoroughly reacquainted with it. A glorious prospect for me who had been brought up in the cult of Rome. My mother had met my father in Rome and had spent her early married life there. Her whole attitude towards Rome and its past was of the purest Germano-Romantic type. She told me of how she had sat on a bench in the Villa Ludovisi weeping over its destruction while all around her the trees were being felled. Of course I had been to Rome again and again but this stay with the Berensons was to be the longest I ever had. Part of it we spent in the Rennell Rodds' apartment in Via Giulia which gave one a wonderful sense of intimacy with old papal Rome and its population. From the end of September to early December scarcely a day passed without our going to visit museums, churches, excavations and driving out in every direction. Mary was soon reconciled to "flat old Rome" and loved "exploring" the Roman *campagna*. Very often a specialist in one or the other fields of art or archaeology would accompany us. Arduino Colasanti—then director general of fine arts—showed us restored early Christian churches, Adolfo Venturi—the dean of Italian art historians—met us in the Vatican library to look at illuminated manuscripts, Monsignor Weigelt—the early Christian archaeologist—took us to the small museum near the catacombs of Praetextat and lectured to us as if we were schoolchildren if we failed to guess whether two clumsy feet were fragments of a Saint Peter or a Saint Paul. Eugenie Strong drove with us to Città Lavinia and to Gabii and showed us the underground basilica at the Porta Maggiore.

We saw a lot of Ernst Steinmann, the head of the Hertziana Library and a friend of long standing, typically German in the best sense of the word, well-bred, courteous, hospitable, helpful, with an exquisite sense of fun and a scholarly yet never pedantic knowledge of Renaissance Rome. Of Roman society or of diplomatic circles we saw relatively little, B.B. being at that time already too much considered an outspoken anti-Fascist to make contacts with him desirable.

More than once I heard B.B. say that until 1914 he had bothered very little about current politics. It was the First World War which made him keenly aware of world events and being a resident in Italy ever since 1888 it was natural that the Italian post-war problems should take a dominant position on his political horizon. Some of his friends abroad criticized him for being too vehement in expressing his opinions and thought that as a guest of Italy he should have been more impartial. Already in Paris during his activity as political adviser to the American embassy he had been accused of being anti-Italian (even by so close a friend as Carlo Placci) because he saw clearly what the megalomaniac ambitions of Italian nationalists would lead to. His ideal for Italy was a very lofty one. After achieving its political union it should have become the leader and protector of smaller nations striving to become independent instead of pretending to be a great power with dreams of territorial aggrandisement. Consequently the whole squalid horse-deal over Yugoslavia filled him with impotent rage and in 1919 on his return from Paris he would burst out with it at the slightest provocation. Being a coward by nature I dreaded his clashes with Italian nationalists and proto-Fascists while at the same time I felt in absolute harmony with him over what he considered the right direction of Italy's future development. After the Fascist *coup d'état* things became worse and discussions more heated and bitter until gradually B.B. stopped seeing any staunch upholders of the regime who were probably equally anxious to avoid him. Serious clashes he was more likely to have with foreign visitors who had been taken in by Fascism because of the apparent order it had brought, the improvements of roads and railroads and generally as a bulwark against Bolshevism. When Thomas Lamont, one of the directors of the Morgan bank, came to Italy to negotiate a loan to the Fascist government and stayed at I Tatti before going to Rome, B.B. did his best to put him in touch with well-informed anti-Fascists in the hope of their opening his eyes. Lamont was too thoroughly indoctrinated as to the regime's stability and his faith could not be shaken, although the reaction to the Matteotti murder had been so intense all over Italy that it looked for a while as if the new government would not be able to hold out against it. But the opposition played their cards very badly and the support given by the United States and Great Britain to what they considered a bulwark against communism made the Fascist regime stronger and fiercer than ever.

During our long stay in Rome we saw a number of friends who were not only in full agreement with B.B. but —as in the case of Salvemini—more vehement than he ever was. Lina Waterfield, who was working for the *Observer*, took me to the journalists' box in Montecitorio to have a look at Mussolini and I was duly horrified by his truculent expression. Giovanni Amendola, the leader of the opposition, Victor Cunard, the *Times* correspondent, Enrico Visconti Venosta, the son of the former Italian minister of foreign affairs, all came to our apartment in Via Giulia. A young attaché of the French embassy to the Quirinal, Jacques Truelle, who took an intelligent interest in the Italian political situation, was asked by B.B. to meet Amendola and Salvemini. He told me later that when he left the house two policemen in plain clothes were at our door and followed him to his lodgings.

Of the many anti-Fascists I have met, Giovanni Amendola was by far the most outstanding personality. A tall massive man with the powerful head of a Roman bust of the Republican era, very quiet and measured in his speech, without any over-expressiveness or gesticulation although a native of Campania. He had been a member of the Cabinet at the time of the march on Rome and described to us the night before the march when he and his colleagues accompanied the heads of the general staff to the Quirinal Palace and tried to get the king's signature to a decree imposing martial law all over Italy. The king refused stubbornly and said that he could not bear the thought of any more bloodshed. In Amendola's opinion it was the fear of losing the throne that prevented him from taking any action. Pro-Fascist members of the Aosta branch of the Savoias had threatened to take his place if he made any opposition to Mussolini.[1]

Salvemini had many discussions with B.B. in Rome about his own future. B.B. advised him to leave Florence, to teach mediaeval history in one of the northern universities

---

[1] Amendola lived on under strict police supervision until in the summer of 1926 while driving out of Montecatini where he had been taking the cure, his police escort suddenly disappeared, a band of blackshirts stopped the car and beat him up so savagely that he died of the consequences a few months later.

and to keep away from current events. Gaetano was too deeply involved and too passionate by temperament to take such a course. Besides he would have had to leave Italy anyway when a few years later an oath of allegiance to the regime was made obligatory for all university professors.

On our return to I Tatti I found out that many *bien-pensant* Florentines were indignant over the company B.B. had kept in Rome. So our evenings with Amendola that we had been so careful to keep secret were already common knowledge. I was not told how and through whom the news had spread.

AMONG MEMORIES of the early part of 1925 what stands out chiefly is a great deal of political tension, fierce discussions and much anxiety. While he was staying with friends in Rome Salvemini was arrested and then transferred to Florence where his case came up in the early summer. He told us later that when he arrived in Florence in the early morning at the small station of Campo di Marte, his escort of two *carabinieri* was very much at a loss as to how to reach the prison, having never been to Florence before. So it was he who led them to the great prison of the *Murate* in Via Ghibellina. Friends who got permission to see him—like Ugo Ojetti—told us that Gaetano's sonorous irresistible laughter could be heard in the street on approaching the prison. After his acquittal he stayed for a while with friends in southern Italy and then left clandestinely for France and England, later for the United States not to return until the Second World War was over.

For us Salvemini's arrest had one positive and far reaching consequence. A few days after the news of it had reached us and while he was still in Rome, Placci sent us a young man, recommending him warmly. The object of his visit was to ask B.B. whether he would put aside any notices he might find in the foreign press of Gaetano's arrest. From the first moment there was such a feeling of warmth, of mutual understanding between this young man and the three of us that he stayed on to supper that same day and from then on became a constant visitor. His name was Count Umberto Morra di Lavriano, the descendant of an old Piedmontese family of military traditions and no doubt he too would have been brought up for service in the army had he not been struck by coxitis as a small boy. Tall and slender he would have been well made but for the lameness that this illness had left him with. His subtle intelligence combined with great sensitivity showed in his features and in his expression. A great help in his becoming almost a member of the family was his familiarity with the English language, literature and history. For Mary at any rate it was essential. She never felt really at home in another language and probably was never able to think in it. Salvemini to whom she was devoted long before he learnt to speak English was the only exception I can remember.

During a long visit of B.B.'s sister Bessie in the summer of 1925 we went for the first time to stay in Morra's country-house near Cortona.

Nicky to Mary   Cortona   Villa Morra   July 15th 1925
Dearest Mary,
    Here we are in a house filled with old-fashioned furniture and keepsakes and huge photographs of mid-Victorian ladies in court attire and corresponding gentlemen in uniform and decorations. The atmosphere is nice and *gemütlich* and lived-in, the rooms cool and the beds comfortable. . . .
    Morra does not know anything about our friend except that he is provisionally free and hopes that he will come and stay with him.

From Cortona we went on to Perugia and were joined there by Belle Greene and a friend of hers.

Nicky to Mary   Perugia   July 23rd 1925
   . . . Belle Greene and her friend arrived in the afternoon, Belle looking more or less as I remembered her to be
like. She seems jolly and tells amusing stories about her stay
in Rome and her interviews with the Holy Father. We also
talked a lot about her hobby, illuminated codexes and the
Vatican library. At first I could only understand one third
of what she was saying but then got on better. The friend
is young and good-looking but somehow like a calf, quite
uncultivated and barking out remarks in slang. I daresay
she is shy. We will probably go to Orvieto, Spoleto, and
Siena with them. It would be no use taking them to the
Marche. They do not care enough to endure uncomfortable
hotels for the sake of seeing beautiful things and sights.

Nicky to Mary   I Tatti   July 27th 1925
Dearest Mary,
   Just a little scrap of a letter in the middle of a crazy
morning to tell you that we got back yesterday for dinner
after a lovely drive via San Gimignano, Certaldo, Lucardo,
San Casciano, dined in the garden and found it not a bit hot,
on the contrary rather too breezy. The two ladies were in
ecstasy over the beauty of the house and the delights and
civilized comforts of the Ritz Suite. Belle was rather wild
and shrieky the two first days but has been a very pleasant
companion ever since and we get on well together. . . .

   Belle Greene was at that time full of enthusiasm for the
Fascist regime because the steward on her boat had kissed
Mussolini's photo in her presence and had raved about the
Duce. What B.B. or other people had to say on the subject
could not make her change her mind. Like so many Americans she had no discrimination about where information on
European affairs came from. One source was as good as
another and the first one more likely to be preferred. I
remember in this connection how Raffaele Piccoli (professor

of literature at the University of Naples and a member of Croce's circle) suffered bitterly during the visit of his American parents-in-law from their stubborn defence of Fascism based on the information gathered from fellow travellers in the train between Genoa and Naples.

IF ONLY B.B. had limited himself to having outbursts of indignation with his co-religionists and not in the presence of unreliable individuals! It must have been in 1924 that a young member of the Florentine aristocracy was recommended to B.B. and Mary as an excellent general agent and as being particularly anxious to protect foreigners against any form of exploitation. In their usual careless way B.B. and Mary accepted him as an habitué at meals and at tea-time and were amused by his clownish manners. And in his presence B.B. gave vent to rages against Fascist rule without the slightest circumspection. When several years later I discovered that this young man was a real crook and made the most of his position to enrich himself in a shameless way, I could not show him the door as I would have liked to do because the danger of his avenging himself by denouncing us all to the *Fascio* was too great. By good luck an occasion for getting rid of him *in guanti bianchi*—as politely as possible—presented itself at last.[2]

---

[2] After this unfortunate experience I no longer hesitated to accept the proposition made by Mary, already some years earlier, of entrusting the Tatti administration to my brother-in-law Bertie Anrep. Even if he was not familiar with the Tuscan agricultural systems he was sure not to cheat the Berensons. Bertie in his turn engaged an excellent young *fattore*, Geremia Gioffredi, to look after the farms and trained him so well that when he himself became unable to carry on, this assistant took over his duties. Gioffredi's capacities have been recognized by the new management of I Tatti who have kept him on in the same position after B.B.'s death.

In the following years several of Morra's contemporaries who shared his political convictions became friends of I Tatti. There was first of all Count Guglielmo degli Alberti, descendant of the Tuscan Albertis and of the Piedmontese Lamarmoras on his mother's side, at home in French literature as much as in Italian and himself gifted as a writer; Count Alexander Passerin d'Entrèves, a young Piedmontese philosopher, who after World War II taught in Oxford and in Yale University; Pietro Pancrazi, a Tuscan literary critic and writer, later on collaborator of Ojetti in publishing the literary review *Pegaso*. Thus B.B. ended by belonging to a network of anti-Fascist intelligentsia and wherever he went could be sure of meeting kindred spirits. In Naples there was Croce and his circle, in Turin the Visconti Venostas and Lionello Venturi, in Padua the Papafavas (the widow and the son of B.B.'s old friend the philosopher Francesco Papafava), in Rome Papafava's daughter Margherita Bracci and her husband, Duke Giovanni Colonna di Cesarò and his wife, and the house of Luigi Albertini (until 1925, director of the *Corriere della Sera*), one of the strongholds of anti-Fascism. Albertini's daughter Elena Carandini and her cousin Nina Ruffini became devoted friends of B.B. and particularly Elena kept close to him through many years of correspondence.

Also several Italian diplomats shared B.B.'s views and were glad to pour out their fears and grievances into his sympathetic ear. One was Giuliano Cora, first brought to I Tatti by Salvemini. Later on it was Gastone Guidotti (at present Italian ambassador in London), who never failed to get in touch with B.B. when he happened to be in his hometown Florence. Giuliano Cora I remember only once taking an optimistic view of Mussolini's foreign policy. Having spent years at the Italian embassy in Addis Ababa he was well acquainted with the Ethiopian scene, also a personal friend of the Negus and was therefore sent on a special mission there—if I remember right—in 1930. On his return he came to see B.B. and told him about his interview with Mussolini. "Even you," he said, "will have to admit that he is politically more intelligent than we have given him credit for. I gave him a detailed report of my mission and of what in my opinion Italy's policy in Ethiopia should be, very slow and cautious, chiefly commercial penetration. He grasped my meaning with astonishing quickness and agreed fully.[3]

IN THE LATE SUMMER of 1925 I went to stay with my people in Munich and was joined there by Mary and B.B. Almost two years uninterruptedly in Italy and in its oppressive political climate seemed a long spell and we were all in need of some fresh air beyond the frontier. From Munich we went on by way of Salzburg to Vienna and spent most of the autumn there. It turned out just as much of a musical as a sight-seeing experience. German hours, with the opera or concert beginning early and a light supper afterwards, suited both Mary and B.B. and we went out a lot unhampered by social engagements. In Czechoslovakia, where we spent week-ends in the country-houses of both the daughters of Count Luetzow, the impression of acute tension between the Czecho-Slovak government and the German land-owning classes was rather alarming. It reminded me of the contrasts between Esthonian population, Russian officials and German upper class of which I had seen so much in one of my "former" lives. Also in Budapest we spent several days, cordially received and helped by Royall Tyler—at that time

---

[3] Ambassador Giuliano Cora is to this day a personal friend of the Negus and persona grata in Ethiopian official circles. In our foreign office he is considered as the best adviser on questions relating to Ethiopia.

American adviser to the Hungarian government—and his Italian-born wife.

At I Tatti we found Senda and Herbert Abbott already established in the house and Senda in her element, seeing all her former friends again and being invited by them. She was really made to be a successful and popular hostess. For me there was the joy of finding my sister representing the Kurt Wolff publishing house in Florence. My brother-in-law and my nephew followed her at Christmas and early in 1926 they moved into a quaint old house in Borgo Santo Spirito, supposed to be haunted and in which not only my sister—who had good qualifications for being a medium—but my very sceptical brother-in-law heard the strangest things.

CHAPTER XI

Attributions of Pictures and the "Lists"

To my working in the library, to my helping B.B. with his work and Mary with the household, a fourth and rather irksome task was gradually added, dealing directly or by letter with owners of pictures who applied for B.B.'s attestations.

The attributions that he was expected to approve of were generally as high-sounding as possible—Botticelli, Raphael, Giorgione, Titian, Correggio. Like Midas, B.B. was supposed to have the power to change whatever he touched into gold. Sometimes I managed to get rid of particularly insistent postulants by asking them whether a price had already been offered for their picture and if they said yes, I urged them to sell it as quickly as possible and before running the danger of getting an adverse opinion from B.B. In a few cases this worked very well.

During our stay in Naples in 1926 the concierge begged me to receive a woman who had the most urgent need to speak to me. I tried to put her off but one day as I was entering the hall of the hotel there she was waiting for me. A handsome woman in deep mourning who said she would treat me as if I were her sister, and out came a tale of misfortunes and losses and at the end the request that Mr.

Berenson should come once more to see her precious collection of paintings. "When he came last year he admired them greatly but I was then not yet ready to sell them." But excuse me," I said, "Mr. Berenson has not been in Naples since he sailed from here for Egypt in 1921. How could he have seen your pictures last year?" "But I assure you he did and was so kind and promised to come again." "What did he look like?" "A tall dark handsome gentleman."

While stopping over in Berlin on our way to Scandinavia in 1927, I was pursued by one of the then prominent American collectors. He had bought a doubtful Titian without anybody's advice and wanted B.B. to bless it. As B.B. refused to see him he went down on his knees before me entreating me to make B.B. change his mind. A ludicrous spectacle, all the more so as he was physically very unattractive.

Another comical incident I remember in connection with a group of Russian refugees with whom the Anreps and I had become very friendly. There was an older couple called Volgine (he formerly a member of the Synod and a deeply religious man) and a young woman married to one of the Narishkines with her mother, Madame Stepanov. We took them all to I Tatti and B.B. had excellent talks with Volgine but was also very much struck with the glamorous young Narishkina. Both she and her mother found B.B. fascinating and when told of his Jewish origin denied it flatly, declining to admit that there was anything Jewish either in his looks or in his manner. Then came the unlucky day when invited to I Tatti for luncheon they produced the photo of a picture and wanted B.B. to confirm its being a marvellous Velasquez. B.B. looked at the photo and asked them whether they had already had an offer for it. They said yes, twenty-five thousand lire, at that moment a considerable sum. B.B., greatly relieved, urged them to sell it for that price, but as they had hoped to hear that it was worth millions they were bitterly offended. The next time we met them somebody started

131

again discussing B.B.'s origins. *"Comment, pas juif,"* yelled Madame Stepanova. *"Mais naturellement qu'il est juif! A Odessa j'ai vu des quantités de juifs qui lui ressemblent."* With stories of this kind I could make B.B. laugh but others were anything but comical.

As B.B.'s violent outbursts against the Fascist régime got talked about there were inevitably disagreeable consequences. Once on landing in Naples the New York banker Otto Kahn went around from one antique shop to the other and saw a small Sienese picture which took his fancy. He asked for a photo and sent it to B.B. begging for his confidential advice. B.B. answered that the picture seemed to him heavily repainted and that he could not recommend its purchase. Otto Kahn told the dealer that Mr. Berenson had discouraged him from buying this picture. For over a year B.B. kept getting letters from the Neapolitan dealer threatening to have him expelled from Italy on acount of his well-known anti-Fascist attitude.

Another time when B.B. had refused to look at the photo of a so-called Raphael the owner sent up his lawyer accompanied by a Fascist militia-man in full uniform, a notorious bully and leader of punitive expeditions. When I repeated B.B.'s refusal to look at the photo he began to mutter threats of having B.B. expelled from Italy. Unable to get rid of them I finally had to call B.B. himself. He turned to the lawyer and asked him whether he was obliged by law to accept the defence of a case. "Certainly not. I am perfectly free to refuse it." "Then so am I free to refuse looking at a picture or at a photograph and expressing my opinion. I am not a public official and I will not let my hand be forced in the exercise of a free profession." These words had a marvellous effect and both men took their leave quietly and politely. I daresay B.B.'s "aura," something about him that inspired and even commanded respect, was the chief reason for their suddenly becoming so meek.

The same thing happened again a few years later with the difference that the accompanying militia-man was a very decent person who seemed half-ashamed of having been sent on such a silly errand.

It HAPPENED VERY RARELY that serious collectors approached B.B. directly and he certainly did not encourage them to do so, as he much preferred the indirect and strictly businesslike approach through a dealer. One of these exceptions, an appeal from a well-known collector and client of Duveen's, I remember very vividly, as it was the cause of a ridiculous incident.

The picture—the bust of a youth—was sent up by one of the forwarding agencies. I showed it to B.B., who confirmed his attribution already made on the basis of a photo. I wrapped up the panel and left in the office, telling the servants to give it back to the messenger who was to call for it. We happened to have in the house at that moment Degas' enchanting copy of Bellini's *Sacra Conversazione* which Marie-Laure de Noailles had brought down as a special treat for B.B. It gave him the chance of taking it to the Uffizi and looking at it side by side with the original. She deposited it with us when she left and said that her chauffeur would call for it. A few days later returning to I Tatti from having spent the week-end in Florence I found B.B. in a towering rage, Logan—who adored any kind of rumpus—in peals of laughter and Mary rather apologetic for having not only opened a telegram addressed to me but shown it to B.B. It was from Marie-Laure, who protested against having been sent a *Quattrocento* portrait instead of her precious Degas. On the Saturday evening during my absence the Noailles chauffeur had appeared in a fearful hurry, had seen the wrapped up picture waiting to be called for, had snatched it declaring it to be undoubtedly the picture prepared for him and an idiotic servant had allowed him to take it without making any protest or asking for further instructions.

For B.B. the whole subject of picture attributing was a very sore one, almost a complex, made worse by his natural tendency to suspicion. If new acquaintances went out of their way to receive him hospitably he was at once on his guard and thought that they wanted to worm an authentication out of him. Sometimes he was right and sometimes not, but he tended to remember only the cases in which his suspicion had been justified and not the other ones.

Whenever I visited a private collection with him he was extremely careful in expressing his opinion. He had probably been more outspoken in his younger years with unfortunate results. Only in public galleries could he let himself go and express his opinion freely or when pictures were shown to him by one or the other of the dealers with whom he had definite arrangements.

Sometimes I felt quite desperate over this curse of attributions chiefly because of the bad effect it had on B.B. "If only he could cut himself off completely from it," I would say to myself. Followed at once by the reflection that had his profession not brought him in a good deal of money there would have been no I Tatti and no library and no need for a Nicky.

B.B.'s CONNECTIONS WITH DEALERS were very correct, particularly those with a very dear old man in London called Sully, with the Steinmeyers in Lucerne, with the Seligmans in Paris, with Luigi Grassi in Florence and later on with the Wildensteins. More complicated and sometimes tempestuous were his dealings with the house of Duveen, because of Sir Joseph's character and his unpredictable caprices and tantrums. B.B. was half repelled and half fascinated by him. When they met, B.B. could not resist Sir Joseph's vitality, his sense of fun, his clowning, perhaps also his flattery. He was an incomparable teller of stories and never afraid of making fun of himself. At a distance B.B. almost loathed the thought of him and suffered bitterly from the humiliation of having to wrangle with him over payments due to him and not unfrequently retarded or contested. When in 1927 the whole Benson collection was bought by Duveen and a lump payment was offered to B.B. instead of single percentages, things became much easier, for this arrangement led to a very satisfactory one, a retaining fee that was paid out punctually at definite intervals with no further discussion over a picture having or not having been sold. I only wish this agreement could have been reached earlier, for it would have spared B.B. much exasperation and even anxiety and made our life more peaceful.

Of course it could be argued that B.B. was free to give up his professional work in order to dedicate himself exclusively to his reading and his publications. It would however have meant losing all that he had gradually built up. Mary and he had been very extravagant in their expenditure, in the rebuilding of I Tatti, in the laying out of the gardens, in travelling, in buying books, in being fabulously hospitable and very little of what B.B. had earned professionally had been put aside. It was only in 1927 (as a consequence of the agreement over the Benson pictures) that B.B. started making provisions for the future and had his will drawn up for the first time by Duveen's legal adviser, leaving his whole estate to Harvard University.

It was not a decision that could please Mary. She was deeply disappointed and instead of showing her usual exuberant optimism she was almost panicky for the future of her children and grandchildren and would have liked to provide for them in a generous, not to say extravagant, way.

Egged on by her sister Alys, who was a fanatical feminist, Mary had built up a grievance against B.B. for not having shared every penny of his professional earnings with her. I had endless discussions with her on this very point and tried hard to convince her that he practically did share everything with her, as there was nothing he spent money on—acquisitions and improvements in house, library and garden at I Tatti, extensive travelling, long stays in foreign countries—that she did not enjoy with him. What he had done for his own people, creating a family trust that provided them all with a decent but certainly not lavish income, was very little compared to the vast sums she had spent on her children and grandchildren. My efforts to get Mary over this particular grievance had generally a good effect momentarily but after a few days or even hours she would snap back into her former attitude.

Nicky to Mary   Poggico allo Spino   July 30th 1930
   . . . The feeling that a good deal of extra expenses keep on being made out of his account and in a half-hidden way creates a state of irritation and suspicion on B.B.'s side and if that could be somehow changed and made clearer and more open it might operate, in my opinion, a great change in his attitude. He *ought* to be more philosophical about it, I grant you, but a man who has made his money himself has very rarely the same attitude than one who has grown up in relative opulence. Having no children of his own it seems so natural that he should want to leave something that will honour his name and his activity. I remember that when three years ago he made his will for the first time and settled money on your grandchildren you were simply radiant and told me and even wrote to me that you would be delighted to help him with his plans for the future. I cannot see what has been changed since then to make you feel so differently about it.
   But I daresay many things have been said in years gone

by that I do not know and cannot really judge. What I have been successful in making him understand is that the only way for letting you have a peaceful *Nachkur* which he so sincerely wishes you to have is to give you some peace of mind about money.

Nicky to Mary   Poggio allo Spino   July 30th 1930
          . . . I found your dear letter of August 24th and am sorry you misunderstood one sentence in my letter. I find it absolutely natural that B.B. should help your children and I would find it just as natural if you had not done a stroke of work for him and he did it only out of love for you. What I meant was that it would be equally natural if in a moment of crisis childless blood relations of theirs, like Alys, like Logan, like Carey Thomas helped them too. But I daresay I had no business to make a remark of that kind.

Now and then I was tempted to remind Mary of her own responsibility in changing I Tatti from a relatively modest house into a big and money-devouring establishment. Keen on creating work for her two pets Goeffrey Scott and Cecil Pinsent, Mary had probably been the initiator of it all. It seemed to me not unlikely that B.B., so conservative by nature, would have gone on living in a house of more modest proportions. But it is never safe to base one's arguments on something one is not absolutely sure of.

Mary's grievance about B.B.'s professional income was, I believe, based on the assumption that a great deal was due to her because of the advantages his marriage with her had brought him not only professionally through her complete devotion to his work but also socially. The social advantage certainly counted as to her own family and friends in the States and in England but not otherwise, for B.B.'s most important social links—Mrs. Gardner, the Thomas Perrys, Ralph Curtis, Lady Sassoon—were all made independently from his marriage with Mary. That she helped him enormously in his work was absolutely true. Without her driving power behind him he would have achieved much less. It was she who egged him on to write down his aesthetical theories, just as she later pushed and persuaded Geoffrey Scott to write his *Architecture of Humanism*. Mary must also have worked out with B.B. the plan of the "lists" appended to each of B.B.'s four early essays. The discussing and comparing photographs of paintings in connection with the lists went on being one of their favourite pastimes and as an amusing by-product Mary and B.B. tended to see likenesses with types painted by the old masters in the people they met. Mary used to say that she herself had been compared to Giorgione by B.B. when he first met her, then to Titian, then to Palma Vecchio, then to Licinio and finally to Girolamo di Santa Croce.

But already during our first sight-seeing expeditions I had noticed that when it came to looking at the actual works of art there was a divergence between B.B.'s and Mary's approach to the old masters. Mary, faithful to the *Golden Urn* [1] tradition, was interested in what she called "sacred pictures," despised what did not fit into that canon and considered it a loss of time to look at the works of the provincial followers or at the inferior productions of the great masters. B.B. on the contrary was very methodical and slow, almost pedantic in looking at everything, good, bad and indifferent and kept preaching to Mary that only by knowing the smaller masters thoroughly could one build up the artistic personality of the great ones convincingly. Frequently, when we entered one of the provincial museums Mary would begin by walking resolutely through all the rooms and then return to us declaring it to be an N.A., a never-again type of museum. Mary knew a great deal about the smaller masters but was thoroughly weary of them and

---

[1] A sort of anthology put together by Mary, B.B. and Logan of the finest passages in English poetry and drama combined with the first Lists of "sacred" Italian Renaissance pictures.

remained unshakable in her conviction that only the very highest creations were worth bothering about. On our reaching Budapest in 1925 Mary, who was just recovering from a bad cold, asked us to do our sight-seeing without her. "I shall ask Parry to accompany me to the picture gallery just to look at two 'sacred pictures.'" She told us afterwards that when she had explained to Parry that only two pictures were worth looking at his reply had been: "Madam, how would you know which are the really good ones if the bad ones were not there?"

Gradually the meaning of the lists became clear to me and with it the importance of taking note of every word B.B. might say while looking at a picture. It was no use telling him that his former attribution of a picture was different from his present one. "What of it?" he would say. "I have learnt to see more clearly and that alone is important." We used to tease him about certain smaller eclectic masters being like waste-paper baskets for him. Whatever he could not place definitely would be thrown into one of them.

B.B. to Nicky   June 6th 1927
   . . . I am getting on with the lists and am now in the thick of the Piedmontese. They do not excite me. Of course the *Epigonen* will be scandalized at my failing to distinguish between the least of them known to-day and that least's imitator whom they will discover. . . .

All our trips in the years between 1922 and 1938 except those to Egypt, Greece, Turkey and Syria were more or less connected with the lists, with making corrections and additions to them. The agreement over the new edition with the Clarendon Press was reached in 1923, and in 1924 the actual work was started and carried on for several years by Margaret Rickert, an American art student who later became well known as an excellent connoisseur of English illuminated manuscripts. I was at that time too busy in the library to help except by taking notes when we were travelling. When B.B. himself began to go systematically over the material prepared for him I started working with him every morning. Sometimes everything went as if on wheels, on other days there were no end of snags and problems and rages. Once B.B., who generally covered me with butter over the correctness of my English, lost his temper when I pronounced the word allegory with the accent on the second syllable. "Your English will drive me to drink," he groaned. As a matter of fact although I have a fair knowledge of English, my pronunciation will never recover from my having my first English lessons "second-hand." Both my sisters had an English governess to instruct them during a summer that I spent in the Baltic provinces and handed me on what they had learnt on my return.

I worked as hard as I could on the revision of the lists but it never engaged the whole of me as the new edition of the *Florentine Drawings* did years later. Perhaps because the well-defined corpus of the drawings was something I felt I could master while the *olla podrida* of the lists was more than I could cope with, at least not in a way to get real satisfaction and happiness out of it. It seemed like a desperate endless chase to detect double listings, to procure photographs, to look up articles and reproductions.

Nicky to Mary March 1st 1928
> . . . The lists are going on slowly and peacefully as I have learnt to go over them more carefully before I present them to B.B. But it leaves me hardly a minute for anything else for it means hunting up every possible information and reproduction. . . .

I appreciated the lists chiefly as a means, not as a purpose in themselves, as a wonderful excuse for sight-seeing expeditions to remote places. In the course of the years until the revised edition appeared in 1932 we had several other helpers working at them. For instance Barbara Sessions during one of her long stays at the Villino. She and her husband, the composer Roger Sessions, had been introduced to B.B. and Mary by Mrs. Chanler and during the years they spent in Europe came again and again.

Later on it was Evelyn Vavalà who did most of the proof-reading very efficiently. We met her in 1926 in Verona and went around sight-seeing with her there. When she settled down in Florence, Mary took her under her special protection because she considered her ill-used by her husband. B.B. respected her capacity and excellent preparation in art studies but found her rather tiresome and would have preferred not to see her so frequently at his table. His nickname for her was Attila because he said that where she had been harvesting there was nothing left for others to glean.

B.B. to Nicky   May 14th 1930

. . . Yesterday was a Vavalà day and I took her out for a walk. She talked steadily all the time about attributions and their makers, how wonderful Longhi was at the London Exhibition and how dreadful various other people. She sang of the industriousness of Fiocco and was loud in her praises of Offner. She prattled and rattled and tattled and sometimes I did listen and was amused or informed. . . .

Nicky to Mary   August 2nd 1930

. . . With Vavalà who is here we have talked a great deal about Fiocco and Salmi and Weigelt. She is very intelligent and alive but her horizon is about as narrow as Creswell's and sometimes she makes me think of Lopez[2] "nobody knows anything about her." With the difference that there is nothing *louche* about her, only the strange fact that she seems to have no set of friends or acquaintances, no relatives, nothing except art history, attributions and her marital and

---

[2] One of the characters in Trollope's *Prime Minister*.

amorous complications. She has not been a bit gloomy or desperate here and I hope that the change has done her good.

B.B. never had pupils in the accepted sense of the word. He could only work by himself and the help he required was what Mary and later on I could give him, looking up dates, quotations, photos and general information. When I worked with him on the lists or on the drawings it was as an amanuensis, not as somebody professionally trained. He never gave lectures or held seminars. Younger men could only profit by being in touch with him, by meeting him at meals or at tea-time, by walking with him or accompanying him on his sight-seeing expeditions, above all by exposing themselves to his socratic system of asking questions. In a certain sense Geoffrey Scott or Walter Lippmann or Umberto Morra or Harry Coster and later on Arturo Loria and Giovanni Colacicchi were just as much his pupils as the young art historians who came to work at I Tatti.

One of these was a young American recommended by old friends of B.B.'s and Mary's who turned up after our return from Rome and came to work in the library and to join us for meals or for drives and walks. His name was Hyatt Mayor[3] and I remember him as particularly responsive and sensitive and that both Mary and B.B. became very fond of him. There was even some talk of his becoming attached more permanently to I Tatti but other things intervened. Probably he found a job that attracted him more.

In the late summer of 1925 while I was staying with my people in Munich, Mary wrote to me:

September 12th   I Tatti
    . . . Mrs. Ross, Charlie Bell[4] and a handsome Oxford

[3] Now curator of the print room in the Metropolitan Museum, New York.

[4] For many years the keeper of the Ashmolean Museum in Oxford.

boy were coming to dinner but Charlie is ill and only Aunt
Janet and the boy are coming.

September 13th Bologna

. . . The boy turned out a perfect dear. B.B. was enraptured with his intelligence and culture. This morning we
walked over to Poggio Gherardo to see Bell and he was
worse and said he was particularly sorry because of his young
friend. So I said let him come over to lunch and Sidney
Brown[5] will take care of him afterwards and this seemed to
turn out very satisfactorily. But the chief thing was that
B.B. after more talk with him invited him to come and work
under himself for two or three years and the young man
was enraptured. It all depends on his father who wants him
to be a lawyer. He is very rich. You are sure to like him and
he is as keen as snuff on most of the things we care for.
Sidney was going to take him to Pinsent which filled the
youth with pious awe, as Geoffrey [Scott]'s book is his
Bible. . . .

Knowing how easily Mary took an *engouement* I felt
slightly sceptical but when Mary and B.B. arrived a few
days later in Munich I found that B.B. too was very much
taken with the young man and talked a lot about what he
hoped would be a fruitful association. When the young
prodigy Kenneth Clark arrived after Christmas to stay for a
fortnight, what so often happens when somebody has been
praised in superlative terms happened to me. I found him
not too easy to talk to, rather stand-offish and cutting in his
remarks, also not free from conceit for one so young. But
soon I realized that much of all this was a mask for shyness

---

[5] A cultivated and gifted young Anglo-Swiss with whom we had
become acquainted through Byba Coster. He was a great favourite
with both Mary and B.B. and was called by B.B. "gentle Robber
Brown" a quotation, I believe, from one of the Bab ballads. He
is now one of the managers of the Brown Boveri works in
Baden-Aargau.

and that there was much more kindness and softness of heart in Kenneth than appeared in his outward manner. B.B. was delighted with his *trouvaille* and so was Logan, who had arrived almost at the same time with Kenneth. Without being perhaps quite aware of it Logan fell in love with Kenneth and at the table addressed himself exclusively to him. It was arranged that in the following autumn Kenneth would join us in northern Italy, travel around with us and help B.B. with the revision of the lists in view of the new edition.

The plan was carried out and in October 1926 B.B., Kenneth and I set out together while Mary left for a short stay at I Tatti to attend to various improvements in house and garden. When she joined us at Verona she became at once aware of Kenneth's nervousness about the post and about where letters could reach us and told me that this was not natural and could only be explained by his being desperately in love. Keen as Mary was on any possibility of that kind she managed to find out the truth very quickly. Kenneth was indeed deeply in love with a young Oxford student of history, of Irish origin about whose charms we had already heard, as one of Lina Waterfield's sons was also in love with her. Kenneth considered himself engaged to her and Mary thereupon encouraged him to go home for Christmas and to get married as quickly as possible. Then to return with her and to inhabit the San Martino house, an old monastic building close to our parish church of San Martino a Mensola which had been added in 1920 to the Berenson estate. All this was arranged without B.B. being told a word about it and when he at last heard what was being planned his disappointment was great. "I counted on having an assistant free from family ties," he said. "And now it is bound to be a completely different thing." Although fully aware of Jane Clark's unusual charm and glad to have the young couple as neighbours in the Chiostro di San Martino,

B.B., Poggio allo Spino, 1931

*Edith Wharton at
Sainte-Claire-le-Chateau,
1934*

Arturo Loria

it took him a long time to digest his personal grudge. B.B.'s connection with Kenneth might have become a humanly closer one if Kenneth had stayed unmarried for a few years longer, but I doubt whether it would have made a great difference.

Nicky to B.B.   Merano   June 5th 1927
Dearest B.B.,
I have not seen your big sprawling handwriting yet. It always looks as if your pen was a horse galloping along without minding rider or reins.

You will have seen in my first letter to Mary that I had a very pleasant time with the Clarks. He talked freely about you and the work he would like to do for you and I feel very hopeful about it. After all, the fact that he has a great deal of affection for you means a lot for any kind of collaboration. . . .

Temperamentally B.B. and Kenneth were not made for working together, partly because both needed solitude and concentration to do their best work, partly because B.B., as I have already said, had a disconcerting way of throwing cold water on whatever suggestion one tried to make while he was grappling with a problem. If one could manage not to mind (which I admit was not easy) and stick to one's opinion or idea, he would not infrequently end by taking it into serious consideration. Kenneth was both too shy and too proud to defend his position successfully. Of course there were many occasions when they saw eye to eye and when B.B. rejoiced in the richness of Kenneth's cultural foundation. In later years, when Kenneth had already made his reputation as art critic and writer and as museum director, B.B. and he found themselves again and again in complete harmony while looking together at works of art and particularly so in the contemplation and discussion of classical art.

IT WAS SEVERAL YEARS after Kenneth's return to England that John Walker, warmly recommended by Paul Sachs after his brilliant graduation from Harvard, came to spend a period of study first in Florence and then at the Villino. He fitted into our circle like a cog in a wheel with his charming responsiveness and quick sense of humour. B.B. called him *Cherubino* and loved to tease him over his being almost uninterruptedly in a state of infatuation with one young woman or another, if not with more than one at the same time. B.B. had gradually become milder in his attitude to younger art students and readier to enjoy their company and the stimulation of their talk without trying to discourage them from what seemed to him irrelevant pursuits.

AGAIN A FEW YEARS LATER it was Benjamin Nicolson who came to spend a winter in Florence, worked almost every day in the library and joined us at the lunch-table or for week-ends. B.B. did not feel very hopeful about his having chosen the career of art historian and considered him more gifted as a writer on literary subjects but did not discourage him and liked talking to him and getting his reactions, slow and halting ones but always absolutely truthful. B.B. used to say that Ben was like a deep well of crystal clear water and that it was worthwhile making the effort to draw it up.

TWO YOUNG AMERICAN ART STUDENTS with whom B.B. was in contact between the late twenties and the early thirties were Alfred Nicholson, a relation of Mary's, who following B.B.'s advice had spent a year in Oxford and had then taken art courses at Princeton, and his friend Rensselaer Lee.[6] Alfred stayed for several years at the Villino with his attractive wife while the Lees lived in Poggio Gherardo as paying

---

[6] Now dean of the art department at Princeton University.

guests. Both worked in the library and were considered very promising by B.B.

A little later on B.B. acquired another semi-pupil in Daniel Thomson, a young Bostonian scientist who having become interested in scientific methods of restoration worked for some time at the Fogg Museum and was sent from there to I Tatti, where B.B. liked him at first sight and found his caustic combative turn of mind intensely stimulating. Between 1930 and 1939 Daniel came several times to see him and many letters were exchanged between them.

Among B.B.'s younger English colleagues the one he saw most frequently either in London or when he came to Italy was W. G. Constable.[7] B.B. could invariably count on his help, on his procuring material or information for him and W.G. became one of his most faithful correspondents.

Perhaps of all these men the one B.B. talked to most during his frequent visits to I Tatti and to Poggio allo Spino was Umberto Morra. He had a special gift of drawing out B.B. and acted as B.B.'s temporary Eckermann by noting down many of his conversations with him.[8] Nothing could give a more vivid picture of the variety of his interests, of his erudition, his witty paradoxes, his sense of fun. B.B. had no notion of Morra's having the habit of noting down each evening all he could remember of the various subjects touched upon during the day. And perhaps it was better that he did not know. It might have embarrassed him somehow and kept him from letting himself go without any restraint.

---

[7] After being keeper of paintings at the National Gallery, London, from 1924 to 1931, W. G. Constable was from 1938 to 1958 curator of pictures at the Fine Arts Museum, Boston.

[8] These annotations have meanwhile been published under the title *Colloqui con Berenson* (Garzanti, 1963), and in English as *Conversations with Berenson* (Boston: Houghton-Mifflin; 1965).

CHAPTER XII

Travel in Italy

WHAT MEMORIES the title of this chapter awakens! I see ourselves rolling along on the white and dusty roads of Italy in our heavily loaded Lancia car. How Parry managed to get such quantities of luggage evenly distributed on its roof remains a mystery. Inside endless rugs, shawls, maps, guidebooks, Mary's special voluminous book-bag, plus the precious tea-basket had to find their place. Nevertheless we were very comfortable in this old-fashioned diligence-like contraption which allowed a full view of the landscape through its large windows. Often as we approached our destination I could have wished for a magical change of its size allowing us to spend the night in it. Our arrivals in hotels—except where we were already well kown—tended to be stormy. B.B. suffered acutely from what he called his "xenodochophobia"—horror of inns—even for a stop of one night. His chief preoccupation was about the size of the room, the right kind of light for reading in bed, the general cleanliness. Once on reaching an inn in the southern Tyrol late in the afternoon, I went at once to the dining room to find out what kind of a meal we could get. Then I went to B.B.'s room to tell him about the delightful impression the whole house with its huge stoves and old-fashioned furniture had made on me. "I am afraid you are far too optimistic," he said. "Look what I have discovered." And lifting himself up on the tips of his toes he managed to reach the top shelf of the cupboard and showed me that his fingers were covered with dust.

Mary's preoccupations were of a different kind. She would start inquiring whether the rooms to right, to left and above the one proposed to her were or were not occupied, whether the lift or the waiter's office were in its neighbourhood and sometimes ended by choosing a small and badly appointed room on the assumption that it would be particularly quiet. In a large and luxurious hotel Mary once refused to occupy an excellent room on the front end because she had found an ideally quiet one way at the back. In the early morning hours it turned out to be over the kitchen entrance where heavy vans drove up to deliver provisions.

Added to the problem of the room there was the arduous question of the mail. Had it arrived? Was the concierge a competent man? Were there any family letters for Mary and daily and weekly papers for B.B.?

Also the choice of a suitable place for a picnic at lunch-time or tea-time was apt to become a dramatico-comical episode. No agreement could be reached and when a site that seemed attractive to both Mary and B.B. was at last spotted, Parry had a perverse way of rushing past it before he could be stopped. On a long drive from Syracuse to Enna B.B. noticed a solitary almond tree and proposed, although it was a bit early for luncheon, that we should take advantage of its shade. "Nonsense Bernard, we are sure to find a grove by a lovely spring later on." B.B. begged her to remember that we happened to be in a particularly arid and stony part of Sicily and that the chances of hitting the kind of place she had in mind were slight. She would not hear of it. When it was almost two o'clock and all of us were a bit famished we ended by spreading out our food on the bank of a dried up stream without a tree in sight and under the stinging sun of a *scirocco* day.

B.B.'s curiosity about fellow travellers, their racial type and what their profession might be was inexhaustible. Once on reaching the Albergo Nettuno in Pisa in the early autumn we found it full of English people, a whole party of them and in the evening we saw them all dining at a long table, exchanging noisy jokes and throwing rolls and oranges at each other. B.B. was fascinated. "Who can they be? What are they here for? They are not ordinary tourists and belong to the small bourgeoisie. If they took a trip to Italy at all they would not be spending the night at Pisa." Next morning he received me with a beaming smile. "There is only one explanation. They must be undertakers on their way to choose marble for funerary monuments in Carrara or Pietrasanta and have used the occasion for making a jolly party of it. Please go at once to the concierge and ask him." "*Sissignora*," said the concierge, "*sono partiti or'ora per Pietrasanta a comprar marmi*"—they have just left for Pietrasanta to buy marble.

Sometimes he would say of people in museums or restaurants: "They look like unknown old friends." When we travelled by train or by boat he got into conversation with his fellow travellers chiefly to satisfy his curiosity about the books they were reading and not infrequently got a lot of fun out of such chance encounters. In this craving for direct contact with other human beings B.B. was like a character out of a Russian novel. Mary often told him that it was safer for him not to meet people against whom he had a well-justified prejudice because he might end by finding them very attractive. "For instance, Mussolini. Who knows how you would react to him personally?"

OUR TRIP all around Sicily in the spring of 1926 was a particularly happy and carefree one and equally delightful our long stay in Naples. For me it meant getting thoroughly acquainted for the first time with my "home-town," for in 1898 when we left it I was only familiar with our house, the garden, the terrace, the little port of Mergellina, the walks along the Posillipo and the Corso Caracciolo, the view of the gulf and of Vesuvius. Our new friend Morra came to meet us in Naples and accompanied us on many of our excursions. Aldo de Rinaldis, the director of the museum and his chief assistant, Dario Ortolani, were constantly at B.B.'s disposal. In Pompeii it was Matteo della Corte, the archaeologist, who looked after us. With Morra we went for the first time to see the Ruffinos at the Capo di Sorrento, Salvemini's friends with whom he had stayed after his release from prison and where he was much later to spend his last years. The three of them, Titina (Ferdinando Martini's daughter), her husband Carlo Ruffino and Titina's daughter from her first marriage, Giuliana Benzoni, became real friends and B.B. used to call La Rufola, their enchanting home in Sorrento, by the title of one of Turgenev's novels, *Dvorianskoe Gniezdo*—a nest of gentlefolk. At the Rufola we also met the Braccis, Margherita, the daughter of B.B.'s old friend Francesco Papafava, and her husband, Lucangelo. It was while staying with them that Salvemini had been arrested in 1925. With this whole group one could feel in perfect harmony not only for political reasons but for their quality as highly civilized and cultivated human beings.

On reaching Naples I had rung up Benedetto Croce's house and had introduced myself as the daughter of Croce's old friend Raffaele Mariano. On being cordially invited I asked whether I could introduce B.B. to him. Croce accepted readily and from then on we never stayed in Naples without calling on him. The afternoon gatherings in Croce's studio were very informal. He would go on with whatever he happened to be doing, proofreading or tying up a parcel or looking for some manuscripts in a drawer and accusing his wife or the servant of having mislaid them, then would interrupt himself and take part in the conversation of his little group of friends. As each visitor came in a maid carrying a small tray with a cup of coffee would appear. I remembered Croce, from having seen him in my mother's salon, as rather elegant and was amazed to find him not only aged and thickened up but very slovenly in his appearance. Handsome he had never been but was saved by his fine intellectual forehead, the penetrating intelligence of his expression and his small elegant hands. The intercourse between him and B.B. was based on agreement in political questions and on human sympathy rather than on direct intellectual contacts. Croce's Abruzzese accent was not easy for B.B. to follow. Just as B.B. thought very little of Croce's approach to aesthetics and considered him incapable of looking at a work of art except from a literary point of view, so Croce had probably little use for B.B.'s theories of aesthetic enjoyment. But while B.B. had the highest regard for Croce as historian and knew all of Croce's historical publications, Croce had probably never taken the trouble to read any of B.B.'s books. Only quite late in his life did he come across B.B.'s four early essays on Renaissance painting and was sufficiently impressed to write a short appreciation of them for the *Critica*.

We returned to Florence by an unusual route, visiting Gaeta and Cassino, spending an icy cold night at Roccaraso on the high plateau of the Abruzzi and another at Francavilla, on the Adriatic coast whose praises were sung by D'Annunzio, where the squalor of a highly advertised hotel drove B.B. into one of his worst rages. Also the inns at Ascoli and Macerata were dark and depressing but at least free from any false pretence. The small beautifully clean inn at Loreto repaid us for these hardships. The Marche like the surroundings of Siena had a special place in B.B.'s and Mary's hearts, reminding them of their early jaunts in search of Lotto's paintings.

ON MY RETURN from my summer holiday in 1926 I found
that Mary had already left for England and that B.B. was
expecting Belle Greene to stay with us. She arrived full of
zest for sight-seeing and altogether at her best, *bon-enfant*,
gay, quick and responsive, ready to enjoy whatever we were
looking at under B.B.'s guidance. We spent several days in
Ravenna with her and then accompanied her to Genoa where
she was to leave on a brand-new Italian transatlantic liner,
the *Roma*. The date of its departure for its maiden voyage
had been fixed by the *Duce* but she turned out to be so far
from ready that relations and friends of the passengers were
not allowed to accompany them on board. While we were
saying good-bye to Belle, furniture and rolls of carpets were
being hoisted up. A disappointment for me who had never
seen one of these floating grand hotels but a source of satisfaction for B.B. as another proof of Mussolini's arbitrary
power. All the more so as the only squabbles between him
and Belle were over Fascism.

During these two trips I had twice to share a room with
Belle and discovered how chock-full of dealer's gossip she
was, and how angry over B.B.'s being—as she assured me—
shamefully exploited by the Duveens. She explained to me
that Mary's and B.B.'s stay in the Hamilton flat in 1920–21
had been nothing but a trap skilfully arranged by Duveen,
who, realizing that Hamilton was not solvent any longer
and would sooner or later return his treasures to him, wanted
the pictures to be well advertised through B.B.'s staying
there and talking about them to his numerous guests. When,
after Belle's departure on the *Roma*, I told B.B. all this he
took it very calmly. "I doubt her being even partly right in
what she has reported to you," he said. "I know for certain
that Hamilton was still on the crest of his wave of financial
success when we stayed in his apartment. Besides his pictures
were good enough not to need much advertising. You must

remember that nobody in any prominent position can escape having dirt thrown at him. It is the price one has to pay for being in one form or another in the limelight and exposed to malicious insinuations."

IN TURIN we met Mary, back from England with her hair cut, and there was much laughter over B.B.'s not noticing this transformation for several days although he had previously strictly forbidden her to think of such a drastic change. At once we were plunged into our usual list-correcting activities. Lionello Venturi, who was then still teaching at the University of Turin, went about with us and invited us to spend a whole day in the Gualino house looking at the collection gathered with Venturi's help and advice. Riccardo Gualino—a fascinating type of self-made business man —had ambitious plans for raising the level of Turin's cultural life. Adjoining his house he had built a small elegant theatre for concerts of classical and modern chamber music, for *avant-garde* plays. His wife, a gifted artist and highly cultivated woman, was able to encourage him in carrying out his program. It was all done without ostentation or fuss.[1]

From Turin we went on to the Gazzada, Don Guido Cagnola's property near Varese, and I had a last glimpse of what the autumn season in these sumptuous Lombard villas used to be like. In Milan we were joined by Umberto Morra and later by Kenneth Clark. To Mary, who had gone to Florence, I wrote:

---

[1] A few years later Gualino lost his fortune, got into trouble with the Fascist regime and spent several years *al confino*—in exile—on the island of Lipari. His collection was sequestered by the government and now forms part of the Turin picture gallery. Later on, undaunted, Gualino remade a considerable fortune and went on collecting. At his death in 1963 he left a fine villa at Arcetri above Florence and a palace in Rome both filled with works of art, antique as well as modern.

Hotel Cavour   Milan   October 24th 1926

Our news is good and Kenneth seems to be a most delightful sight-seeing companion and from what I watched at the Ambrosiana while B.B. and he were looking at drawings together I could see that he would be what B.B. needs for getting that work into shape.

Yesterday we went to Sant'Ambrogio and saw the doors uncovered and the treasury and in the afternoon we looked again at the collection of illuminated mss. bought by Hoepli from Fairfax Murray.[2] We had quite a dinner-party in the evening, really more people than we wanted because the Rosselli couple had changed the date at the last minute. So we had them and Mario Borsa and a friend of Morra's from Turin. Borsa was delightful, something like a bourgeois Don Guido, very spontaneous and hearty and speaks excellent English. You would have enjoyed meeting him and hearing him talk. The Rossellis [Carlo Rosselli and his English wife] were very pleasant. Friday we had Ojetti to dinner and Kenneth had an occasion for getting accustomed to the sound of Italian. He understands more than I thought and his accent is very good. The way he has got hold of German is amazing for he has read and enjoyed very difficult things like for instance Woelflin's books.

When a few days later B.B., Kenneth and I started out on our trip the beginning of it was not auspicious. Already at Brescia, three days after our departure from Milan, we found ourselves arrested for theft. Late at night Elizabeth knocked at my door in floods of tears and told me that we were wanted by the police. My heart sank. I thought of our dinner-party in the Hotel Cavour in our private sitting-room, of the talk with such passionate anti-Fascists as Carlo Rosselli and Mario Borsa and felt sure that it had been somehow overheard or registered. "What do they accuse us of?" I asked. "Of having stolen something in a church." I laughed out-

---

[2] Now in the Giorgio Cini Foundation, San Giorgio Maggiore, Venice.

right, to Elizabeth's amazement, so great was my relief. The men who came into my room turned out to be of the Fascist militia, not of the regular police, and seemed determined to take us right off to prison. With the help of the hotel owner I persuaded them of the impossibility of our running away with our car in a distant garage and made them wake up the director of the museum who had been with us all through the afternoon. Nevertheless they insisted on making a thorough examination of all our things in the hope of finding the stolen *arredi sacri*. Also Kenneth had to submit to the search in his room. Actually there had been a theft in a church in Treviglio that we had visited on our way to Bergamo and the thieves had paid the sacristan to denounce us as the culprits to the police.

But after that flurry all went smoothly and most enjoyably. As usual B.B. did not confine himself to the revision of the lists but looked at sculpture, architecture, illuminated manuscripts, church treasures. Drives to distant shrines were taken in horrible weather and over the worst possible roads. On an icy day we went up from Parma to the Bardone Pass to look at one early Romanesque relief. While on our way to Feltre I remember Mary asking B.B. whether he also would look at the picture belonging to the lunatic asylum. "Of course," was B.B.'s answer. "Splendid," said Mary, "then I can have a good look at the lunatics too." Kenneth, who knew nothing of this particular propensity of hers, was aghast. Great was Mary's disappointment when it turned out that the picture had been removed from the central hall of the lunatic asylum to the chapel.

What B.B. was able to achieve on these trips in spite of his delicate constitution beggars description. He would spend hours in a museum without sitting down once, he would prowl around churches and climb up shaky ladders to see frescoes or pictures more clearly. If some world-forgotten chapel could not be reached by car he would walk for miles.

Tea helped to keep him going and we never moved without a tea-basket. We were supposed to find a lovely spot but often ended by having it in the car, even in a crowded street, gaped at by the local population like strange animals. It was his self-discipline and the passionate love of his pursuit that made him get the better of his bodily ailments. Sometimes he overdid it and more than once I have seen him faint away after a day of intensive sight-seeing. But he knew how to relax completely and recovered quickly.

Many years later in the spring of 1945 after the liberation, B.B. fell ill with bronchitis and his cousin Robert Berenson (then A.D.C. to General Clark) insisted on bringing down from the Gothic Line two American specialists serving in the army. They overhauled B.B., said he was threatened with pneumonia, prescribed various drugs and had some talk with him. As they were walking away I heard one of them say, "He does not act sick," and the other answer, "Yes, he ought to act sicker." B.B., in order to "act sick," had to be very sick indeed.

We took a number of shorter trips in Italy between 1924 and 1931, with and without Mary, who frequently went off to England or to try a new cure. I see one picture after the other before me. Siena and San Gimignano in 1924 with Eric and Helen Maclagan. Siena had been one of the centres of B.B.'s and Mary's early wanderings and B.B. had a special tenderness for it, not only for its school of painting but for the town itself and the country around it. His delight in looking at things tended to be combined with a nostalgic wistfulness over not being able to communicate fully to others his own aesthetic experience. Yet he had the capacity of making one see more clearly and feel more intensely without saying a word himself. It was as if his rapt absorption in the work of art communicated itself to his companions without any need for explanation or instruction.

Both the Maclagans were most appreciative and congenial people to sight-see with, but between Eric and B.B.
there was a special bond created by their sense of quality,
even if B.B.'s reactions were more spontaneously sensual than
Eric's. Vary rarely have I seen them in disagreement over
what they were looking at and one followed the other's lead
in what was his special field, painting for B.B. and sculpture
for Eric.

In July 1924 and in full summer heat another long stay
in Siena with almost daily work on the illuminated codexes
in the Piccolomini library and excursions in the late afternoon through the scorched almost spectral landscape of the
crete—the white chalk hills—to Asciano and Monte Oliveto
or through the ilex woods to Lecceto, San Leonardo al Lago
and Celsa, or to Pienza and Montepulciano, or around the
Monte Amiata to Montalcino and Sant'Antimo, or down to
Paganico, San Galgano and Massa Marittima. I remember the
light being so intense at midday when we used to step out
of the *duomo* that B.B. would keep his eyes shut and I would
lead him like a blind man over the *piazza* to the shelter of
one of the narrow alleys. After dinner we would return to
the *duomo*, sit on the marble bench along the side of it,
enjoy the evening breeze and the children playing up and
down the steps and watch the curve of the unfinished aisle
against the evening sky.

In May 1928 we set out all three for Siena and Massa
Marittima and on to Grosseto and Civitavecchia where
Placci, accompanied by his Sicilian valet Giuseppe, came to
meet us from Rome. As we were getting ready for the excursion to Tarquinia, Elizabeth implored us not to leave her
alone "with that awful Giuseppe." In Tarquinia B.B., Placci
and Parry went to look at the so-called "indecent" frescoes
and both Placci and B.B. came back disappointed because
they remembered them from previous visits as being of larger
size. Parry made no comment.

Later on in 1928 I see B.B. and me on our way to San Pellegrino in Alpe above Pistoia and from there driving through the Garfagnana to Aulla where the old fortress La Brunella with its four massive towers watches over the confluence of the Aulla and the Aulella rivers. In the fortress lived our friends the Waterfields and we stayed with them in an easygoing and picturesque atmosphere. Aubrey Waterfield, who tended to be peevish and dissatisfied at Poggio Gherardo (perhaps because everything there reminded him of his antagonist Mrs. Ross, who had died in 1927), was at his best at Aulla, looking after his garden, painting his lovely flower compositions and living the unconventional kind of life he loved. One thing however followed the lines of a well-established tradition—the food was excellent. Dinner was served at a rustic table on top of one of the towers with the full view of the Apuan Alps before us. To call for the second course Aubrey would blow into a huge conch like a sea-god.

It must have been in 1927 that we all three went to Urbino and Rimini and met Adrian Stokes in the Tempio Malatestiano. Then going on towards Ravenna we stopped at the church of San Giuliano outside Rimini to look at Paolo Veronese's altarpiece there. It was a lovely morning in May, the church wide open, the altar decorated with a row of vases with white lilac in them. Not a soul in the church, not even a sacristan. While B.B. was trying to find the right place for looking at the picture, placed behind the high altar, Mary discovered a small ladder, climbed up on it and sat down on the back of the altar so heavily that all the flower-vases on the front fell down with a terrific clatter. Mary, quite unconcerned, boasted of having found the best place from which to see the picture and teased us for being so unenterprising. Then as she wanted to use the ladder again it collapsed under her with more deafening noise—but no harm done. B.B. rushed away in despair, saying he could not stay another minute in such an *inferno*, and we after him. The sacristan on returning must have thought that the devil himself had visited the church.

Early in June 1930 Mary decided that she would try out the cure in Fiuggi and we both accompanied her, stayed first in Montepulciano with the Braccis in their *palazzo* with the heavenly view over the small lakes of Chiusi and Montepulciano, the Trasimeno and the dark shape of the Subasio behind it. Then to Assisi and further down to Rieti and Palombara and so we reached Fiuggi without touching Rome. While Mary had her cure in the morning B.B. and I took walks in the chestnut woods or read together. In the afternoons one excursion followed the other, to Anagni with its fortress-like cathedral, to Alatri with its cyclopic walls, to Frosinone and Ferentino with the Cosmati altars and pulpits in their churches, to Segni with its church built into the walls of an antique temple, to Fossanova, the abbey where Saint Thomas spent his last years, to Subiaco with its ilex groves, to Filettino at the top of the Aniene valley where the river gushes down in small waterfalls along the road. It was all as it must have looked when Ferdinand Gregorovius wrote his *Lateinische Sommer* almost sixty years earlier.

Years later on my arrival in Sorrento I wrote to B.B.:

> . . . Our journey gave me a most delicious sense of being close to you, so many and sweet were the recollections of you every time I looked out of the window. Perhaps some day, if you should have to leave me I could spend my time just driving about in Italy to remember and to dream. There was the Trasimeno that enchanted us a few weeks ago and the level crossing at Castiglion del Lago where we sat in the sun and the road to Amelia running up the hill and Fara Sabina with its meadows stretching down to the river, and Velletri and Cori and Norma; the brigand country between Itri and Fondi and the buffaloes on the banks of the Garigliano. It is all of it doubly beautiful for having seen it with you. . . .

CHAPTER XIII

Half a Year
in Northern Europe [1927]

THAT IS WHERE WE WERE in 1927, leaving home early in
the summer and in our usual style, snug and compact
in our mastodontic Lancia car with Stockholm as our chief
objective. We reached it by slow stages, stopping in Vienna,
in Loûcen (the country seat of Princess Thurn und Taxis),
in Prague, in Dresden, in Berlin, in Stralsund, where B.B.
and Mary had their first rages against windows devoid of
dark curtains or blinds of any kind. How my father used to
curse those "white" northern summer nights and the strange
northern habit of providing no protection against them.
When we landed in Trelleborg I felt completely at home.
The light, the smells, the tall birches with their white stems,
the wooden peasant houses and barns and fences, the food—
everything reminded me of my second, my lost, homeland
Esthonia. If only I could have spoken the language! From
our first stop, Hälsingborg, we paid a visit to the crown
prince in his summer home, Sofiero. On reaching the gate
of his property we found the crown prince himself, in a white
summer suit, waiting for us. There was something delightfully Hans Andersen-like in this reception. The same uncere-
monious atmosphere during dinner and while walking about
out-of-doors in the soft light of the northern summer evening.

At the Grand Hotel in Stockholm we had a rather unfriendly reception and in spite of our previous correspondence there seemed to be no rooms available for us. Finally B.B. had to make, in Casanova's phrase, *un tapage de grandseigneur* and refer to his friendship with the crown prince. This had an immediate effect and very nice rooms were put at our disposal. It must be a time-honoured practice of hotel managers the world over to keep some good rooms in reserve for unexpected important clients. B.B.'s rage on this occasion was as usual out of proportion to the cause and made our arrival and settling in comically dramatic.

Between B.B.'s colleagues at the various museums and court officials to whom the crown prince had recommended us and Naima Löfroth and various friends of hers, we saw a good many people, were taken out on excursions, invited to excellent meals, and of course accompanied through the art collections. But now after almost forty years it is not the people nor the meals nor even the art treasures that I remember most vividly, but the light, the blue-greyish, almost steely colour of the water, the forests, the smell of the freshly cut timber, the majestic trunks swimming down the rivers, the sense of space, the long stretches of wild uninhabited country. Both B.B. and I went on and on talking about what reminded him of New England and me of the Baltic provinces. As a child I used to be shown a book by my mother called *Im Fluge durch die Welt*—On a Flight through the World. One of the large illustrations was of Stockholm, and although my mother had never been there she described to me the loveliness of the town in a way I have never forgotten. Like many Balts of her generation she hated the Russian rule and longed for her homeland to be reunited with Sweden. Of course the Stockholm of the early nineties as represented in my picture book had changed a good deal by 1927, yet no modern constructions can ever spoil the essential beauty of its being embraced by the sea.

We left Stockholm by way of Karlstad and the Värmland —Selma Lagerlöf's country—and through endless forests reached the Norwegian frontier and drove down to Oslo along the Glommen. Already in Stockholm we had suffered from what B.B. called the Tower of Babel torture because only a few of the people we met spoke any of the *table d'hôte* languages with any ease. It was worse in Oslo. The archaeologist who accompanied us to the Oseberg ship was unable to answer any of B.B.'s questions. Remarkable was the amount of alcohol consumed on every occasion at Oslo. Even in a motor boat that took us around the bay magnums of champagne were produced and many skoals drunk before we reached land again. Invited to dinner by Jens Thiis, B.B.'s old friend and at that time director of the picture gallery, I counted no less than seven glasses for each guest and when we left about eleven the real fun was only just beginning. For the following morning Jens Thiis had arranged a visit to a famous collection of Impressionist paintings. When we got there the owner of the collection (one of the guests at dinner the night before) and Jens Thiis were both there to receive us but barely able to stand upright and utter a sensible word. Again I was reminded of how birthdays, marriages, and holidays generally used to be celebrated in the Baltic provinces.

As we reached Copenhagen by way of Hälsingborg and Elsinor the Danish coast appeared to us like one great rose garden. We were lucky in having really enchanting summer weather for our northern trip as well as smooth weather between Mary and B.B. As usual we spent our days visiting museums and private collections and driving out to Fredericksborg, Roskilde, and Nievagaard. At Kronenborg the keeper, an elderly man with very courtly manners, accompanied us. He kept looking at Mary and finally asked her where she came from. "Philadelphia in the United States," she answered. "But before that, where did your family come from?" "From Yorkshire." He beamed. "Yorkshire was settled in by Danes and nobody could have more nobly Danish features than you, Madam."

On our last day in Copenhagen the crown prince came to join us at the National Museum and later had lunch with us in a restaurant. The waiter, to show he had recognized him, put a small Swedish flag on our table.

THEN B.B. AND I met the Kingsley Porters in Hamburg while Mary went off to England. Our first excursion with Kingsley and Lucy was to Kiel, where B.B.'s old friend, Arthur Haseloff, the mediaevalist, was at that time teaching at the university. He and his family had lived for years first in Rome and then in Florence and both he and his wife had repeatedly been guests at I Tatti. A gargantuan Italian lunch had been prepared for us in the Haseloff house and right after it we were taken to the museum and to a private collection where a large tea-table was ready for us. Late in the afternoon, with the light already failing, we finally reached what B.B. had chiefly come to see, the small archaeo-logical museum with a Viking boat in it. But there was some-thing else there to fascinate B.B., the so-called *Moor-leichen,* early mediaeval corpses dressed in cassocks of loosely woven wool, completely preserved through having been buried in a special kind of peat-earth. B.B. wanted detailed informa-tion about their dates and their miraculous preservation and there was nobody who could satisfy his curiosity. Meanwhile he had got to the point of almost collapsing from sheer fatigue and we decided to leave. Just as we were getting into the car the specialist for the *Moor-leichen* who had been called appeared on a bicycle, overjoyed at having such a rare visitor and eager to give us a learned and probably very long lecture on the subject. His disappointment as he watched us driving away was pathetic and neither B.B. nor I could ever forget it.

Unforgettable, although not pathetic at all, is the long afternoon we spent at the Warburg House in Hamburg, being shown the magnificent library and meeting Aby Warburg himself, his secretary Gertrud Bing, and a number of young art historians working in the Institute. Ludwig Heydenreich, later well known as a specialist for Leonardo studies,[1] and Fred Neumeyer, now teaching at Mills College, California, were among them.

From Hamburg the Kingsley Porters, B.B., and I took a tour through northwestern Germany dedicated to mediaeval monuments and church treasures. When looking at mediaeval architecture, sculpture, or art objects B.B. and Kingsley were in perfect harmony. No anti-classical bias on Kingsley's side and no censorious endeavours of B.B.'s to get him out of it.

Nicky to Mary   Minden in Westfalen   August 28th 1927
Dearest Mary,

B.B. has gone to take a rest while the Kingsley Porters are already starting for Paderborn, as their average pace is slower than ours. We had great fun yesterday at Hildesheim and wonderful food, *Rebhühnchen mit Sauerkraut* that made me long for your presence to enjoy it with us. Kingsley was able to photograph a tombstone that seemed extremely ugly to us but made him very happy. We saw some really beautiful objects among the church treasures and some good manuscripts and B.B. and I were again struck by Kingsley's slightly *meschugge* method. He just goes for one thing he has in his mind and does not look right or left at anything else. However, thanks to this obstinate hunting-dog system, we saw several remarkable things in Hildesheim we did not know and also came here at his instigation to see a fine eleventh-century bronze and a Carolingian ivory. The drive from Hildesheim this morning was delightful not only because the weather is clear at last (though pretty cold) but

---

[1] Now head of the Zentralinstitut für Kunstgeschichte in Munich.

because we drove through one of the small ex-principalities,
Schaumburg-Lippe and its quiet charming capital, with the
women coming out of church wearing the *Tracht,* red skirts
and enormous black bows, like windmills on their caps. It
is one of those *Fürstentümer* where you might smell the
coffee being toasted in the *Nachbarland.* Tonight we are
going to sleep at Paderborn, the stronghold of German
Catholicism, in an inn called Loeffelmann, probably a real
Locanda di Preti, with good wine and good food. Kingsley
is as concientious as ever about his bacchic habits and orders
excellent wine at every meal. B.B. keeps well and achieved
a real stunt yesterday. We raced about Hildesheim from
10 till 7.30 with only a short rest in the afternoon!

Nicky to Mary   Muenster in Westfalen   August 31st 1927
Dearest Mary,
    Arrived here yesterday and were delighted to find your
letters and such good happy news. It was altogether a pleasant arrival, nice cheerful rooms, nice dinner, no unpleasant
letters, no telegram from Sir Joe, and everything smooth.
Yesterday in Düsseldorf while B.B. went to see the few
Italian pictures and drawings with the help of a stone-deaf
keeper I got some letters off and the Kingsleys rushed on
ahead of us to a Benedictine abbey where we found them
still happily taking photographs at three o'clock. Then on
to Essen where the cathedral has been as usual horribly
repainted but has a wonderful treasury.

IN HOLLAND after looking together at the famous Psalter
in the library of Utrecht, Kingsley and Lucy left for Paris
while we met Mary in Amsterdam and with her went on
visiting museums and private collections in Holland. Particular attention was given to the Teyler Museum in Haarlem.
The revision of his *Drawings of the Florentine Painters* was
beginning to be uppermost in B.B.'s mind and a good deal
of preparatory work had already been done in the summer

in Vienna, Dresden, Berlin, Stockholm, Hamburg, and Bremen. Later, in London, Kenneth Clark joined in most of our visits to the print room of the British Museum, to Windsor, to the Ashmolean in Oxford, and to the Oppenheimer Collection. He took admirable notes on everything and they were of invaluable help during the final revision.

But before getting to London we had an interesting *intermezzo* staying with the banker Adolphe Stoclet and his wife in Brussels. Their house had been built by the Viennese architect and decorator Klimt in what seemed a derivation from the *Judgendstyl* with a curious circular pseudo-mycenean design repeated everywhere on bed and table linen, on forks, knives, plates and glasses. Except for a dancing figure of the Khmer period in the music room and some charming scenes from the life of Saint Catherine of Siena by Giovanni di Paolo, no works of art were on show. Pictures and *objets d'art* were brought out from cupboards and drawers for the visitor to look at quietly and concentratedly in the presence of Stoclet and his wife, who both enjoyed showing and discussing their treasures. This is at least what they did for B.B., who considered Stoclet one of the most intelligent and sensitive collectors he had ever met.

For the month we were to spend in London B.B. had taken things into his own hands and with the help of Lady Colefax had secured Lady Horner's house in Lower Berkeley Street (now Fitzharding Street). We could not have been more comfortable, with an excellent Scotch cook and a priceless parlourmaid, a great character who knew everybody, remembered every engagement, and corresponded to B.B.'s ideal in doing her work with real *passione* and superior intelligence. There was a continual coming and going of guests, while relatively few invitations were accepted by B.B. and Mary. Among these few I remember two in particular.

One was a luncheon party at the house of Henry Harris, the amateur and collector. On the morning before, Harris rang me up and told me that he had asked Roger Fry to meet B.B. after years of coldness between them and would it be better to warn B.B. or not? I felt very doubtful but decided to say nothing. It went off beautifully. The charm of Roger Fry's manner and voice were irresistible and B.B.'s prejudices melted very easily when a personal contact could be established. I will not say that they became intimate friends again, but they met repeatedly in London and both Roger and Helen Fry came to stay at I Tatti a few years later. Mary was very fond of both and particularly happy over this reunion with them.

I never found out what had been the cause of the quarrel between B.B. and Roger Fry. Presumably a question of professional jealousy. Perhaps a picture discovered by one of them and snatched away by the other or an attribution that both claimed to have been the first to make. Whatever it was, Mary must have made things worse by repeating to the wrong person offensive words said by B.B. in a fit of rage or despair. More than once I have seen her creating a lot of unpleasantness by taking B.B.'s often quite irresponsible utterances at their strictest face value.

The second memorable occasion was a luncheon party in Lady Cunard's house—another of the prominent London hostesses, if not the most prominent one. I was seated next to Sir Austen Chamberlain, who, as soon as he discovered my being Italian, started talking about the Fascist régime and Mussolini's character. He told me how shortly after Mussolini's usurpation of power he had been sent to Rome for the signing of a commercial treaty. He had started out with his wife and children, planning to deposit them somewhere on the Riviera and to proceed alone to Rome. When they reached Rapallo his children caught the grippe and he did not feel like leaving his wife alone with them. So he rang up Rome and begged Mussolini to meet him in Rapallo. Mussolini arrived, spent hours with them, sat by the beds of the children, and showed himself as the most charming, easy-going, fatherly friend. At tea-time in their private sitting-room the agreement to be signed was handed to Chamberlain and he read it over twice to be quite sure he had understood all its implications. When he lifted his eyes from the paper the smiling agreeable man opposite him had changed into a scowling truculent one with protruding chin and rolling eyes. For a moment Chamberlain felt frightened and wondered whether his wife had said anything to upset Mussolini. Then he realized that the waiters by opening the double doors of the room to carry out the tea things had exposed the Duce to the eyes of the crowd already assembled in the hall and waiting to cheer him. This story and his way of telling it delighted me and made me take a different view of a man whom I had suspected of being pointedly pro-Fascist.

IT WAS DURING our stay in London that I saw Geoffrey for the last time, just before his sailing for New York, where he had accepted Col. Ralph Isham's proposition to edit the newly discovered Boswell papers. It was a happy and harmonious meeting. After the lunch at Lower Berkeley Street we walked to his flat and had a long talk. He was at his best, witty, playful, detached from himself. We touched on the past only in discussing B.B. and Mary and their relations to each other. He told me that Mary at the time of her infatuation for him had filled him with a strong prejudice against B.B. Curiously enough I met a few days later, when Geoffrey was already on his way to New York, the woman who years earlier had replaced me in his affections. She was a proud and shy woman, difficult to approach, but having heard so much about me from Geoffrey she behaved as if we knew each other well, began at once to talk about Geoffrey and told me how after a first period of complete abandon she had got tired of his neurasthenic egotism and had been in self-defence obliged to break off the relationship with him.[2]

As IN 1923 our stay in London was followed by several weeks in Paris, again at the charming Hotel Beausite in the rue de Presbourg with the old waiter coming up each morning to take our orders and serving us excellent meals in our sitting-room. We worked regularly with Kenneth Clark in the Louvre print room and found time to return to museums and churches in and around Paris. Seymour de Ricci accompanied us to Chantilly, Louis Gillet to Saint Denis and Senlis.[3] When I look back on our trips what I feel most grateful for are B.B.'s slow and thorough sight-seeing habits, his going to places of interest again and again, his allowing for so much time in the important cities that a sense not only of intimacy with the works of art but with the town itself and its human atmosphere was gained by it. Remarks like "We have already done that" or "We need not go there again" did not exist for him except in very rare cases for things that bored him, like collections of armour or porcelain or costume. He had the gift of approaching a picture, a statue, a building as if he were taking it in for the first time. It was what turned sightseeing with him into an exciting adventure. A small particle of B.B.'s receptive mood communicated itself to his companion even if he himself did not utter a word.

---

[2] On his way to the United States in 1929 Geoffrey caught a chill and died of pneumonia in New York.

[3] Seymour de Ricci (1881–1940), French bibliophile and art connoisseur. Louis Gillet (1876–1943), French professor of art history whom B.B. had met during one of his voyages to the United States, when Gillet was going to teach in a Canadian university; remained a close friend and faithful correspondent until his death; translated B.B.'s early four essays into French.

CHAPTER XIV

Friendship with Edith Wharton

F ROM THE VERY BEGINNING of my life at I Tatti I heard
Edith Wharton, her gifts, her character, her books, her
background, her whims and caprices being discussed until
she became for me an important figure on the Berenson
scene. I heard B.B. tell the story of how on meeting her for
the first time he had disliked her thoroughly and how their
friendship had grown out of a later meeting arranged by
Henry Adams (see *Sketch for a Self-portrait*). I heard him
describe a motor trip he took with her in 1913 through
Germany and what he had to go through owing to her
sudden changes of mood. Several years went by without her
coming to Italy nor my accompanying B.B. and Mary to
France or England. At last in the autumn of 1923 during
our stay in London she came to lunch accompanied by one
of her closest friends, the ex-diplomat and painter Robert
Norton. The first sight of her was rather disappointing. A
conventionally dressed woman, jerky in her movements,
somehow ill at ease, with an ugly mouth, shaped like a
savings-box. The eyes were fine, her voice agreeable, and
when she laughed there was something very engaging about
it. My negative impression may have been partly due to the
fact that she never addressed a personal word to me. And
yet she knew that I had been for four years closely associated
with the Berensons. Perhaps she thought that it was just one

of Mary's usual *engouements* that would not last much longer. Her companion, Robert Norton, I found on the contrary most attractive, a member of what Edith called the Society of Charm, Inc.

Later that same autumn she came to stay at I Tatti and there, listening to her during quiet evenings in the library and watching her, I began to see her in a different light. Besides, my *amour propre* was satisfied by her giving now and then a little attention to me and by her asking me to accompany her on a tour through the Florentine shops. It required a good deal of patience to comply with her fastidious and often surprisingly capricious demands.

In the following years she came repeatedly to stay at I Tatti but never made me feel that I was anything more than an outsider to whom one had to be polite. A sudden change came in 1926 when during our stay in Naples she landed there with her yacht and sent a message to our hotel asking us to come and inspect the boat. We found her and her party of friends in very good shape and delighted with all they had managed to see during their Mediterranean tour. I asked Edith how her maid Elise was and whether she had enjoyed the trip. I knew Elise well from her having accompanied Edith to I Tatti. My question made Edith's face suddenly light up and she begged me to go down to the cabin deck and to have a little chat with Elise. From then on I became aware of a complete change in Edith's manner to me. There was a warmth, a tone of intimacy that I had never heard before. A gesture that was natural to me had let down the drawbridge leading into the fortress of her small intimate circle.

Our next meeting that same autumn could not have been more delightful. She and Walter Berry were on their way back from the lakes while B.B. and I were visiting Piedmontese sights and we met in Aosta. Already during our first dinner *à quatre* I understood how different Walter Berry could be from what I had seen of him in Paris, and surrounded by his super-chic lady friends and a slave to their values and tastes. He was gay, entertaining, easy to talk to. When on the following morning B.B. sent me with a message about our plans to Edith's room I found her in her bed in an elegant wrapper with a coquettish lace-cap on her head, books and writing things spread all around her, her pekinese doggies asleep at her feet and Walter Berry seated near her, in excellent spirits and she as happy as a young girl to have him all to herself and to let herself be teased by him.

It was to be her last trip with him. In the spring of 1927 he had a stroke, lived on at half-cock for a few months, and died in the autumn while we were again in London. B.B., who knew what losing Walter meant for Edith, felt desperately sorry for her and decided to propose himself as her guest for the Christmas holidays. So from Paris Mary and I accompanied him to Hyères and stayed for a few days with him in the Château-Sainte-Claire, an enchanting old house, low and long-stretched with a crenellated roof, a long sunny terrace with a wide view over the little town of Hyères to the sea and the peninsula of Giens. A terraced garden all around and above the house, beautifully kept, almost too much so. A certain wilderness and *laissez-aller* would have been more in harmony with the landscape. But the orderliness of the garden corresponded to the exquisitely furnished and appointed rooms, to the definite and strict ritual that regulated the house's daily life.

Again in 1929 on our return from Spain we deposited B.B. there and from then on it became his habit to spend a few weeks with Edith at Christmas time. Generally I would accompany him, stay for a few days and then hurry back to what B.B. called Mary's and my "tribal rites," she with her daughters and grandchildren and I with my three Anreps. And for both of us it was certainly easier to give ourselves

up wholeheartedly to the enjoyment of our families without having B.B. with his restless activities and numerous
demands to pull us away from them.

The Christmas party at Sainte-Claire was composed of
Robert Norton and Gaillard Lapsley, the latter a thoroughly
Anglicised American and don of Trinity College, Cambridge,
a great stickler for ritual and traditional good behaviour.
In former days Percy Lubbock had belonged to the group
but had then deserted it by marrying Lady Sybil after her
divorce from Geoffrey Scott. Passionately possessive as Edith
was in her friendships she never forgave him this betrayal.

B.B. to Nicky   December 23rd 1929
. . . here it has been pouring boisterously since night
before last and neither Edith nor Norton or I went out at all.
Lapsley did and with him John Hugh Smith who arrived
in the morning. He is a banker of the Tom Lamont kind,
collects books, reads and takes a great interest in the latest
archaeological finds. . . .

B.B. to Nicky   December 27th 1929
. . . Edith gave me for Christmas a marvellous bed-jacket
the like of which Bilkis could not afford to give Salomon.
And what a hostess she is! Of us four guests three have
separate régimes and she sees to it that most scrupulously
each gets his. And she watches lovingly what one eats and
offers more appetizing alternatives if she sees that one eats
listlessly. Her last book absorbed me so much that I did not
put it down till after one in the morning. . . .

B.B. to Nicky   January 4th 1930
. . . Here the uneventful hours pass too quick. Yesterday
both Edith and Norton were busy and I walked with Lapsley
through lovely valleys. We reminisced about college days
and Boston and common acquaintances of my spring time.
Like all *salonfaehige* men of a certain age he has no little
to give if one knows how to get it. . . .

174

Nicky to Mary   January 8th 1930
Dearest Mary,

It seemed a bit unreal to find everything so unchanged and quiet and unruffled in this household yesterday evening, the little dogs with their red curly tongues and Edith in her elaborate tea-gown and the ritual of dinner presided over by Fabre after all our holiday irregularities. It feels like having eaten a good thick *minestrone* even with garlic in it and I am sure we have both digested it very well. So has B.B. his more refined dishes and he seems well and not nervous and looks forward to his work. . . .

Nicky to Mary   December 19th 1930

. . . It is enchanting here, so warm and sunny and our walk along the sea at Giens with the waves dashing against the rocks and the stems of the pines golden in the sunset light made one dream of the road from Eleusis to Corinth. Edith seems better than she was at this time last year and full of energy and invariably grumbling over poor B.B.'s little nap. She will protest against it as long as there is life in both of them. To-morrow John Hugh Smith is arriving and on Monday I am going to leave her to the full enjoyment of her "male wives." Norton is going to take me to the Connollys' to-morrow and on Sunday the Huxleys are coming to dinner here. Edith has had both couples here lately and liked Cyril but not as much as Huxley. She says that Cyril's wife is an awful lump but her descriptions of people cannot be trusted especially if they are young and conceivably intimidated by her not always reassuring manner.

B.B. to Nicky   December 26th 1930

. . . Here Christmas passed planturously.[1] There was plum pudding, *soupe à l'oignon* and other dishes the mere sight of which affected my digestion. Edith and her three

---

[1] *Plantureusement* is a French word meaning "plentifully, abundantly, richly," which B.B. has, so to say, anglified.

cavaliers sang the praise of good food and of the restaurants all over France that provided it. I envied them. Why have I lacked the belly and members for a rich animal life? . . .

Complicated and sometimes dramatic were Edith's relations to her neighbours at Saint Bernard, Charles and Marie-Laure de Noailles. She was very fond of Charles and shared with him a passionate interest in gardens and gardening but could not stand Marie-Laure's eccentricities nor her group of friends, mostly *avant-garde* artists and writers. On one of his first visits to Sainte-Claire B.B. had a rather upsetting experience at Saint Bernard.

B.B. to Nicky   December 31st 1929

Dearest Nick,

I feel bruised and tattered in much the way that I was after having been all but killed by a mob at Aquila a few days after Italy went to war with Austria.

It happened like this. I was lunching with the Noailles. She sat between me and Cocteau and Rivière sat a little further away. We fell into a discussion about art over a creation of Picasso's that had just arrived and hung in the sitting-room. This masterpiece consisted of a surface about the size and shape of the London *Times*. Not far from the top was a circle of sepia about five inches in diameter. Under it to the left was a column of small print looking as if it had been photographed from a newspaper. To balance this there was fixed with thin headless nails a piece of brown sacking.

Cocteau insisted that this was as complete and satisfactory a work of art as any Raphael and with every logical right to be so considered. I tried to make him consider the matter in detail and with the least possible irony. It infuriated him but he kept up a certain appearance of calm while pouring out a lava torrent of sheer verbiage that physically overwhelmed me. My hostess trembled with rage and her

Casa al Dono, Vallombrosa

B.B. with King Gustav VI Adolphus and
Queen Louise of Sweden, I Tatti, 1952

eyes flashed fire and to relieve herself she kept powdering her cheeks and painting her lips. Rivière agreed entirely with Cocteau. The company behaved towards me as if I were Edith's Mr. Blandhorne and had in a Zaouiah insulted the Prophet and blasphemed the Koran.

I had never been treated as such an outsider, never made to feel so helplessly hopelessly in the presence of a world which knew me not.

When later I described the scene and the occasion thereof, the Picasso, Norton swore that it was all a *burla* from beginning to end. I wonder. . . .

Later on Marie-Laure and B.B. became very good friends and in moments of coldness between her and Edith B.B. tried again and again to mediate between them. Once on my arrival after Christmas he came to meet me in Toulon and told me of how he had persuaded Marie-Laure a few hours earlier to break the ice by inviting Edith and her guests to lunch and of how he had taken the message to Edith and that it had been graciously received. But next morning the sky was clouded over. Edith declared that an invitation sent by word of mouth was an insult to her and that it should have been a written one. This was clearly Gaillard Lapsley's doing. He had anyhow little use for the Noailles and, being a rigid upholder of protocolled behaviour, had persuaded Edith to refuse the invitation. It was an easy thing to do as she had a sort of complex about not being treated as an equal by French titled society. Robert Norton, who had lived for years in Paris, was of course entirely on our side in finding all this perfectly ridiculous. He was one of the most enchanting friends and companions, gifted as artist and poet. He too had to suffer from Edith's possessive and jealous friendship, particularly when the time came for his changing over to the Polynésie, his second Riviera home. La Polynésie, a modern house filled with exotic works of art, in a marvellous position, on the peninsula of Giens, belonged to Madame de Béhague, a devoted friend of Norton's and definitely not in Edith's good graces. For Percy Lubbock's book about Edith Wharton I wrote:

> In the autumn of 1931 while staying at I Tatti Edith suddenly proposed to me to come and spend a week with her in Rome. My first reaction was a certain apprehension of a prolonged tête-à-tête with her. She easily gave me on such occasions the sense of being "weighed in the balance and found wanting," as if I were not coming up to her expectations and did not entertain and amuse her enough. A pleasant sense of familiarity that I felt between us in the presence of others would suddenly disappear and leave me inwardly struggling to recapture it. B.B. would not hear of such silly scruples on my part; he urged me to accept the invitation and off we went, she, her beloved maid Elise, Linky, her little Pekinese dog and myself.
>
> My parents were not dog-fanciers and in my grandmother's and brother-in-law's Baltic homes I had learnt to be very fond of huge Newfoundland dogs and other out-of-doors pets. The lap-dog and its cult were a new experience for me and already in the railway carriage I found out that between Edith and her maid it formed a real bond and kept them happy and occupied.
>
> Everything went off very well during the first days in Rome. Edith wanted particularly to see early Christian churches and being fairly well prepared on that subject I made out various programs of sight-seeing and they seemed to be just what she liked. We drove about in a taxi-cab, the oldest and dirtiest and most ramshackle one in the whole of Rome with a driver whose black coat had turned greenish with age. I asked Edith whether she would not allow me to procure a car more in keeping with her station in life. She said no, she would stick to this man and engage him again because he looked as if he would be kind to her little dog while we were inside a church. It was quite true: he was tender with the little creature and it gave me an insight into the quickness of her perceptions. She noticed details

of expression and subtle nuances of mood in a flash while apparently rather bored or otherwise preoccupied.

On the third day she asked me whether there was any chance of hearing some good church music, or at least of watching one of the more important religious functions. As it happened the feast of the consecration of the churches of Saint Peter's and Saint Paul's was quite near and I learnt that a Pontifical Mass would be sung by the Benedictine Fathers at San Paolo fuori le mura in celebration of it. I expected a refusal from Edith on account of the rather early hour; but no, she accepted with alacrity and both she and her maid (a very pious Catholic) were ready before nine. So was the taxi-driver with the greenish coat and we were there in good time. In the dim light of a muggy November morning the Basilica looked even vaster and emptier than usual; a small group of poorly clad parishioners from the quartiere San Paolo were waiting before the Central apse and watching the candles being lit by the sacristans. Never have I been present at a more magnificent and sumptuous and yet dignified and even severely classical ceremony enhanced by the smallness and quietness of the congregation which helped one to concentrate on what was going on in the apse. I felt deeply moved and at the same time acutely aware of Edith's presence—the presence not as I had feared of an impatient and rather spoilt woman, easily bored and anxious to move on, but of someone quite close to me, carried away with me and like me into another sphere, with no stiffness or impatience left in her, no thought of the passing hour or of other plans. We stayed to the very end and followed the procession carrying the Blessed Sacrament all round the Basilica until it had disappeared into the sacristy and the bell had stopped ringing and the candles had been put out.

That same day at Vesper hour we went to Saint Peter's and watched the relics being exposed there and during the following days we assisted at various other functions and loved it all and felt in great sympathy, but the particular "Stimmung" of that dim November morning at Saint Paul's

179

never came back. It left me in the belief that Edith may perhaps have been much nearer to actual conversion to the Church than any of her friends ever thought. When I once told one of her *intimes* about this experience I found him sceptical. He admitted that she was very sensitive to the beauty of ritual, but could not imagine that there could be more than that in it. "Anyway," he said, "if Edith should be converted to Catholicism, my heart would go out to her confessor."

And yet I still believe that if the two humble and pious women near her and devoted to her, her maid and her housekeeper, had not died shortly afterwards and had continued to exert their influences over her it might have happened and might have been the source of great happiness to her, helping her to let herself go more easily and to let the soft and tender notes in her being be heard more clearly. Whenever in later years we happened to be alone together and I touched upon recollections of those Roman days, it brought an immediate response of sympathy from her and even of wistfulness as for something lost.[2]

As I think of those far away days with Edith in Rome a comical incident comes into my mind. We both were invited by Ugo Ojetti to the autumn opening session of the Italian Academy. Edith did not feel like accepting but encouraged me to go to it by myself. I objected that I had nothing elaborate to put on for the occasion. She said she would lend me her black coat. It was very elegant and fitted me perfectly. Thus clad in foreign feathers I presented myself in the assembly hall of the Farnesina and took a seat in one of the back rows. To my amazement there was a certain commotion all around me, more and more people turned around to look at me and whispered to each other. Then I was asked to take a seat in one of the front rows. Suddenly I understood

[2] Reproduced from Percy Lubbock's *Portrait of Edith Wharton* (London: Jonathan Cape; 1947) by kind permission of the publishers.

that it was not me people were staring at but my coat and looking down on it I saw on its lapel what I had not noticed before, the *cocarde* of the Legion of Honour, a decoration bestowed on Edith in recognition of her philanthropic work during the war in France. I felt like the donkey in La Fontaine's fable before whom people prostrated themselves because it was carrying the Holy Sacrament.

B.B. to Nicky   Christmas day 1931

. . . Here it continues to be very beautiful and gently delicately wintry as if winter had to put in an appearance for form's sake but did not want to tisturb in the least. I must tell you about my fellow cavaliers. Lapsley yesterday did not utter one word. He morosely munched or read or meditated. Norton was scarcely better. He too spends most of his time when indoors reading by himself. Last night both men fell upon the two last numbers of *The Times* that had just arrived while Edith whirled through *Punch, The Times Literary Supplement* and the illustrated papers. So I went to bed directly after swallowing my Camomille. I don't think it is more than "Angry-Saxons" being *in confidenza*. With Norton I have had only one talk and he was, for him, so unreasonably French in his attitude towards every international trouble that I could only hasten to talk of something else. It is I daresay hard to resist the opinion of people you see most and now that he lives altogether in France they are French.

I feel lazy and let myself idle away the hours, musing, reading drivel, wondering. . . .

B.B. to Nicky   December 28th 1931

I have often half reproached myself for making more fuss over Edith than over other guests. I gather from Elizabeth that she is the same over me, that no other guest is so pampered, no other of whom all and sundry stand in such awe. I asked her whether it was the tips. She thought not but that I was supposed to want everything of the best in the best way. My own reading of the matter is that it is the tips plus the fact that of all Edith's cavaliers I alone have an establishment big enough to impress the *valetaille*. . . .

Later on the circle was enlarged through Edith's new friendship with a member of the English Colonial Service, Simon Nicholson, who had looked after her and her party in Cyprus during their trip in a yacht around the Mediterranean and while he was representing the absent governor in Nicosia. Edith invited him to stay at Saint Brice, liked him better and better and considered him already as one of her stable group of friends when to her disappointment he announced his marriage. Edith feared the worst—a complete outsider—but was won over on their first meeting by Molly Nicholson's charm, her excellent mind, and incomparable sense of humour. And thus we met both the Nicholsons at Sainte-Claire in the spring of 1932.

Nicky to Mary   March 31st 1932
    . . . We took a lovely walk in the Gapeau valley yesterday and saw the brown fields overspread like by a pink veil of flowering fruit trees. It is an experience in itself to see this garden and this landscape for once in the spring. Our fellow guests the Nicholsons are very pleasant and so easy to talk with. She has a lovely figure and fine open features and clear green eyes. She might be the heroine of one of Edith's novels. He is not handsome but so natural and straightforward. He talked a lot about Cyprus yesterday and we gathered that there is no love lost between him and Ronald Storrs. Most of his official life has been spent in Africa and I felt that many good talks are in store for us. . . . Edith has been reading excellent short stories by Somerset Maugham in the evening, excellent but very gruesome mostly about secret murders committed by haughty and unapproachably well-behaved women.

Later in 1932 we met Edith in Rome. It was not altogether easy.

Nicky to Mary   Rome   May 21st 1932
      . . . B.B. has just gone off to the Borghese Gallery with
Mrs. Garrett[3] (what will he not say about her exquisite
understanding when he comes back!) and I have done a few
errands and got some flowers to cheer up our rooms and
now I am sitting by the open window with the view over
"flat old Rome." A lovely breeze is blowing in and I feel
very happy and full of leisure. There are very thorny
moments with Edith but on the whole it goes better than
I expected. She delights in sideswipes at our friends and at
our sociability and when she heard that B.B. had asked the
Duchess of Cesarò to lunch she was extremely annoyed and
said she would her lunch at another table. I talked her
into staying with us and they got on so well together that
we are all three lunching with the Cesaròs to-day. Edith says
she did not know how to refuse! The curious thing about
her is that she seems almost provincial in her awkwardness.
A simple excuse or innocent social lie seems never to be at
her disposal. That the two dinners we have had to accept,
one with the Garretts and one with the Pasolinis, were her
arrangements she does not seem to realize. Yesterday morning I went with her to the Palatine and she appeared to be
overwhelmed because of too much sun and heat, yet she
said afterwards that it had been heavenly.
      Yesterday we went to Grottaferrata, visited the Abbey
and the museum and then drove up to the Monte Cavo
where it was heavenly with the yellow broom just out and
the plain half veiled in a blue haze and the Capo Circeo
rising up beyond the Pontine marches. We had a *panne* on
the way back and Edith's nervousness about being late for
dinner was indescribable. She does not realize how *alla
buona* an old-fashioned Italian household like the one of
the Pasolinis is. It was a pleasant evening, very quiet and

---

[3] Mrs. John Garrett, wife of the American Ambassador.

gemütlich. We talked a lot about Miss Paget to whom they are all so devoted.

Nicky to Mary   Rome   May 31st 1932
      . . . This morning when I went into B.B.'s room with his cut orange soon after eight I found him on his terrace with the whole of Rome spread out before him, reading *Faust* and enjoying himself hugely. Edith left yesterday morning. She was so delightful these last days, so *bon-enfant* and pleased with everything, almost tender in her demonstrations of affection that I felt ashamed of ever having uttered a word of grumbling in spoken or written form. However you know her and understand how difficult she can be.

Nicky to Mary   Sainte Claire   January 17th 1934
      . . . we paid a pleasant visit to the Huxleys yesterday in spite of a raging mistral. The coast where they live is very wild and unspoilt and we took a lovely walk along the cliffs. Mrs. Huxley wore grey flannel trousers and an engaging white Chinese sheepswool jacket and looked I thought very charming. But heavy criticism came down on her from our severe hostess. Huxley turns out to be a painter and not a bad one. They live in a semi-artistic but not uncomfortable nor squalid way in a charming white Algerian-looking house.

Life at Sainte-Claire could be most enjoyable and restful if one was ready to submit to its ritual on one side and to Edith's incalculable whims on the other. I was amused to notice that B.B. with many years of marital discipline behind him was much more submissive than her bachelor friends who frequently rebelled against her orders and counter-orders about going or not going out for a picnic or a drive.

Edith's fixation on picnics was closely connected with an important part of her domestic ritual, namely, with her scrupulous respect for the servants, for their hours or days of liberty. By going out she wanted to spare them. And this was not only a programme to be dutifully carried out. She looked after her servants with affectionate zeal and took a lively interest in all their joys and sorrows. I remember how once during one of our excursions with her, she was deeply hurt and angry when on leaving a villa near Siena after a prolonged visit she discovered that neither her maid nor her chauffeur had been asked into the house.

Nicky to Mary   January 7th 1933
> . . . The situation between our hostess and her two bachelor friends is sometimes very funny especially when they get restive under her persistent domination. I am sure if their temper were not kept in check by iron rules of good behaviour they would end by quarrelling like Mabel Dodge Luhan and her friends. B.B. is the most submissive but perhaps also the one she is most afraid of. Morra fits in very well and enjoys it all and sometimes he and I have a good laugh by ourselves.[4]

Edith's relationship to B.B. was like that of a somewhat older, loving and pedagogical sister. During all his visits she never stopped chiding him about his afternoon nap and its robbing him of the best and sunniest hours of the day. He was for her like a lovable and amusing but very naughty child that should never be left unwatched nor unadmonished.

Nicky to Mary   January 16th 1934
> . . . I am really mad this morning, mad in the American sense of the word. Edith in her obstinacy has decided to go out for a picnic to a place just five miles from here and hardly as delightfully sunny as the terrace of this house and B.B. is to have lunch by himself as he very wisely refused to run the risk of another cold. Why can't she do without picnics for the 17 to 18 days that he is her guest? I think

---

[4] Umberto Morra had joined us for the last part of our stay at Sainte-Claire.

I shall talk to her about it and warn her that he will not come back if she goes on letting his need for an afternoon nap weigh on him in this manner. Otherwise she has been very sweet all these days and the weather is perfect, very still and sunny. The Cambridge "don" has left which lightens up the atmosphere considerably. We had a lovely walk yesterday and saw the sunset from a small homeric bay, lighting up the rocks and the stems of the pines. We are reading Trollope's *The Duke's Children* again, that is to say, Norton reads it to us to perfection. We have heard some quiet and reasonable and some uproarious communications about the Saar yesterday from Germany. . . .

Nicky to Mary   January 27th 1934

Our stay here is a very harmonious and pleasant one, perhaps more harmonious with the Nicholsons as fellow guests than with the old boys who have got into the habit of letting Edith's whims and caprices get too much on their nerves and of grumbling about them. I confess that it was my habit too but I feel quite differently now, rather like what I used to be in my grandmother's presence. Great affection mixed with a slight fear of meeting with disapproval and a temptation to giggle over it all like a silly school-girl. This mood is much encouraged by Molly Nicholson's presence who is very fond of Edith yet with her exquisite sense of humour and power of observation does not miss one of Edith's comical little provincialisms and "Junkerisms."

. . . No picnics have been proposed yet and B.B.'s frequent visits to Saint Bernard have been accepted in a meek and gentle spirit. Edith does try to keep more quiet and not to fuss herself and her guests with too many plans. She looks much better than she did a week ago and Mr. White[5] thinks it does her a lot of good to have a congenial party of guests in the house. I am afraid, we two alone would not have achieved these pleasant results. It was only possible with the help of the Nicholsons who are both delightful.

---

[5] For many years Mrs. Wharton's general agent.

Edith started reading the continuation of her last novel *The Buccaneers* after dinner to us but found that the possible corrections and alterations excited her too much and kept her from sleeping. So we have changed over to Stevenson's *The Ebb Tide*.

THE CHARM OF THE Pavillon Colombe, Edith's summer residence near Paris, was somewhat diminished by the endless drive through dreary suburbs, but once inside the enclosure and protected by the plane trees in the garden one found oneself in an enchanted world of its own. An eighteenth-century house of exquisite proportions even more cosily furnished than Sainte-Claire. During our various stays in Paris we drove out repeatedly but only once, in 1932, stayed for several days. It was a house all concentrated on itself, not open to the sun, the view, the landscape like Sainte-Claire and therefore well suited to its original purpose, a *nid d'amour* for Mlle Colombe, the eighteenth-century actress.

EDITH WAS AT HER BEST in the evening with the draw-bridge of her fortress pulled up and no fear of intrusions from the outer world. Then she could get rid of her "offensive-defensive" type of shyness that under adverse circumstances seemed to encase her like the scaly shield of a tortoise. Then she could be really *gemütlich* and easy-going, clad in an elaborate tea-gown curled up in the corner of the sofa by the fireside reading aloud beautifully and then stopping to discuss the plot of the story and its handling with her listeners. Occasionally she would read something just written by herself but as a rule preferred stories by other authors that would stimulate her critical capacity.

The change in her if anybody from the outside world turned up was almost unbelievable. From being simple, gay, ready to tease her friends and to let herself be teased by them she became stiff, conventional, almost frozen up, and created an atmosphere of *gêne* all around her. Personally I had no longer any difficulties with her.

Nicky to Mary   January 23rd 1936
    I had an extraordinary experience yesterday and one I am very grateful for. While B.B. and Norton went out for a walk Edith invited me to pay her a visit in her room.[6] There we were, she in her bed and I stretched out by the fire and it was perfectly enchanting. We talked and talked without any of those maddening "I can't see why" and "I don't understand how people" and those freezing silences. She was gentle and sympathizing and human and I understood as I never had before what she must have been for her friends when moods like that were frequent with her. I never had it out with her about B.B.'s naps because B.B. told me it would be no use. Now I am glad I did not try to fight it out with her. Her misfortune is that she will not let herself grow older comfortably, will hold out against it and rushes about, gets tired and then again will not give in and becomes peevish and fussy and deprives her friends of the real treasures that her friendship can produce for them. It is very sad but too deeply rooted in her to be changed. . . .

The news of Edith's death reached B.B. while I was away on my holiday.

B.B. to Nicky   Poggio allo Spino   August 12th 1937
Dear Nick,
    So poor Edith is dead and I feel dumb and numb and as if my bodily temperature had lowered to the freezing point. . . .

B.B. to Nicky   August 13th 1937
    . . . I feel Edith's departure more and more each hour. *The Times* has a very stale and dull obituary notice of her. I am receiving letters of condolence which will have to be

---

6 Both Edith and myself had been laid up with the grippe.

answered. Of course Ojetti was among them. He is perhaps the only pure Italian who has ever heard of her. . . .

Nicky to B.B.   La Rufola   Sorrento   August 14th 1937
Dearest B.B.,

My writing to-day is almost senseless, to-morrow being the *Ferragosto* with no postal service but I am writing all the same because my heart is full of the sad news your letter contains. One would not have wanted her to live an invalid life, especially if her head was no longer clear, yet to know for certain that she is no more, that these two houses have shut their doors for ever, that we shall never again be able to grumble over her whims and caprices only to enjoy her good and delightful moods even more, is difficult to realize. And if I feel it who have known her only for ten years what must it be for you. . . .

Nicky to Mary   La Rufola   Sorrento   August 18th 1937
Dearest Mary,

Before leaving this enchanting place I want to send you a word of love and tell you that B.B.'s accounts of your health make me very happy. He too seems to be getting out of his black mood and to take his present incapacity for work more philosophically. The news of Edith's death must have made him very sad. It is *wehmuetig* to think of the exquisite small world created by her and now disappeared and I find myself thinking of her and of her difficulties and her lovable sides much more now that she is dead than while she was still alive. The owners of the land all around here come to bathe every day in our little bay at the foot of the garden and bring a Pekinese doggie along. Watching the little creature running along the rocks and standing there like a small lion and barking at its mistress in the water makes me think so much of Edith walking swiftly up and down her lovely garden with her doggies before and behind her. I am sure as time goes on her friends will forget all about her tantrums and only remember what she could be in her really delightful moods. . . .

CHAPTER XV

B.B.'s Orchestra

ALREADY BEFORE MEETING HIM I had been told about B.B.'s flirtatious, not to say amorous, temperament. Perhaps it was Hermann Keyserling, more likely Geoffrey Scott, who spoke of it. When I saw him for the first time he seemed so intimidating and aloof that I could only regard these reports as grossly exaggerated. Yet as I watched him in the company of women he admired, as I sensed the currents of delicate understanding and intimacy between him and some of them I came to a different conclusion and suddenly almost without being aware of it I found myself caught in the net of his subtle charm. He did not make any particular advances and left all that to me. Nor do I think he would have paid much attention to me if I had remained a casual visitor. It was all due to my being there day by day, to my getting interested in his work, to my gradually becoming indispensable to him; not through any peculiar ability but through my eagerness to please him and to serve him. He loved to tease me mercilessly about my being like the woman in Chekhov's story "The Darling" and assured me that, like her, had fate made me the companion of a musician or a politician or a philologist or a historian, I would have become interested in their work just as I had become keen on art and art history.

Mary, when in a good mood, could be full of mirth and

laughter over B.B.'s variety of amorous and semi-amorous attachments.

Mary to Nicky   August 9th 1921

    . . . Poor B.B.! He had arranged his various honeymoons with his various ladies so very carefully—Mrs. Lanier in Venice from the 20th to the end of the month, and Baroness La Caze from September 12th till I came back and now suddenly the Baroness writes that she is coming to Venice on the 20th and that upsets all his plans. By the way a sweet young creature to whom he writes that the thought of her is like a gold thread woven through the unrolled tapestry of his life while she writes to him that his words are like a music her ears are almost too gross to hear is coming to us in October. I too thought her delightful, when we met her in Hyères. . . .

Mary to Nicky   Salsomaggiore   October 2nd 1921

    . . . The lady B.B. claims to have discovered in Venice seemed to us a perfect goose when we met her in New York. As she appears to be coming to us you can judge for yourself. B.B.'s views on women are not to be trusted. . . .

Of some of his former loves, like Gladys Deacon or Lady Sassoon, I only heard him speak again and again; others like Belle Greene, Gabrielle La Caze, Natalie Barney I met when they no longer played a prominent part in his life. The only one with whom the flame of their former love was kept up in a sublimated nostalgic way was Countess Hortense Serristori. And what his feelings for her were comes out clearly in his diary of the last years.[1]

Naturally I was interested in meeting his former loves and watched him being absorbed by one or other of them without feeling the slightest pangs of jealousy. Absurd as

---

[1] *Sunset and Twilight* (New York: Harcourt, Brace & World; 1963).

it may sound it never occurred to me that new stars might rise up in his sky and the first time it happened I went through agonies of despair and doubts and feelings of intense inferiority. When I look back on it all now I see clearly how ridiculous and unreasonable it all was. But can jealousy ever be reasonable? The delicate threads of mutual understanding that I felt were being spun between him and his new pet weighed on me like chains of iron. It helped of course to talk to B.B. about it and his patience and sweetness were endless. Nobody could be freer from any hypocrisy or desire to represent himself as different from what he was. It was all the more absurd of me as I knew his many-faceted nature well and how much he had to give, much more than I alone could absorb.

When the next star rose up I did have a relapse but got over it much more quickly and from then on was free from any doubts. It ended by my enjoying—as a mother enjoys a new toy for her baby—a new half-amorous friendship of his.

Nicky to B.B.   La Rufola   Sorrento   August 1934
> . . . The thought of X's charming presence near you makes me happy while ten years ago such a thought *aurait fait noircir le monde à mes yeux*. And yet I do not love you less, on the contrary more, much more.
>
> I have finished Anne Lindsay's and Benjamin Constant's letters and found a passage in one of Julie Talma's letters which would fit you rather nicely. *"Ce que je vois clairement c'est qu'avec le sentiment que vous conservez pour Madame de Staël et celui que vous portez à Madame Lindsay il vous serait très facile d'en aimer une troisième."*

In later years it happened not infrequently that after coming to an end of his absorption he would leave it to me to look after his neglected lady-love. He became lazy about reading his letters himself and generally put them aside for me to read to him. One day having torn open an envelope

addressed in a to me unfamiliar handwriting I started reading and realized that it was a passionate love letter. "B.B."
I said, "this is not a letter that I should read." "Oh, my dear,"
he said with a sigh, "having got as far as that you might
just as well go on to the end."

VERY CLOSE TO B.B. and very dear to both of us were two
Italian young women, the one Florentine and the other Neapolitan, brought up in the same convent school. The Florentine, Pellegrina Del Turco (later married to Marchese
Paulucci de' Calboli), we met through Byba Coster and she in
her turn introduced us to Clotilde Marghieri, the *ninfa del
Vesuvio,* as B.B. called her, because of her home near Torre
del Greco, at the foot of Vesuvius, in a Pompeiian landscape.
If Mary's yearly expedition to England and my holiday
happened to coincide it was generally Clotilde and Morra
who would keep B.B. company at the Consuma and if Pellegrina could tear herself away from her high-strung Romagnol
husband, Marchese Paulucci, and her equally high-strung
mother-in-law she would join them. Pellegrina was a charming creature, graceful, gay, quick-witted with a natural gift
for appreciating art and poetry. Clotilde being a born intellectual had serious talks and discussions with B.B. She had a
definite gift for writing and her attempts to develop it were
steadily encouraged by B.B. For Pellegrina it was enough to
listen to him, to breathe in an atmosphere that took her away
from the complications of her family life. She belonged to
the category of what B.B. called a "work of art," people,
women (but also men) whom he enjoyed not so much for
their physical appearance and elegance—although that too
had considerable importance for him—but for their being
completely integrated and absolutely natural human beings.
There was something of the brother-and-sister relation
—but less intimate than in the case of Edith Wharton—

between B.B. and "Addie" (Mrs. Otto H.) Kahn. They were devoted to, and at the same time rather critical of, each other but she was more cautious in giving expression to this criticism than Edith ever was.

Charming was his flirtatious relation to his contemporary Katie Lewis[2] whose nimble mind and witty repartees he found adorable. Her letters were a constant joy to him, for she had a Jane Austen-like gift of weaving a delightful story out of her quiet daily life in a Worcestershire village.

Another correspondent of B.B.'s was for several years the Venetian novelist Paola Drigo. B.B. had read one of her short stories in *Pegaso* and had expressed his admiration for it to Pietro Pancrazi, the editor of the review. He repeated B.B.'s words to the author and she wrote a playful witty letter to B.B. He answered and they went on exhanging letters without ever having set eyes on each other. She seemed to be reluctant about meeting him and it was explained to us that having been a famous beauty in her youth she felt shy about presenting herself as a middle-aged woman. Finally during our stay in Venice in 1935 she invited B.B. to spend a day at her villa near Bassano but insisted on his coming alone.

Nicky to Mary   October 3rd 1935
    . . . I am taking the lists along to the Titian exhibition to-day to do a bit of controlling although B.B. says that he is beyond all that, beyond attributions, and G.P.s and P.s and S.s and wants only to enjoy himself. Our great joke is that B.B.'s unknown literary friend Paola Drigo wants to make his acquaintance but refuses to meet him *in mezzo alla gente* (the *gente* being Morra and myself) and proposes to come and fetch him one day and to take him for a drive on the mainland. As we hear that she is a big masterly type of

---

[2] Daughter of the English jurist Sir H. P. Lewis. Her mother's— Lady Lewis'—salon was known as a centre for writers, artists and particularly musicians.

woman we wonder whether having taken B.B. off she means to return him. If you get a telegram saying "B.B. swallowed up by Drigo" you will know what it means. . . .

Nicky to Mary   Venice   October 9th 1935
Dearest Mary,

Here I am in B.B.'s deserted room enjoying the lovely view over to San Giorgio Maggiore and wondering whether he will ever come back from this independent adventure. He left at 9.45 this morning for Bassano and was to be met there by the unknown one and taken to her house. . . .

He did come back very well satisfied with his new friend who finally consented to pay us a visit in Venice. She led a quiet retired life in the country and had like Katie Lewis the gift of making her uneventful days charmingly alive in her letters.

Of course B.B. tended to be more tolerant with women's weaknesses than with men's. When Countess Blandine Gravina[3] appeared and bored the rest of us with her high-brow dribble and her blind adoration of whatever had to do with Bayreuth, B.B. would always be ready to engage her in conversation, to listen to her patiently and he assured us that he never failed to get some interesting information out of her. He called her a "foolometer."

Another member of the Wagner circle and intimate friend of Houston Stewart Chamberlain, Edith de Gasparin, was introduced to B.B. by Countess Gravina and became one of his adorers and faithful correspondents.[4] She too belonged to the "lovingly pedagogical sister" category. Many of her letters contained reproaches or at any rate laments over B.B.'s far too widespread curiosity, over his not sticking

---

[3] One of Cosima Wagner's daughters by her first mariage with the pianist Hans von Bülow; married to a Sicilian nobleman.
[4] Several of B.B.'s letters to her appear in the selection of Berenson letters published by Houghton-Mifflin (Boston, 1964).

exclusively to the great classics, over his being too frivolous, over his not taking Indian philosophy seriously enough. She was admirably educated and well-read and B.B. got a great deal out of his spoken and written discussions with her.

B.B. COULD BE ADAMANT in his negative attitude if one of his pets had done or said something that in his eyes was definitely offensive. I remember how shortly before World War II we met a very charming and stimulating Central European woman and how B.B. took to her at once and how she came to stay with us at I Tatti and at Casa al Dono and how on these occasions she was most congenial to both of us. Then the war separated us. When she appeared again she was still good-looking, still graceful, still gay and agreeable, but alas on the first evening talking about the war she loudly proclaimed that nobody in Germany or Austria had been informed about the concentration camps and all the other horrors and could therefore not be expected to have any reaction to the whole question. B.B. froze up in an almost frightening way as if he had retired to a distant star and remained so towards her for the rest of her stay. How she was able to endure it I never understood. Being a guest at I Tatti was evidently more important to her than her friendship with its guiding spirit.

Thus it might be said that Sylvia Sprigge preferred writing and publishing B.B.'s biography against his wish to his warm and sincere affection for her. She appeared at I Tatti in 1945 as a war correspondent and this led to B.B.'s seeing a lot of her during our stays in Rome and to her being his guest at I Tatti any number of times. B.B. enjoyed her company and particularly the political information she brought him and the interesting letters he kept getting from her. By the time she was asked by a publisher to write his biography he was too old and tired to refuse her insistent appeals but he never stopped regretting the half-hearted permission he had given her.

IN ROME during one of our long stays he once became interested in the housekeeper of the hotel who from time to time would come to ask if all was as it should be in our rooms. A middle-aged Sicilian, not beautiful except for her large luminous eyes and her radiant smile. B.B. was fascinated by her poetical almost mystical way of expressing herself and encouraged her to talk. It was one of the instances where his charm worked just as much on a simple uneducated woman as on a highly trained and sophisticated one. She again was in her way a complete "work of art."

Numberless were the women who had what I would call a semi-flirtatious relationship with him, enjoying his presence, his understanding of their problems, his playfulness but without the lyrical overtones of his intimate friendships. They were almost like the body of strings in an orchestra as compared to the soloists. He was a master in getting the best out of each of them.

In 1938 after the *Anschluss* I was rung up one day by a twittering English voice with the most perfect clipped accent. The voice gave a confused account of what had happened to Jewish friends in Vienna and seemed to be the bearer of a message from the famous laryngologist Neumann who had been looking after B.B. in the preceding autumn and about whose fate we were very anxious. I invited the lady belonging to the voice to come up and tell us all about it. She came and turned out to be a typical *pazza inglese*— an eccentric Englishwoman—very sportive and wiry, gallant gay impulsive, pouring forth twittering sounds that did not always make sense. Never were we able to make out what the message sent by Neumann really was. I came to the conclusion that it was not Neumann who had sent her but a photo of B.B.'s she had seen in Neumann's waiting room. Having decided that she wanted to meet B.B., Neumann and the persecution of the Jews served her as a good excuse. She came again and again before and after the war, adored the garden and the whole countryside and would suddenly appear from behind a hedge during B.B.'s morning strolls through the garden. B.B. called her Sylvan and was amused by her and by her poetical letters. Whenever we asked one of our English friends whether at home they knew anybody like her they would deny it. So she must have been *einzig in ihrer Art* like a "sport" in a breed of flowers.

A BY-PRODUCT of B.B.'s post-war publications were the number of fan-letters that women began writing to him. He had never had them before and felt almost overwhelmed by their generally very gushing style. Both the *Sketch* and his war diary had brought him to the attention of readers who had probably never heard of his art historical publications. Some of these ladies had found extracts from his books in a magazine handed to them at the beauty parlour, others had read him during a journey. One of them, the daughter of a well-known actress, wrote rather fascinating introspective letters. B.B. had thanked her for the first of them and a long correspondence was the result. Finally she came herself to pay him a visit and disappointed not only B.B. but the rest of us as well in her appearance and manners: she was too much of a *cabotine* and unable to fit into our circle.

More serious and lasting was the correspondence and friendship with Mally Dienemann which also grew out of a very fine fan-letter. Mally was the widow of Max Dienemann, rabbi of Offenbach, who had suffered so cruelly in Buchenwald that when he left Germany he died soon afterwards in Israel. Mally had transferred herself to Chicago where one of her daughters lived. She was a very unusual woman.

Behind her mouse-like unassuming appearance one discovered not only the possessor of a distinguished mind and of
a vast culture but a powerful dialectician. How she would
fight with B.B. over controversial aspects of the Israeli
government! She came several times to stay at I Tatti and
he was touched by her devotion and full of admiration for
her combative spirit.

DEFINITELY A "SOLOIST" in B.B.'s orchestra, perhaps a
flute, was an unusually sensitive, delicate, highly cultivated
American, Frances Francis, the wife of Henry Francis, curator of pictures in the Cleveland Museum. She belonged to
the last period, after the Second World War, and there was
a charmingly filial quality in her devotion to him. To this
last period belong several other women, like the traveller
Freya Stark, the novelist Rosamond Lehmann, the poet
Catherine Biddle, with all of whom, if he had met them
earlier, the lyrical overtones would have been very audible.

B.B.'s last conquest was a young nurse who looked after
him during the last year and a half of his life. She was a
perfect darling, quick, sensitive, musical, in her way a "work
of art" herself, devoted to her job and wonderfully skilful
and inventive in alleviating pain and discomfort. Her devotion to B.B. was so great that she had to be forced by me
into taking a day or at least a few hours off. When I said
to B.B., "Do you realize that this young woman is quite dotty
about you," he just smiled and said, "Of course."

CHAPTER XVI

Around the
Mediterranean [1928–31]

THE YEAR 1928 has become identified for me with the magical word "Constantinople." B.B. insisted on using the classical name and not the Turkish mispronunciation of the Greek *iz tin Polis*—to the town—whereby it became Istamboul. From the middle of September to the end of November we stayed at the Pera Palace Hotel with the full view of the old town from our windows, its sky-line gently descending towards the Bosphorus, accentuated by the cupolas and minarets of the great mosques. As the season advanced it would be wrapped in mists in the morning and only gradually emerge from the greyish blue vapours as the sun touched it.

Rudolph Meier-Riefsthal, the excellent connoisseur of Seljuk and Ottoman art, had paved the way for us, ordering our rooms, procuring a car and a driver and putting us in touch with his friends at Robert College and with Aga Oglu, a young Turkish art historian. Riefsthal himself was on the point of leaving for the United States but managed to come with us on our first expedition to Adrianople. A rather strenuous one as the heat inland was still grilling and the incredibly squalid inn at Adrianople provided no protection against it. But the sights we had come to see were worth the effort. Besides several early Ottoman buildings there was the finest of the great mosques built by Sinan Pasha, the sixteenth-century Turkish architect, who carried the formula of Santa Sophia to its complete and perfect solution. At sunset time we went back to it and were allowed to sit quietly in a corner while the worshippers recited the sunset prayer and the sound of their voices rose up into the vast cupola.

While Riefstahl caught the Orient Express towards Europe we took it in the opposite direction and had the surprise of finding Eric Maclagan in it. We knew he was coming but expected him a few days later. As keen as B.B. on missing nothing, be it classical, Byzantine, Seljuk, or Ottoman, he was a wonderful companion for us and we spent hours at Santa Sophia, in the museums, walking along the great wall or finding our way from one of the smaller mosques to the other (many of them former Byzantine churches) in the dusty lanes of the old town. We ended by becoming well-known customers at some of the small cafés where fragrant Persian tea was served in small glasses. One I remember with particular nostalgia, at the corner of the Bayazid mosque under a spreading plane tree and wonder whether it still exists or whether the *esigenze della vita moderna* have made away with the exquisitely simple unostentatious pleasures of Turkish life.

Through Sibyl and Arthur Colefax, who were staying at the British embassy, we met the British ambassador Sir George Clark, who could not have been more courteous and hospitable. The United States ambassador, Mr. Joseph Grew, was on the point of leaving when we arrived and B.B. was only just able to see him and his wife, the daughter of B.B.'s old friends and protectors in Boston, Tom and Lilia Perry. Mr. Grew left instructions for the embassy launch to take us all along the Bosphorus to the mouth of the Black Sea. As we got in sight of the open water it looked indeed almost black, for a storm was gathering and we could see the fishing boats bobbing up and down dangerously on the waves. The embassy *kawass* advised us to turn back. Mary was bitterly disappointed at not being allowed to go further out into the open sea. "Mary dear," said B.B., "what did you expect to gain by getting further out?" "Well, I hoped I would be able to see something of the Crimea." Like many Americans of her generation she had only studied American geography and her ideas of European sites in relation to each other were surprisingly vague.

Accompanied by Aga Oglu we ventured as far as Konia and got a sense of the desert-like vastness of central Asia Minor. The visit to the Seljuk monuments of Konia was made difficult by the military authorities and we had to leave without seeing the finest of them. B.B. was sorely disappointed and got it into his head that the superintendent of fine arts in Constantinople was behind all this and had been instructed by Mr. Thomas Whittemore to let B.B. see as little as possible of Seljuk antiquities. Whether B.B. was right in having this suspicion I cannot say but several baffling experiences we had at Yildiz Kiosk and later at Brussa seemed to give support to it. What Mr. Whittemore could have been afraid of is difficult to imagine, for although B.B.'s interests were very widespread he had no thought at that time of publishing things outside his own parish. Many years later he did discuss other periods of art in *Aesthetics and History* and in the *Arch of Constantine* but certainly never with the purpose of announcing some newly discovered treasure before anybody else could do so. Perhaps it was simply a question of personal antipathy or jealousy going back to the days when Whittemore had been at the feet of Isabella Gardner and had resented her great regard and affection for B.B.

A new and interesting experience was seeing so much of the Robert College and Constantinople College groups, American men and women devoted to their task of teachers

like missionaries and invaluable in their thorough acquaintance with the country and its inhabitants. Theron Damon,
the brother-in-law of Mr. Huntington, the president of
Robert College, and Laurence Moore, one of the teachers
at Robert College, became our guides on many of our expeditions. Particularly Damon, who had more time at his
disposal, became a close friend and my memories of our trip
to Turkey are linked up for ever with this delightful companion, so easy-going and humorous, full of unexpected bits
of information, never opinionated or pedantic.

Constantinople was at that time full of Russian refugees
and a group of them was managing a restaurant in Pera,
the Topaz, where excellent Russian food was served. But
most of them were threatened with expulsion from Turkey
and having read in the papers about their plight two youngish American women had given up their comfortable home
in the United States to devote themselves to this cause.
Through their office in Constantinople they managed gradually to get a number of Russian refugees settled elsewhere,
particularly in the Balkan states. We met these two charming
women repeatedly and heard a great deal about their work
and their experiences.

The old town had not yet been spoiled by ugly modern
apartment houses but the local colour was already gone.
European dress had been imposed by the Gazi and wagonsful
of second-hand European garments were arriving daily.
Nobody cared about their being even approximately good
fits, about sleeves or trousers being too long or too short.
Anything would do. Caps were generally worn with the flap
at the back of the head so as not to interfere with the saying
of prayers. Long lines of men could be seen crouching along
the pavement in these haphazard accoutrements poring over
small pamphlets. They were learning the Roman alphabet,
for that also had been imposed by law and created absurd
misunderstandings and delays.

On our way home we spent a few days at Salonica looking at Byzantine churches and mosaics. As we were being shown the restoration going on at Saint Demetrius we were joined by a Russian Byzantinist who had been given a short leave for studying Byzantine monuments in Greece. He looked like a ghost, haggard and emaciated, and we did not dare to ask him any questions. But when B.B. mentioned Santa Sophia he almost broke down. The Russian boat he was scheduled to take was not going to stop in Constantinople even for a few hours.

The loveliest impression we had of Salonica was in the old upper town, where in the tiny church of Hosios David we looked at a remarkable mosaic representing the vision of Ezekiel. The priest invited us to his house and there from a ramshackle wooden balcony we saw against a stormy sunset sky the bold outline of Mount Athos.

Our friends at Robert College had asked us to get in touch with a young American social worker who had chosen Salonica as her field of action. When Mary invited her to supper we found her very attractive but were surprised by the candour of her approach to the Mediterranean world and its ageless customs and traditions. B.B. asked her what she was really trying to achieve and she said she wanted to teach Greek women to make their homes so cosy and attractive that the men would give up their habit of spending hours at the café. Mary afterwards recited the nonsense rhyme to us:

> There was an old man from Dundee
> Who taught little owls to drink tea
> For to sit and eat mice
> Is not proper and nice
> Said that curious old man from Dundee.

Athens we found flooded by the first almost tropical autumn rains and the streets leading down from the

Lykabettus changed into torrents. But as it cleared up the purity of the sky, the crystalline outline of the hills, the intensely blue distances showed us Attica as we had never seen it in the spring and returning to our old haunts was like seeing them for the first time.

THE MOST OUTSTANDING FEATURE of our trip to Palestine—described by Mary in her *Modern Pilgrimage* (London: Constable; 1932)—was our stay in Jerusalem. I remember finding Mary's rationalism and her continual half-sneering and half-censorious condemnation of what she called "pagan forms of worship" (like the kissing of stones and relics) not easy to bear. B.B. tried in vain to convert her to his own indulgent attitude towards such childlike and touching manifestations of faith. B.B. felt the sacredness of the whole place as the centre of worship of three great religions too intensely to be shocked by them. Watching the Sabbath prayer at the Wall of Wailing he was deeply moved by the venerable figures of old men wrapped in their prayer shawls and looking like the prophets in one of Titian's or Lotto's altarpieces.

B.B. was not a Zionist in those days. He had to go through the Hitler years before he could feel real sympathy with the heroic effort of the Israelite state builders. Only the danger of orthodox Jewry having the upper hand in Israel filled him with horror and became a sort of obsession with him during his last years. Of course he had to admit that Zionism could only have grown out of a century-old religious tradition and that therefore the orthodox party had a firm basis to stand on. Nevertheless he regarded the strict observance of Jewish law as an unacceptable incongruity in an otherwise modern and highly developed state.

An episode not told by Mary is what happened to us in Nablous, the ancient Samaria. As we were approaching it by car, Mary noticed a line of people climbing up like ants toward the top of the mountain just above the small town and wondered what they were up to. Suddenly B.B. became interested. "To-day is the Jewish Passover," he said, "and in this place there must be still a small community of Samaritans who celebrate it in the ancient way by sacrificing a lamb on the top of Mount Gerizim. These are probably the worshippers going up for the celebration."

A little later, as we were having our evening meal in the small inn, an elderly English couple came in and sat down at the table next to us. They seemed to have been on a long tramp and looked tired and dusty. B.B. jumped to the conclusion that they had been watching the Passover feast on Mount Gerizim and started asking them about it. Yes, they had been to the very top but had felt shy about staying to watch the actual sacrifice and had come away before it took place. Gradually B.B. managed to get their life story out of them. Established as tea-planters in India they had stopped in Palestine on one of their trips home. The atmosphere of the place and its history had impressed them so deeply that they had decided to sell their property in India and to settle down in Tel Aviv. "With what object?" "To convert the Jews." "Have you been successful?" "Well, not really. We have been received very cordially and our neighbours like to drop in and to have long discussions with us but so far we have only made one convert, a young man who wants to marry a Christian girl, and we are afraid that that is his only reason for wishing to become one too. We drive all over the country in a small truck filled with copies of the Gospels in several languages and we distribute them freely. Whenever we stop near a field where people are working they all come running along at the sight of books and they accept our gifts but nothing further happens."

IN THE EARLY AUTUMN of 1929 we set out again with Spain as our main objective, preceded by a run through the whole of Provence in the most glorious September light. We met Mary in Toulouse and Morra in Pau, had a sight of the Atlantic at Biarritz and spent a quiet morning at Bayonne looking at the drawings in the Bonnat collection. From Pau Mary insisted—very much against B.B.'s grain—on taking an excursion to Lourdes. It was a radiant day and as we watched the processions following each other and mounting the steps to the church and heard the feeble voices of the sick on their stretchers reciting the responses to the prayers read out by a priest, B.B. was suddenly overcome with emotion and burst into tears. Mary was horrified and thought he was going through a second conversion. What had moved him was the thought of how suffering humanity's search for supernatural help goes back to the earliest civilizations. Lourdes appeared to him as one of the bridges that still connect us with antiquity.

Morra accompanied us on most of the trip, sometimes driving with us, sometimes going by train to places not included in our programme. A delightful companion and a helpful one too through his fair knowledge of the language. Again, as on all our journeys, B.B.'s general plan gave us time to get a real feeling of familiarity with the sights, the people, the landscape. We were able to visit out-of-the-way places (perhaps no longer out-of-the-way now!) like Cuenca and Jativa where B.B. was attracted by the paintings of Leonardo's Spanish followers or Ubeda on account of Sebastiano del Piombo's Michelangelesque *Pietà*. During our long stay in Madrid B.B. was in touch with Spanish art historians like Gomez Moreno, Sanchez Canton and Beroqui and both Morra and I accompanied him when he called on Manuel Cossio. Already an old man but still full of fire and noble eloquence. In Sevilla we were looked after by a charming young art historian, Diego Angulo, who is now the head of the Istituto San Fernando in Madrid. We got as far south as Cadiz and Algeciras and I remember the startling impression on our drive from Cadiz to Tarifa, of suddenly seeing the outline of distant hills and then only realizing, as the blue expanse of the straits appeared before us, that we were in sight of the African shore and that those hills belonged to another continent. In Sevilla and Barcelona there was the added interest of the two great exhibitions, the first remarkable for the Central and South American precious objects and textiles, the second for the treasures of mediaeval art. I ended by feeling thoroughly at home in Spain. But in which European country have I not felt that if I could master the language it would be easy to make my home in it?

Mary also enjoyed the trip enormously and went in for a great many gastronomic experiments. B.B. teased her about being "verbo-toxic" and unable to resist the fascination of the exotic name of a dish. She accused us of being "sticks-in-the-mud" if we refused to follow her example. More often than not the appearance of the dish she had ordered would horrify her. "This looks black and too disgusting for words. I cannot eat it."

It was already December and the days were getting short when we re-crossed Provence in a raging mistral to return to the luxuries of Sainte-Claire. Again Mary and I deposited B.B. and Elizabeth there and hurried on to Florence where I found my people comfortably established in their new apartment on the first floor of one of the old houses in Borgo San Jacopo that seemed to be growing out of the river. It was to be their home until the house was blown up by the Germans in August 1944.

OUR TRIP TO TUNISIA and Algeria in the spring of 1931 —described in detail by Mary in her *Across the Mediterranean* (Prato: Giachetti; 1935) was a perfect one, very restful and free from social ties. Except for a few people in Tunis to whom B.B. had letters of introduction, we knew

Domenico Veneziano's St. John the Baptist in the Wilderness

B.B., Diana Menuhin, and Bessie Berenson, Casa al Dono, 1952

Hamish and Yvonne Hamilton and John Walker,
Casa al Dono, 1952

nobody. There was no hitch in carrying out our programme and no bad consequences from spending some bitterly cold nights in very primitive inns. In one of these I remember a comical scene. B.B. had insisted on visiting the classical ruins of Sbeitla although the place was difficult to get to and the inn definitely not recommended by the travel agency in Tunis. When we reached it in the gloaming after an endless drive over the desert-like high plateau of central Tunisia it seemed little better than a faintly lit cave. An almost inedible meal, small cubicles without windows and a huge bed in each was all we could get. When I woke up next morning in my dark cell I went at once to see what sort of night my "old birds" had passed. Mary I found in the best of moods and enjoying her breakfast. "I have never had such a quiet room and such a refreshing sleep." B.B. also in the midst of his breakfast seemed very gloomy. "Have you had a bad night?" "Oh no, but it disgusts me to come across such carelessness." And saying this he pointed to the milk jug. The handle was broken off.

What added greatly to the enjoyment of our trips beyond the Italian frontier was being rid of the incessant apprehension about the Fascist regime. On the other hand it was often annoying to meet with total incomprehension of what conditions in Italy really were, to be asked—as happened to me more than once—whether I was not proud of having a man like Mussolini at the head of our government. But it could also happen that abroad one met with a sudden wave of understanding and sympathy as if two members of a secret society had given each other the sign of recognition.

Among the letters of introduction for Tunis was one to the commanding general of the garrison, at that moment Count Chambrun (one of Lafayette's descendants), married to Alice Longworth, a highly cultivated American. They asked us to lunch in a fine old Turkish house with lovely

old tiles and magnificent Senegalese servants walking noise-
lessly around the table like elegant panthers. I found myself
next to a French lawyer and amateur archaeologist, Monsieur
Saumagne, and soon discovered that he knew a great deal
about Italy and the Fascist regime. He ended by telling me
how in the summer of 1929, while he was temporarily
replacing the chief of police during the latter's holiday, on
a Saturday evening the arrival of a motor launch had been
announced to him with people in it whose papers were not
in order. Were they to be arrested? He had felt instinctively
reluctant about taking any action and when on Monday
morning he finally gave the necessary dispositions the launch
had left. It was the boat that had carried out the daring
exploit of liberating Carlo Rosselli and two other anti-
Fascists from their exile on the island of Lipari and whose
first refueling station had been Tunis.

THIS NORTH AFRICAN TRIP was to be the last in the old
style with the Lancia car, Parry, Elizabeth, and mountains
of luggage. In the autumn of 1931 Mary insisted—against
the advice of Giglioli, the family physician, and without con-
sulting any other specialist—on going through an operation
which would have been an easy one for a young woman but
not for somebody of Mary's age. It was carelessly done or in
her undisciplined way she insisted on getting up too early.
I remember finding her out of bed two days after the operation and when I asked who had given her the permission to
move her answer was: "I would have yelled the house down
if they had not let me do what I wanted." Whatever the
reason she returned home in rather poor shape and lingered
on for a while, then developed a violent infection which
took her to death's door from which she was only just pulled
back with the help of powerful drugs. From then on she
led an invalid's life interrupted by periods of apparently

complete recovery and almost alarming euphoria. One never knew when the next cloud of depression, misery, and pain would come over her. All sorts of cures were tried to improve her condition—treatments in Swiss and Austrian sanatoriums and watering resorts, new drugs, healers, rays. Each of them helped for a longer or shorter time until the next collapse. There was at least one compensation: no more quarrelling. B.B. was too upset by her suffering condition to have any serious arguments with her. Mary's lack of physical self-discipline got on his nerves but he did his best not to show his impatience with her.

One of Mary's consolations was the recollection of our journeys around the Mediterranean which led her into reading extensively and also into writing about them.

CHAPTER XVII

Poggio allo Spino
and Casa al Dono

THE FIRST TWO SUMMERS (1917 and 1921) that Mary and
B.B. spent at the Saltino on the slopes of the Prato
Magno, staying in a hotel convinced them that this was the
ideal region to escape to from the worst heat, ideal for air and
temperature, for walks and excursions and particularly for
being so near to I Tatti that in a couple of hours books and
photos that B.B. might require for his work could be fetched.
So they started looking for a house to rent and settled on
one near the Consuma pass. Its name was Poggio allo Spino
in a wonderful position surrounded by beechwoods and with
a superb view towards the Mugello and the high Apennines.
It was not an attractive house, a square block, badly built
so that the slightest noise, even a sneeze, echoed through it.
Also very primitively furnished and far from comfortable.
Only one bathroom for all of us and one felt like pinning
up a notice begging the occupier not to stay longer than ten
minutes in it. Yet B.B. and Mary loved the place and with
the exception of 1927 when we went north and 1936 when
we went to Yugoslavia we spent every summer in it till 1937.
Moving into it was quite an elaborate affair, as so much had
to be carried up to make it a little more habitable. Regularly
every year the move was put off for different reasons until

the heat became unbearable and then in a great rush and going through an intense sweating cure everything had to be made ready.

B.B. to Nicky   August 4th 1924   Poggio allo Spino
Darling Nicky,
    But for its being so icy in the evening it would be perfect here. For I do enjoy the silence, the comforting solitude and the soughing of the wind in the trees, the abstract beauty of the opalescent mountain shapes. I feel frightfully lazy, heavy and irresolute. I have lost interest in the Domenico Morone article and feel I ought to turn to grass. I know it would be a good investment. And yet like a petty shopkeeper who prefers a penny today to a pound tomorrow I want to go on giving myself the illusion of getting something done every day.

With the exception of Countess Serristori who owned a villa at the Saltino and came over very frequently, we had no neighbours. One summer long the Costers rented a villa not far from us and the same house was occupied for several years by the Spelmans. But even without neighbours Poggio allo Spino was not exactly a hermitage. Somehow by telegram, by letter, by telephone messages through the post office of Consuma, friends managed to announce or to propose themselves and there was the usual mixture of guests staying in the house and others coming for lunch or to spend the day. Old friends like Trevy or the Perrys or the Hands[1] came for longer stays. Morra appeared regularly during my holiday and so whenever possible did Pellegrina Paulucci and Clotilde Marghieri. Logan came several times and once accompanied by Desmond MacCarthy, the Anglo-Irish man of letters and one of the most delightful and stimulating *causeurs*. Friendships that lasted to the end of B.B.'s life began at Poggio allo Spino, like that with the Mongan sisters,

---

[1] Judge Learned Hand and his wife, from New York.

Agnes and Betty. Sent by Paul Sachs they turned up one day, very late for lunch and rather flustered. B.B. liked them both from the first moment and very quickly made them feel at their ease with him.

Hortense brought over her guest, Riri Visconti Venosta (his official title was Marchese di Brelio), son of the former minister of foreign affairs and a descendant of Cavour on his mother's side. When still a boy at Sankt Moritz he had become attached to B.B. and we had seen a lot of him in Rome in 1924. Tall, elegant, very much *fin de race*, he was even more of an anti-Fascist than B.B., haughtily intransigent and full of bitter irony. It was a pity he did not settle down to write more seriously. The one small book published by him about the United States, *America, An Atmosphere*, has real quality both as psychological penetration and as poetical feeling. At Poggio allo Spino Riri met the Hands and a real friendship grew up between them, reinforced during Riri's long stays in New York.

B.B. to Nicky   August 17th 1925   Poggio allo Spino
. . . Mary has written to you about the Hands. He is the sort of person who can make me say things I would not even think when alone. And that is a fundamental weakness of mine. I cannot by myself produce myself. And that is why I have in one respect made a fatal mistake in drifting into such an isolated mode of existence.

Mary to Nicky   Poggio allo Spino   August 16th 1926
. . . We had a visit yesterday from the Guggenheims, the people who give those scholarships on one of which Sessions is now living. Guggenheim is known in America as the Copper King. He owns almost all Chile and Alaska and is not a millionaire but a milliardaire. To look at, he is a rather ordinary little man with a kind smile and a gentle voice. The wife was nice and wore gorgeous pearls. The son was refined-looking but had a terrific American accent. They were not at all stuck up and rather respectful to B.B., who

214

came out with some of his most exciting and horrifying paradoxes, which they seemed to enjoy immensely. They had been to I Tatti and said they had never dreamt of such a beautiful house to live in. They are just beginning to collect and have fallen into the hands of somewhat doubtful dealers with indifferent results. . . .

B.B. to Nicky   Poggio allo Spino   August 17th 1926
    . . . Sybil Colefax has arrived yesterday with her second son in a Rolls-Royce. She looks springy and uses her hands and arms elegantly, but her eyes are rusty and dim all of a sudden like those of an old woman. The Countess Hortense arrived only a minute later for lunch, and I got Sybil to tell her and us all about the cinema city in California and Mary Pickford and Co. and something about her other adventures in America. She recounts them well, and I am sorry you are not here to enjoy it all. . . .

B.B. to Nicky   Poggio allo Spino   August 19th 1926
    . . . Lady Colefax talked and talked and talked. At times her voice sank and I could not follow and missed a lot. Her curiosity is universal and with regard to people perfectly disinterested although avid. She told us everything about all acquaintances in America and about nearly all in England.
    About English politics she was really informing and illuminating, but not very consoling. No real leaders in sight. As for the attitude towards Germany, the die-hards and sentimentalists were still hostile, but no others. Her boy told me that the youngsters at Oxford had a good deal of ill-will against France but none against Germany.

B.B. to Nicky   August 21st 1928   Poggio allo Spino
    . . . Ralph Perry pumps me on the more conversable parts of my studies and is eager to have me drop lists and drawings and plunge at once into the "decline and resurrection of form." He is stimulating because intelligent enough to ask questions and ignorant enough not to know how hard they are to answer. . . .

B.B. to Nicky   September 5th 1928   Poggio allo Spino
   . . . The Perrys left day before yesterday and as they
went I became aware of how much I had enjoyed Ralph
and how he had endeared himself to me. He did everything
to draw me out and make me talk, effacing himself. I felt
that Rachel did not like this and that my talk bored her.
She preferred reading Trollope aloud to us which she did
extremely well. In many little things she got on my nerves
as I no doubt on hers. I felt a growing tension between us
although of a nature not easy to define. And as always before
I conclude that I love but do not like her.
   Work is getting forward. I have just finished the Bas-
sanos. Leandro will take a bit more time verifying dates in
Hadeln's edition of Ridolfi.
   Du Bos on Gide is a bit slow but full of delicate observation. Lionello Venturi's last has a number of essays defending
Ruskin, Fiedler, Wölfflin and Berenson against Croce. I did
not imagine that Croce on this particular subject was as
wooden-minded as Lionello makes him out.

Various visits of Duveen at Poggio allo Spino took place
during my absences and were described to me in Mary's and
B.B.'s letters. It sounded like a series of breathless rushes,
one excursion following the other. Only once was there some
quiet talk.

B.B. to Nicky   September 2nd 1928   Poggio allo Spino
Dearest Nick,
   Sir Joseph had been and is going in an hour. Mary is
to take him through the Uffizi Pitti and Bargello before his
train leaves. He says that he came not to talk business but to
consult me about his own concerns rather than affairs. He
wanted to know whether he should work first to be trustee
of the National Gallery or to be a peer. I advised him to
try for the peerage because if he got that all else would be
added unto him. Then he asked what I thought of the School
of Art Studies to be established at London University for

which Lord Lee of Fareham was trying to engage his assistance. I told him that if he wanted to help study he should endow one chair at Oxford and another at Cambridge and in each a school in the sense of a historical or classical school. And that he should further endow two fellowships in each university for study at I Tatti when that becomes a training ground for freemen of the city of art.

Joe also wanted to know what to do about contributing to the enlargement of the National Portrait Gallery and I unfolded the scheme I proposed to Lord d'Abernon some time ago, of removing the gallery to a place where it could be enlarged into a museum and Academy for the study of Anglo-Saxon biography down to 1800 as well as to British in the narrower sense after that date.

All my suggestions found favour *mais Allah est le plus savant!*

B.B. to Nicky   Poggio allo Spino   July 28th 1929
Dearest Nick,

Vavalà and Rensselaer Lee are here. She is a pleasant enough guest, being, like most English people, well trained for visiting. In conversation she takes little interest in any topic that is not gossip about the people she knows and shop-talk. The abstracter and more historical and literary subjects reduce her to silence. Lee is a very different matter. One could address one's whole self to him. I want him to write about the revival of the taste for the *primitifs* and I already talked at length about it a week ago and I am doing it again. It should be a readable as well as interesting book.

B.B. to Nicky   Poggio allo Spino   August 4th 1929
. . . I am working as hard as I dare and am getting on fairly well with the lists. I still feel utterly unfit for any other work. Of the Venetian fifteenth century I have only Antonello and followers and Montagna and followers to do. Then comes the Giorgione quicksand.

I am so glad to have Alda—who is looking well and

pretty—and Bertie. Alda has been reading aloud to us a very good Ojetti in *Pegaso* on the real titles of Italy to the attention of tourists. Last night she read us a short story by Hello, far more terrible than Hoffmann or Poe because of its greater moral bulk. Curious how that form of embodying an abstract problem in a short story lasted as a literacy form till Villiers de l'Isle-Adam and then disappeared. For myself I have been reading the second volume of Michaud's *Histoire des Croisades*. Not brilliant, but informing and decently told.

We revel in your letters from London and in all of yours and Cecil's doings. What fun you must be having taking such a big small boy to his first circus of London. . . .

Nicky to Mary   August 12th 1930   Poggio allo Spino
. . . Moravia turns up almost every day at tea-time. He is an amusing mixture, so mature and yet such a child and so straightforward and passionate in his opinions and ideas. He implores you to think of a family that would take him as a paying guest when he goes to London this autumn. He wants them to be intelligent and wants them not to mind if he makes a few inkspots on his sheets as he generally spends his morning in bed writing. Something in the direction of Bloomsbury I should think!

Nicky to Mary   September 1st 1931   Poggio allo Spino
Dearest Mary,
I am giving this letter to Trevy to post as you will get it quicker. He is leaving in 20 minutes the dear old poet and is already in a state of wild excitement, looking at his watch, comparing it with all our watches, taking advice now from Alda and now from me on the question of tips. He has been very sweet and I am sorry to see him go. . . .

B.B. to Nicky   Poggio allo Spino   August 14th 1933
. . . Alys Russell has arrived and is pleasant enough, although I always feel with her as with an enemy during a truce. At bottom we are at war, for she is and remains an

-ist of every kind, feminist, prohibitionist, philanthropist, pacifist, and she despises me or at least disapproves of me for being such a pagan. . . .

B.B. to Nicky   Poggio allo Spino   August 21st 1933

. . . Here it is so drafty that one does not notice how warm it is. Alys is amiable and uninteresting, but her beautiful wavy hair getting grey and covering a well-shaped skull is some compensation. Andrew Green puffs and pants on, and I cannot help liking him. Yesterday he asked me in a whisper how it was that no man had walked off with you. I answered softly: "*Unberufen,* she always preferred me." He nearly fell over with surprise. What an acute observer!

Have finished *Sons and Lovers* and am grateful that you made me read it. I certainly know no attempt comparable to get to the bottom of the flood that runs between man and woman. . . .

Nicky to Mary   September 16th 1934   Poggio allo Spino
Dearest Mary,

For once you would be thoroughly *einverstanden* with our way of living and its quietness and regularity and especially with the lack of all intrusion from the outside. But already I am caught saying a lie for we had an intrusion yesterday afternoon in the form of Robert Lehmann and his new wife, a rather Scandinavian-looking flapper but already burdened with three children and a divorced producer of same. They came up in a magnificent car furnished with a wireless set, which filled our servants with pious admiration. They listen to it even while they are driving. He wants to collect drawings and brought up photos of Mantegna's Credis and Pisanellos which under B.B.'s magnifying glass dwindled down to "school of," "close to," and "probably a fake." He bore it with fortitude and both were very pleasant. . . .

B.B. to Nicky   Poggio allo Spino   August 9th 1935

. . . You ask about Morra. He is simply perfect and I feel not a thin sheet of paper between us. He takes almost

as much interest as your darling self in all that pertains
to me.

Nicky to Mary   August 14th 1935   Poggio allo Spino
   . . . B.B. says that his *tête-à-tête* with Morra has been
perfect, in fact so perfect that I might have prolonged my
stay in Sorrento. But he never took the trouble to inform
me of this by letter! However, here I am very much refreshed
by those wonderful swims and ready to bury myself in the
drawings. There is still a lot of work to be done on them. . . .

Nicky to Mary   August 24th 1935   Poggio allo Spino
   . . . I am deep in the work on the drawings again and
so is B.B., but we work separately at different ends and when
he wants something he gives a kind of howl in his room and
stamps his feet and I hear it and go up to see what sort of
tangle he has got into. It is a blessing to have something
that for part of the day absorbs us completely for the general
outlook is beastly and seems to get steadily worse. . . .

Nicky to Mary   September 11th 1935   Poggio allo Spino
   . . . To-day we are expecting John Shapley with the
Breasteds. The fire is lit both here and in the dining room
for it has become very cold. Guglielmo Alberti is sitting by
the fire and from time to time we exchange a few words.
He has been a perfectly charming guest, most companionable
and his reading aloud, in Italian as well as in French, is
too beautiful. . . .

IN THE SUMMER of 1937 Duveen sent up one of his
important clients who wanted to meet B.B. It was Samuel
H. Kress and he and B.B. took to each other at once. B.B.
had expected the "greenhorn" type of collector and found on
the contrary a shrewd old man, simple and straightforward,
Germanic in his heartiness. Out of this first meeting grew
the interest of Samuel Kress and later of his younger brother
Rush Kress in B.B.'s publications, the distribution of the

new edition of the *Florentine Drawings* to a number of American university libraries and later the subvention for the new illustrated edition of B.B.'s *Renaissance Painters* and *Renaissance Pictures.*

It was in the same summer of 1937 that the connection between B.B. and the firm of Duveen Brothers came to an end. The cause was the *Nativity* from Lord Allendale's collection, traditionally attributed to Giorgione, which Duveen had bought.[2] It was deposited for several days at Poggio allo Spino so as to give B.B. full leisure to study it. B.B. came to the conclusion that it was painted by the young Titian and Duveen would not accept his verdict. Duveen turned out to be right, for during his last years while working on the revision of the Venetian lists B.B. ended by considering the *Nativity* as painted by Giorgone with the help of the young Titian. But it was just as well that his stubborn opposition freed him from a task that had become very irksome for him.

Nicky to Mary   August 2nd 1937   Poggio allo Spino
Dearest Mary,
        I have just been reading some of those enchanting letters of A.E. to the Kingsley Porters in which he makes fun of Kingsley's love for the rain and the mist and the storms of Ireland. Kingsley would have been absolutely happy here these last days. We have had nothing but storms and lightning and thunder and now we are entirely wrapt up in the clouds. B.B. is depressed and worries a lot. I don't know whether it is his way of getting acclimatized to this air or whether it is his way of getting older and of suffering from his diminished power to work and to concentrate. He has really so much to be grateful for, keeping his body so light and nimble and his capacity to walk and his immensely varied interests. But when people are depressed it is no use

2 Later on sold to Kress and now at the National Gallery, Washington.

221

calling their attention to what they ought to be thankful
for. I remember trying it again and again with Geoffrey
and with no success. Don't think though that B.B. is as
melancholic as Geoffrey tended to be! At meals and with
guests he is very lively and "conversationally inclined"[3] like
with Doro and Anna over the week-end and with the
Guidottis yesterday, but he worries a lot *dans l'intimitè*,
about you principally and about other things too.

. . . I have begun to work on the index for the drawings,
that is to say, on the additions and corrections, for the index
of the first edition is done beautifully by you and by whoever helped you. I wish you were here to help me, for this
is my first experience in index making. A better place for
working undisturbedly does not exist in the world. . . .

IN THE EARLY AUTUMN of 1937 we left Poggio allo Spino
fully expecting to return to it the following summer. But
in the spring of 1938 just as we were getting ready to start
on our trip to Asia Minor, news reached us that it had been
sold to a Florentine nobleman. B.B. felt utterly hopeless
about finding another place with the same advantages of
height and view and closeness to I Tatti. We knew only one
house half way to Vallombrosa and considerably lower, from
having called a couple of times on its owners, the Corsinis.
Alda and I drove up on a dismal rainy day in April to have
a look at it. If I had followed my judgment nothing would
have come of it, for my impression was of a gloomy, damp,
and altogether unpromising house. But my sister, having
much more flair for houses and for what can be made out
of them than I have, was of a different opinion. She said
the old house had a lot of character and with a few improvements could be made habitable and attractive. So B.B. rented

---

[3] That is what Captain Elgood, Bonté Elgood's husband, used to
call Mary and B.B.

it from the Corsinis and two years later when it came up for sale encouraged me to employ the small capital I owned in buying it.

The lower part of Casa al Dono had been one of the farms belonging to the Vallombrosan monks, formerly the owners of the whole forest. It was they who had in the tenth century opened up the wild region of the Prato Magno, the mountain fortress that seems to grow out of the Apennines under the Falterona forcing the Arno to run all around it in order to reach the sea. After the suppression of the convents around 1860 some of the convent land must have been sold and Casa al Dono was acquired by a Marchese Peruzzi, whose wife was William Wetmore Story's daughter. It was she who built up the second story in the same local stone as the former peasant house, who furnished it and spent many summers there. Her father, William Wetmore Story, stayed with her frequently and died at Casa al Dono. According to B.B. he was a typical product of the United States of his time, unable to make up his mind whether he wanted to be a sculptor, a poet, or a novelist. A novelette of his, *Fiammetta*, placed in the Vallombrosa region, had been a great favourite of B.B.'s in his youth and later influenced him in choosing Florence as his residence.

The rustic charm of Casa al Dono with the apple orchard and farmland at its feet and the forest as its background revealed itself to us only gradually. Ralph Perry, our first guest there, could not get over the loss of Poggio allo Spino. B.B. was soon reconciled to the change and loved the spacious rooms, the quaint old-fashioned furniture, the views from his windows, the quality of the water, the quietness. Then we began to discover walks within easy distance of the house, a great help during the following years when petrol was scarce and a car only occasionally at our disposal. At Poggio allo Spino we used to take a special walk to get the full view of the sunset. At Casa al Dono we could see it from the house itself or from the little pine wood close by where later our *casiere* (housewarden) built up a hut of dried broom to give B.B. some shelter from too much draught.

The view was not as grand and sweeping as from Poggio allo Spino yet very lovely, down to the Arno at Pontassieve and further to the curve of Le Sieci, then over the hills surrounding Florence to the Modenese and Pistoiese high Apennines and in clear weather to the craggy blue outline of the Carrara mountains.

Nicky to Mary   July 23rd 1938   Casa al Dono
Dearest Mary,

I can hardly believe that we should be already settled in so comfortably here and feel quite at home. It is a much more home-like place than Poggio allo Spino, at least for us. It is less convenient for the *famiglia* with a longer way between kitchen and dining-room and various other difficulties but they seem to take it all very cheerfully. . . . The paths that lead up into the forest behind the house are delightful and we have discovered a *Belvedere* under pines with the view of the Monte Morello and the profiles of Monte Ceceri and Fiesole nearer to us. . . . I cannot say that Addie Kahn and Ralph Perry make a perfect harmony. She tends to drift into personal gossip very easily and he resents it if people he does not know are talked about. Yesterday things went better as we talked only about Russia in spite of our limited knowledge of what is really going on there at present. . . . To-night Doro and Anna are coming to spend a few days with us. They had a really miraculous escape last week. Having booked their seats on the Cagliari–Ostia airplane for a given day they found them snatched away by some *pezzo grosso* and did not insist on having other passengers left behind but decided to wait a day. That airplane crashed and everybody was drowned or eaten up by sharks. The corpses were brought back to Cagliari with heads and arms and legs missing. . . .

B.B. to Nicky   August 11th 1938
Dearest Nick,

   It has cooled, the air is from the north and brings the swish and rattle from the highroad above us. It is more idyllic than ever this morning. It was always so when Rome was burning. Thousands and thousands of spots like this with people in them too close to the ground to be much affected.

   . . . Had Margaret Barr to dinner. Her flimsy evening dress brought out something Chinese-Japanese in her look. She told me a great deal of what was being done for painters and the theatre world out of relief funds and we discussed whether the results would be good or bad. She spoke with assurance and emphasis . . .

Meanwhile at Poggio allo Spino the new owner, a Florentine nobleman had settled himself in with his family. He was a man well known for his unshakable belief in Fascism. Countess Serristori was surprised—when she called at Poggio allo Spino for the first time—to find him changed from his usual buoyant optimism to a far more cautious and critical attitude. It clearly proved that strong currents of anti-Fascism had been left in the house by so many years of subversive talking and thinking.

MARY BEGAN by refusing categorically to join us at Casa al Dono. Having been miserably ill at Poggio allo Spino in 1934 she blamed it on the altitude and the climate, spent the summer of 1935 in a Viennese sanatorium and the four following summers in England with her family. At last in 1940, finding herself cut off from England and crushed by the news of her daughter's death, she changed her mind and decided to come up. It was a great success from the first day. The house had meanwhile become my property and this was a particular source of pleasure for her. When I accompanied her on one of her short walks she would point with her stick to a stone and say: "Look, Nicky, even that stone belongs to you."

OUR ONLY CLOSE NEIGHBOURS at Casa al Dono were the keepers of the forest administration's nursery garden and the parish priest of San Miniato in Alpe, a small church in an admirable position. The priest, Don Michelangelo Patroni, an elderly Neapolitan, turned out to be a very agreeable, witty, cultivated, even erudite man and an entertaining guest at lunch or tea-time. B.B. could not help wondering why such a gifted scholar and preacher should have been exiled to a small parish of simple-minded mountaineers. Perhaps as a punishment for indiscreet behaviour with women? That did not seem unlikely. His type was that of the vigorously florid, intensely vital southerner. Many years later, after the war, Don Patroni got into a heated argument with one of our guests over the excommunication of Ernesto Buonaiuti. Don Patroni's defence of Buonaiuti was passionately eloquent and made us understand that his allegiance to the modernistic movement had exiled him to San Miniato. This was confirmed by the reaction of the bishop of Fiesole, who while at lunch at I Tatti was asked by me whether another climatically more suitable destination could be found for the ageing Don Patroni. The eyes of this usually very kind and courteous man became cold and stern and his only answer was: *"Don Patroni sta bene dove sta"*— Don Patroni is well employed where he is.

Through Don Patroni we were put in touch with our Sicilian neighbours, the ex-prime minister Vittorio Emanuele Orlando and his family. In the early thirties Orlando had bought the pseudo-mediaeval castle of Campiglioni across the ravine opposite to us, built by and for a number of years inhabited by Julian Story, the painter son of William Wet-

more Story. Among all the children and grandchildren that
surrounded the old man during the summer the most remarkable figure was his daughter Carlotta Garabelli, an unusually
gifted woman. She had inherited her father's dazzling eloquence, his passionate interest in politics and his energetic
stocky figure. B.B. took to her at once but also to her father
and although Orlando and he could never agree on any question regarding the end of the world war and the so-called
Peace Treaty of Versailles they could find themselves in complete harmony in their aversion to Fascism. When the circulation of cars was forbidden Orlando would let himself be
transported on a motor-furgonette to the path that led down
to the bottom of the ravine and up to the church, would
climb down and up, would go to mass then have lunch at
Casa al Dono. Don Patroni, who was proud of his well-pre-
pared and rather elaborate sermons (far above the heads of
his usual congregation), felt rather disconcerted by Orlando's
persistent habit of knocking his stick loudly on the floor as
if to say that the sermon had been long enough.

Mary too found the Orlando family very congenial,
particularly Carlotta, who had lived for years in the United
States and felt at home in the American world. Not to speak
of the heroic side of Carla's nature which appealed greatly
to Mary. After the armistice, when Allied prisoners found
themselves all of a sudden released and roaming about Italy
in the hope of reaching the Allied forces, Carla did not hesitate to receive whoever knocked at her door, to feed these
poor men, to dress them up as shepherds or peasants, and to
advise them about how to reach their goal.

B.B.'s ROUTINE at Casa al Dono was if anything even
more regular than at I Tatti, alternating work with shorter
and longer walks—the latter combined with a drive—and
with pleasant conversation or, when we were alone, with

listening to recorded music or to my reading aloud. Each year he seemed to get fonder of the dear old house and it made me laugh to think of his being described as the most luxury-loving and fastidious of men. There he was blissfully happy in a very simple room containing his bed, his writing table, a chest of drawers, and plenty of room on tables and shelves for his books and photographs. That was exactly what suited him and every autumn when the place became too chilly for him he hated to leave it and yearned to have the same kind of life all the year round. Somehow his affection for Casa al Dono has left an echo there and to this day, inside and outside the house, I feel B.B.'s presence even more than at I Tatti.

CHAPTER XVIII

Janus-faced Years [1931–38]

W HEN I LOOK BACK on the years following Mary's breakdown they appear to me like the god Janus with his
two faces. On one side the constant preoccupation over
Mary's health combined with the worry over the growing
political tension, horror of what was happening in Germany,
fear of what the echo might be in Fascist Italy, acute anxiety
over the fate of Jewish friends in Germany and later in
Austria. On the other side peaceful and concentrated work
on the revision of *Florentine Drawings*, new friends,
various shorter and longer trips.

Work on the drawings was carried on partly at home,
partly in the Uffizi print room, partly in the Buonarroti
house. While handling those delicate sheets and reconsider-
ing his former attributions B.B. seemed to me much happier
than when working on the "lists." Possibly because being
in touch with originals is so much more satisfactory than
working on photographs. Possibly because what little assistance I could give him was of more value to him than my
help with the lists. Not only did I get more interested in
drawings than I ever had been in paintings but my mind
was freer from other preoccupations than in the preceding
years. From 1929 onwards the library had been taken over
by my sister and I was only responsible for keeping the
photographic collection in order.

In the Uffizi print room we found an unexpected assistant in the custodian Ristori, a cross-eyed heavy man with huge clumsy hands. And yet it was enough to describe to him the subject and style of a drawing and he would immediately produce it. He seemed to enjoy particularly difficult problems of location and to have something like a sixth sense about them.

Besides the thrill of looking at the original sheets with B.B., of watching his immediate reaction to them, of listening to his comments, I was able to follow him closely in his work on the various supplements to the text. What I would have liked to achieve and never did was to persuade him to make the original text more readable by cutting out various prolix and no longer necessary passages. He would not accept my criticism which was probably based too much on my personal feelings of boredom regarding these lengthy disquisitions and not enough on scholarly knowledge and preparation. In the third edition of the drawings, the Italian one, Luisa Vertova, the translator, has done a good deal of what I had in mind because she knew how to present her arguments convincingly to B.B. Also in reshaping his *Lorenzo Lotto* with her help all the superannuated parts of the text were cut out.

Countless were the friends among B.B.'s colleagues who procured information and photographic material for him during the revision of *Florentine Drawings*. A friendship that lasted to the end of B.B.'s life, the one with Philip Hofer, grew out of their correspondence about various drawings. Hofer was then on the staff of the Morgan library and Belle Greene introduced him to B.B.

B.B.'s worries over not finding a publisher ready to bring out the revised edition of the drawings were suddenly brought to an end through the help of Fern Shapley (Professor John Shapley's wife), who persuaded the Chicago University Press to handle it, deputing her to supervise the printing of text and plates in Italy. Fern with her two little girls had settled down in Florence in the early thirties and when B.B. and Mary offered her the Villino she began to work regularly in the library and take an interest in the revision of the drawings. A more efficient, quiet, and highly intelligent collaborator would be difficult to find anywhere. *Un pozzo di scienza*—a well of learning—as we say in Italian, yet totally free from arrogance, pedantry, or self-assertion. There was something infinitely reassuring, almost soothing in her way of working, in her presence. She seemed to me like a nun who joyfully devotes all her energies to serving others. John Walker, who used the library during those years, learnt to appreciate Fern and her unusual capactiy just as much as we did and subsequently secured her assistance for the National Gallery in Washington.

Mary too was very fond of Fern and of her girls and called them her second family. It was Fern who did most of the research for Mary's *Across the Mediterranean* (Prato: Giachetti; 1935) and for the *Vicarious Trip to the Barbary Coast* (London: Constable; 1938) and helped her to find publishers for them. John Shapley appeared from time to time to spend his holidays at the Villino and B.B. appreciated his wide learning, especially in the field of Byzantine and Near Eastern archaeology and history.

WHEN IN 1935 John Walker became assistant of the director at the American Academy in Rome we met through him the new director and his sister, Chester and Amey Aldrich. During the years of their residence in Rome, until Chester's death in 1940, we were continually in touch with these two exceptional human beings, exceptional in their combining the highest standards of culture with real intelligence and loving kindness. It also meant a lot that they were politically on our side. Chester left to himself might have been won over by Fascist flattery but Amey, who had the better mind and the firmer character of the two, would never have allowed him to swerve from the right path.

The Aldriches in their turn introduced B.B. to William Phillips and his wife, during one of our stays in Rome. Mr. Phillips was from 1936 until 1941 American ambassador at Rome. They too became very dear friends and stayed repeatedly at I Tatti.

Another acquisition on the American side was the young Harvard professor of classics, Mason Hammond, and his wife Florence. During the time they spent at the American Academy John Walker brought them to I Tatti, and B.B. found them both most satisfactory and attractive. Mason solid and thorough, at the same time rich in New England humour, Florence beautiful and high-spirited and full of feminine charm.

AN UNUSUAL VISITOR was sent to us early in 1933 by Roger and Barbara Sessions, who were spending that year in Berlin, the German orchestra conductor Otto Klemperer. A formidable man not only in stature and in his powerful features, but in his masterful voice and violent way of expressing himself. To our amazement we found him hopeful as to what the recently installed Nazi regime might do for Germany. A few weeks later, having had all his concerts cancelled from one day to the other, he came back in a towering fury and insisted on playing and singing a psalm of hatred against Hitler, composed by himself, on our poor veteran of a piano. (It had belonged to the pianist Hans von Bülow and Mary had bought it from Bülow's and Cosima Wagner's daughter Countess Gravina.) There was something irresistibly genuine, *ursprünglich* about him and the stories told by him. The one B.B. liked best was of how on a voyage to South America Klemperer had been daily sending various delicacies to a group of Jewish emigrants in the third class.

"Do not take him for one of your people," somebody had warned them. "He is a convert to Catholicism." "Never mind," was the answer. *"Er hat sich sein jüdisches Herz bewahrt"*—he has kept his Jewish heart.

A musician, considered a prodigy as a composer, appeared for the first time at I Tatti in those years, Igor Markevitch, under the wing of Marie-Laure de Noailles. He came again with his newly married wife, Kyra Nijinsky, daughter of the famous Russian dancer. Both he and she and their enchanting little boy were to become members of the I Tatti circle during the war.

ELISABETTA DE PICCOLELLIS, the widow of Placci's nephew Lucien Henraux, returned to her home town, Florence, at that time, having taken back her maiden name after a rather disastrous second marriage. Both Mary and B.B. had been very fond of her first husband and welcomed her to I Tatti, listened to her exquisite singing and enjoyed her classical beauty and agreeable atmosphere. Her father, Marchese Ottavio de Piccolellis, a highly gifted musician and conductor, had been the founder of the first concert society in Florence.

It was followed by the one still flourishing, called Gli Amici della Musica, and prominent among its founders were two dear friends of ours, Alberto and Clara Passigli. Alberto's energy and resourcefulness made him an ideal president and the centre of musical life in Florence. On friendly terms with outstanding musicians the world over, he received them in his villa, Il Leccio, whenever they had an engagement in Florence and frequently arranged delightfully intimate concerts of chamber music in his house. Nevertheless he was not only asked to retire as president of the society but forbidden to come to its concerts when the racial persecution set in.

Another friend B.B. loved seeing was Baroness Marion Franchetti, the widow of the Ca' d' Oro Franchetti and owner of the Torre di Bellosguardo. Born Baroness Hornstein (sister-in-law of Lenbach), she was German in the best sense of the word, genuine, artistically gifted, particularly as a gardener, well read, comically careless about her appearance, very shrewd in her summing up of people, warmhearted and hospitable, passionately opposed to Fascism and Nazism. Very much what B.B., inspired by Goethe, called *eine Natur*. Prinz Rupprecht of Bavaria was devoted to her and more than once she brought him to I Tatti or we met him at Bellosguardo.

MANY OF OUR NEW LINKS were with Italians. Through Pellegrina Paulucci we made friends with the Triestine painter and restorer Giannino Marchig, a man of exquisite taste and sensibility. Through Morra a young Italian writer and brilliant talker, Alberto Moravia, became one of our habitués. Either Alda or Olga Loeser (of whom B.B. saw a great deal after Carlo Loeser's death) brought another Italian man of letters to I Tatti, Delfino Cinelli, the son of a straw manufacturer who had developed a delightful gift for story telling and for poetical descriptions of Tuscan country life. His American wife we had hardly any contacts with. Perhaps for political reasons, more likely because being very ambitious socially she wanted to move in more aristocratic circles.

To Placci, who was always generous in sharing his friends, we owed Marilù Stucchi Giuntini, a fine type of Tuscan woman, unrhetorical, clear-minded, and warmhearted.

Through De Marinis we met Aldo Palazzeschi, one of the finest Italian novelists and stylists. We were all great admirers of his books and considered it a privilege to have him as our guest, not because of his fame but because of his delicate wit and his gentle almost prelatic aloofness. He seemed to be an integral part of the world created in his books.

THE AUTUMN of 1932 brought us again to London, where Mary after a visit to her family was expecting us in Mrs. Hammersley's house in Tite Street. A charming house with a spacious and beautifully furnished studio-sitting room, but somehow much less attractive than Lady Horner's house because of a certain stinginess in the appointments and general habits of the servants. Two things stand out most vividly from that visit: Mary's being again miserably ill and B.B.'s heated discussions with many of his guests about the German situation and the Nazi threat. The general indifference to the problem was alarming. "Let them take over power by all means and if they are no good they will have to give it up." That was what Trevy's friend and prophet, Clifford Allen (later Lord Allen of Hurtwood), said and only too many responsible men took the same view.

WHILE HITLER and his party were becoming more powerful Mussolini ended by appearing in comparison—and even in B.B.'s eyes—a little less dangerous. Mussolini was after all—as one of our Jewish friends said—only the monkey who had opened the cage of the lion—*la scimmia che ha aperto la gabbia al leone.*

B.B. was not entirely blind to the material progress made by Italy under Fascist rule but considered it too dearly bought and the actual improvements not superior to what was being done in countries under parliamentary rule. "Autocratic regimes," he would say, "have the advantage of making decisions without having to ask anybody's consent and therefore can carry out material improvements more expeditiously."

What amused B.B. to watch in Mussolini was his having

remained first and foremost a journalist. If criticism or praise of his regime appeared in an obscure paper anywhere in the world he would immediately react and give orders for a suitable reply or perhaps even dictate one himself. B.B. compared him to the cat who asked Venus to change her into a beautiful woman. Venus granted her wish but could not rid her of her mouse-catching instinct. The moment a mouse appeared the beautiful woman had to take on the shape of a cat and rush after it.

With some of his Italian friends B.B. had to be rather circumspect in discussing current politics. Especially after the *Conciliazione* with the Vatican had been stipulated in 1929 there was a tendency to regard the Fascist regime in a more favourable light. To enjoy real mutual understanding and unhampered outbursts of indignation he had to turn to Cagnola, to Morra, to the Braccis, to Guglielmo Alberti, and other younger friends. And sometimes he could get great satisfaction from talking to peasants, workmen, or artisans whose good sense in judging the nationalistic policy of the regime and the disasters it might lead to was infallible. During one of our stays at Edith Wharton's Château Sainte-Claire I remember taking a walk with a fellow guest and how, having lost our way, I stopped to ask an old peasant working in the fields for the right direction. He turned out to be Italian and we got into talking about Mussolini's latest exploits. As we walked on he called out to us. I stopped and heard him shout: *"Chi piscia contro il vento si bagna i pantaloni"*—He who pisses against the wind wets his own trousers.

In 1933 MARY had one of her good intervals and was able to accompany us to the Exhibition of Ferrarese Painting in the Palazzo dei Diamanti and to stay with Don Guido Cagnola at the Gazzada afterwards. It was there that news reached us of Kingsley Porter having been drowned during a heavy storm off the coast of Ireland. It was regarded as a mysterious and incomprehensible accident by many people and legends about his being still alive have been circulated ever since. For us who knew Kingsley's love of dangerous climbs combined with his so easily being lost in a dream nothing seemed more likely than his absent-minded attempt to climb from one rock to the other in spite of the violent storm. Swept away by a wave his body was carried off by the strong current and never found again.

LATER THAT SAME YEAR while Mary had her daughters and grandchildren to stay with her, B.B. and I went for a few weeks to Vienna, to Moravia, and to Istria. The chief purpose was meeting Duveen and his legal adviser in the hope of settling the question of unpaid arrears once and for all.

Nicky to Mary   Hotel Bristol   Vienna   September 3rd 1933
Dearest Mary,
    B.B. is in conference with Sir Joseph and the lawyer and I hope for favourable results. I am to join them at 6 for "high tea" as we are going to the Magic Flute. We had a hectic morning first in the Czernin Collection then in the Picture Gallery with many "next next" from his lordship. B.B. did very well stopping only at the most important things so that we managed to see besides the most beautiful Italians also "sacred" pictures of other schools. At lunch the lawyer recovers from too much sight-seeing and has a lot of stories to tell. In spite of all his qualities and his superior education I prefer Duveen to him. There is something frankly oriental, of the Bazaar and of Hadji Baba about Duveen. If it suited him to be a scoundrel he would be one without any hypocrisy. I do not mean to infer that his legal adviser is a hypocrite but he is a good deal of a philistine. Poor Loewengard [Sir Joseph Duveen's nephew] plays the part of the *Mädchen für alles,* uncle and cousin order him about mercilessly, he

rushes ahead in great agitation, sends telegrams, pays cabs and gives tips. Today at the Czernin he pressed two shillings into the hand of an innocent native tourist whose only likeness with the caretaker of the place was that he wore a similar kind of frock coat.

Later. The "high tea" was announced to me by Sir Joseph's valet, a kind man with spectacles who looks like a parson. The performance at the opera was beautiful and Sir Joseph wild with enthusiasm, like a little boy. Elisabeth Schumann sang the Pamina part.

Nicky to Mary   Vienna   September 5th 1933
. . . We had a very good time yesterday evening at an operetta which is the season's greatest success here. Sir Joseph enjoyed himself uproariously more than the rest of us together. His boyish *joie de vivre* is very endearing. A strenuous time this morning first at the museum, looking at the Cellini salt-cellar, at bronzes, at the Saint Miklos gold treasure and afterwards at the *Estenische Kunstsammlung*. Then lunch at the Sacher with Sir Joseph's noble Austrian pickups. I had an old Hungarian diplomat sitting near me who spent most of the time boasting of his successes with women.

Nicky to Mary   Grusbach, Maehren   September 8th 1933
Dearest Mary,
Here we are, very pleasantly and comfortably settled in, looking out on a rose garden in its fullest second bloom and quaint dwarf-garden statuettes and two magnificent oaks and a pond and steps leading down to it. They have improved the garden since we were here eight years ago or did we come much later in the season? Weather heavenly, the real mild northern September weather. I have left B.B. and old Count Luetzow sitting in the sun and talking politics while Biba and her Russian friend, George Katkov,[1] are playing croquet and five tiny black poodles are in continual danger of being hurt by the balls. We left Vienna yesterday

[1] Now fellow of Saint Anthony's College Oxford and lecturer on Russian history and Soviet Economics.

afternoon and drove in a hired car to the frontier where the Khuen car met us. With us drove Dorothy Palffy[2] and during the drive told B.B. a long yarn about her sister's matrimonial adventures but I got absent-minded when she was half through with it and cannot tell you exactly what it was all about. At any rate Marlborough wants to marry another woman. Here we were received by Biba and her tiny poodles, and met the rest of the party consisting of the old count, the Russian, who seems to be a charming person, and a young woman belonging to the Austrian aristocracy whose name I did not catch. The old man was enchanted at the sight of our beautiful travelling companion and I gather that she has been invited in order to keep him happy and amused. At dinner a young tutor appeared who has just supplanted the little boy's beloved governess. He looked very mild and not like one of Turgenev's fierce nihilist tutors.

This morning the cook appeared in my room to ask whether the menu would suit B.B. Looking at it I realized that it is Friday and that we are in a very *bien-pensant* house but not too *bien-pensant* for having Hitlerish sympathies. Yesterday when the news came through the radio it became clear that opinions are a good deal divided. The old count, the young girl, and Katkov support Dollfuss and hope that he will hold out. Carl Khuen is for Hitler and sees great possibilities for the German race in the success of his regime. Biba is halfway between them. Dorothy does not care one way or the other. I did not find out what the tutor's opinions are.

Our last evening in Vienna was very pleasant. We dined in Sir Joseph's sitting room and he got into a vein of telling us stories, one more Hadji Baba-like than the other, and made us roar with laughter. . . .

Nicky to Mary   Grusbach Maehren   September 12th 1933
. . . Yesterday the old Count, Vika Sprinzenstein (who plays the part of Nicky here), and myself listened to Dollfuss'

---

2 Born Dorothy Deacon and sister of the duchess of Marlborough.

great oration on the *Katholikentag*. It seems that there were 60,000 people assembled from the whole of Austria, which rather contradicts the rumour that the whole rural population is on Hitler's side. The *mise en scène* was very much in the style of other great masters as an art of captivating the crowd but what he actually said was most reasonable perhaps too reasonable and quiet and dignified for our mad world. We three listeners being of the same way of thinking were well satisfied with it. Fortunately our dear *padrone di casa* behaves himself, never bursts out with his mad ideas in the presence of his father-in-law. The young Russian turns out to be a weird combination of reactionary and nihilist ideas. In his opinion lack of spiritual freedom is an excellent thing because spiritual forces thrive particularly under adverse circumstances. As an example he quotes Russian literature at its highest peak under Czarist rule. . . .

Nicky to Mary   Vienna   September 18th 1933

. . . Here we have seen Kirkpatrick and Klemperer and have heard very furious anti-Nazi talk and glowing desire for war, revenge, and destruction. Went to the last Strauss opera, the *Aegyptische Helena,* and found it delightful. We had a *Schinkenbrötchen* and a glass of port in the *entre acte* and no dinner. The only serious economy so far!

Nicky to Mary   Pirano   September 28th 1933

. . . While B.B. is having his sacred nap I am beginning this letter which should have been written yesterday from Parenzo if sleep had not overcome me. It was a long day but a delightful one and one you would have loved. Everything would have been to your taste, the landscape, the weather, the views of the sea, the sights of Pola. The last part of the road running down to Pola gives one a sort of airplane view of the port and the island of Brioni and is lovely not in the Riviera sense, more like the Puglie or like the Maremma, rather wild and solitary. We gathered from the waiter during lunch that Pola has had to pay dearly for its idealism. From being the Kiel of a great monarchy it is

Gaetano Salvemini

Benedetto Croce

B.B. with (left to right) Dario Neri, Nicky Mariano, Alda Anrep, and Luisa Vertova
1948

Hugh Evans Parry, Praia a Mare, 1955

reduced to being a poorly functioning Italian port, and there are many signs of *vergangene Pracht*. The greatest of the *vergangene Prachten* is the Roman one. The museum is full of fragments of fine sculpture. One of the triumphal arches is of exquisite quality, the temple very graceful and unspoilt, the amphitheatre less impressive than the one at El Djem because too much surrounded by houses and lacking the atmosphere of romantic solitude. About sunset time we left for Parenzo, dined out of doors and watched the population walk up and down the pier (like an opera chorus trying to behave naturally) and waiting for the steamer from Trieste. It must be their one daily sensation and amusement. The view from our windows on the small harbour with fishing boats returning into it most idyllic and peaceful, something like a southern Trosa,³ the end of the world. The mosaics in the cathedral of Parenzo are rather rough and considerably restored, but the capitals and the coloured marble ornaments most interesting and closer to Santa Sophia than B.B. remembered. Then we have come on here by a churning road and have "done" Pirano before lunch. Do you remember the old walls and the view from the terrace before the cathedral? They are really the best things here, better than the Carpaccios and they make one dream of the Veneto-Turkish charm of Mudania and Salonika and the Bosphorus. . . .

WHEN MARY REALIZED that strenuous travel was no longer possible for her she urged B.B. to carry on his programme of gathering material in Mediterranean lands for *Decline and Recovery in the Figure Arts* without her. Our first longer trip was to Tripoli and Cyrenaica, where Byba and Harry Coster joined us. Mary used B.B.'s, Harry's, and some of my letters for her *Vicarious Trip to the Barbary Coast* and got a great deal of fun out of it. She meant to do

---

³ A small sea resort to the south of Stockholm where we stopped for lunch in 1927.

the same with B.B.'s letters from Yugoslavia in 1936, from Cyprus, Rhodes, and Crete in 1937, and from Asia Minor in 1938, but did not manage to carry out these plans.

Nicky to Mary   Tripoli   April 5th 1935

. . . We have been about a hundred kilometers inland to a place high up on the *djebel*. The first part of the climb was rather like the country between Sbeitla and Tebessa, fields alternating with desert-like stretches, a few palm trees near a dried up watercourse, a solitary rider in a white *burnous* and shepherds with their flocks. Then suddenly a fortress of grim reddish mountains rises up and an excellent road leads up to a first plateau covered with huge olive trees and flowering meadows and then still higher up to a second plateau where at Kasr Garian there is a military station, a school, a market, and a charming small hotel. If one could be sure of finding anything like that in Calabria or in the Basilicata! We went on about 20 kilometres further south where Guidi wanted us to see the ruins of a Byzantine basilica. Nothing very famous as ruins but incomparable as a site and as a view towards the south. Tell Elizabeth that I took B.B.'s fur lining along in spite of his protests and how glad he was to put it on when we reached the top. She has been most thoughtful in packing and has really imagined every possible emergency. I am so grateful to her. After an excellent *casalinga* lunch we were taken to see some troglodyte habitations in the neighbourhood. Very much like what we saw at Matmata with large skylights cut out of the rock.

. . . What is really astonishing is all that has been done and is still being done in this colony, the first-rate roads, the excellent solid type of governmental buildings and all the simple white bungalows for the farmers in harmony with the landscape. One cannot help wishing them that this huge effort should some day bring its reward. What a difference with the hopeless *squallore* in so many southern Italian regions! It is of coure much easier to make a new beginning than to try to clean up mediaeval establishments. . . .

The archaeologist Giacomo Guidi mentioned in this letter became very dear to us during our days in Tripoli. From the first moment of our meeting him it was as if we had known each other for years. We were not to see him again, for he died suddenly a year later. But we inherited from him his intimate friends the Montezemolo family and kept in touch with them through the years. The eldest son—now our consul general in New York—was then a young boy and very close to Guidi, whom he used to accompany on his archaeological excursions.

AGAIN AND AGAIN we went to Rome, generally staying in a sort of penthouse on top of the Hotel de la Ville in Via Sistina with a large terrace and a view over the whole town. We could look down on our friend Steinmann taking his morning walk on the terrace of the Palazzo Zuccari and wave to him.

Nicky to Mary   Rome   April 21st 1936
Dearest Mary,
   I remember your telling me how once years ago you and Alys had an evening at your disposal and had thought of doing some very interesting things and had ended by having tea with a soft egg and a game of patience and by going to bed early. I too thought of using this evening, while B.B. is dining out on his own, for a variey of things, dining in a restaurant, going to the movies or to a theatre, and instead of that I have put on my dressing gown and my slippers and have mended my stockings and am going to have a chat with you.
   This kind of life would not do for me *à la longue* nor for B.B. either but it amuses him a lot as a change and it amuses me too but for feeling too hurried most of the time. It certainly is the most economical stay we have ever had in Rome. Except for having John Walker one night to

243

dinner and Alberti on another, and the Cecchis[4] with Clotilde and Guidotti on Saturday we have been asked out for
every meal and are already invited for the whole of next
week. My impression is that social life in Rome has been
rather monotonous lately, so many foreigners having left
and tourists being scarce. Consequently people precipitate
themselves on anything new like flies. Also there are many
who want to *sfogare* themselves with B.B., Italian friends
in one sense, English ones in another. I have never been
through such a hailstorm of invitations.

. . . We have not been bothered by fanatical outbursts
as I feared. Wherever one cannot talk openly it is very easy
to keep off the subject. B.B. will have told you about our
having been out with Eugenie Strong to see some recent
excavations. She poured out a lot of bitter things about both
her embassies and their nasty behaviour to her. Altogether
she has been as much as possible her own self, first not inviting us at all and saying we were to "drop in" which is a
difficult thing to manage in a fairly big town. Then she rang
up in a fury and said that she, Eugenie, was much more
worthwhile than all the other ladies B.B. was spending his
time with.

. . . John Walker's best girl at the moment seems to be
one of the Drummond girls.[5] I met her and liked her, in fact
I talked to her without knowing who she was, so I was quite
unprejudiced.

It must have been during one of these longer stays in
Rome that B.B. met the German ambassador, Ulrich von
Hassel, and became very fond of him and of his wife, Ilse,
born von Tirpitz. The critical attitude of both to the Hitler

[4] Emilio Cecchi, Italian writer and literary critic. His translation
of *Italian Painters of the Renaissance* (Hoepli, 1936) was considered by B.B. the best version in a foreign language ever done
of any of his books.
[5] Sir Eric Drummond, later Lord Perth, was at that time British
ambassador in Rome. His daughter Margaret was married to
John Walker in 1937.

regime was surprisingly noticeable, particularly in her. She did not hesitate to express her disapproval in alarmingly imprudent words. He was more reserved.[6] Before leaving Rome they came to see B.B. at I Tatti in 1937 and expressed their growing anxiety quite openly.

A resident of Rome whom we met frequently was Colonel Demetrio Helbig, the son of the German archaeologist and a Russian aristocrat from whom he probably inherited his powerful figure, worthy of a *bojar*. An indefatigable walker and an incomparable guide through the *campagna* and the hills all around Rome, he was an excellent storyteller as well. I vividly remember his account of how he as a young man was sent by his mother—born Countess Shachowskoi—to visit her relatives and friends in Russia and how he got to Yasnaia Poliana just at lunchtime and was very cordially received and taken up to his room. Just as he was pouring water into the washbasin, there was a knock at the door and Leo Tolstoi himself walked in. "My young friend," he said, "you mean to wash your hands and then to empty the water into this pail. Do you really want another human being to be burdened with carrying away the pail? I entreat you to empty your basin out of your window." Then he went out leaving young Helbig utterly bewildered. Another knock at the door and Countess Tolstoi burst in. "Has my husband been here?" "Yes, he has." "Has he told you to empty your basin out of your window?" "Yes, he has." "I entreat you not to do it. The soapy water is poison for the flowers. By all means use the pail which is there for that very purpose." When lunch was served at a long table under the trees, the old count was missing. Then he came carrying a wooden bowl which contained the gruel he had prepared for

---

[6] Ulrich von Hassel ended by being one of the central figures in the clandestine opposition party and was executed in 1944 after the attempt on Hitler's life had failed so miserably.

himself in the kitchen, and this he consumed while the rest of the party enjoyed a meal of several courses.

MARY'S GREAT CONSOLATION during our absences was her "live plaything," as B.B. called him, her small great-grandson Roger, Barbara Strachey's child from her first marriage with a Finlander from whom she was divorced. The little boy spent the greater part of his first years at I Tatti with the result that at the very centre of a rather well-ordered house Mary's room became a sort of gipsy camp, given up to the natural vandalism of a baby. The floor strewn with toys, pillows, broken cups and saucers from Mary's breakfast tray, pages torn out of books or magazines, half-eaten buns or biscuits and Mary on her bed watching Roger's antics with a radiant smile. All this under the protection of Elizabeth Percival, the quintessence of Irish easy-going jolliness.

OUR TRIP TO YUGOSLAVIA in the summer of 1936 had been planned for us by Prince Paul, who was then regent of Yugoslavia, and on his orders we were to be met by two men, both of them journalists, and accompanied by them on the more difficult expeditions.

Nicky to Mary   Dubrovnik   July 17th 1936
      . . . I have just been through the ordeal of unpacking all our things and of squeezing what we absolutely need for twelve days into two suitcases and filling a smaller case with provisions. . . .
      After being at first rather overwhelmed by our reception here and the idea of this officially conducted tour, we have got accustomed to our two companions who are really very kind and agreeable. One is called Mitrovich and comes from Montenegro. He is fat and jolly and cordial and terribly anxious to make B.B. comfortable and to keep him amused. He asks me in loud whispers during our sight-seeing expedi-

tions whether B.B. is interested or not in what he is looking at. The other one, Bralovich, comes from Belgrade, is more reserved, feels the heat terribly, and keeps wiping his forehead. They are both at a loss, I think, to understand what B.B. finds to look at for such an indefinite time in a capital or column or palace front. The guidance of our sight-seeing is entrusted to Mr. Strainic, the curator of monuments here, and he has done it very well, showing us little by little everything, churches, convents, very grand half-abandoned villas with loggias and capitals of exquisite workmanship; he has taken us to a most poetic place where a swift green river bubbles out of the earth. Yesterday by motorboat he took us to the island of Lokrum (Lacroma) just opposite to us, an idyll of pines and rocks and arbutus and laurel with a convent used as a summer camp for children as the only inhabited place. And he promises to take us late in the afternoon to the top of the hill above Ragusa where the view must be heavenly. We simply must come back here with you in September or October. This hotel is not ultra-modern but very clean and comfortable and with a divine view. From the balcony in B.B.'s room we look straight down into the clear green water playing around the rocks. I have managed to get some swimming too and it was lovely—just like at Sorrento. The only drawback is the excessive amount of mature human flesh one is obliged to contemplate. All these people pursue the object of getting sunburnt with such silent solemnity, grease themselves, expose themselves, grease again, expose again, that it makes me think of the midwestern innkeeper who asked some terribly exhausted and dusty trippers, "And be you travelling for pleasure?"

To go back to our new friends the most confusing thing about them is that each responds to a different foreign language. The Montenegrin understands only Italian, the one from Belgrade only English, and Strainic likes to speak German. There is still another very charming man, highly cultivated, who accompanies us, the director of the municipal museum and teacher at the gymnasium who speaks both Italian and German. His Italian is charming with a perfect

Venetian accent and his manners are delightful. He is probably a typical Dalmatian, much closer to Italian than to Slav civilization. B.B. is incapable of remembering their names, although I go on repeating them to him several times a day. . . .

Nicky to Mary   Vysoki Dechani   July 21st 1936
. . . We have been through magnificent scenery yesterday but along rather terrifying precipices and with very narrow turns. Here we are staying in a convent all surrounded by woods and murmuring streams and deliciously cool. Bodily comforts are scarce but we managed all right. Yesterday afternoon we saw the patriarchate at Peč, very close to the Kharie Djami in Constantinople. Peč is already in old Turkey and we got our fill of turbans and veiled women and minarets and swarms of flies and incredible filth and desolation and tottering wooden houses.

My letters to Mary do not contain the description of a curious scene in the church of Vysoki Dechani. As we were going around looking at the thirteenth-century frescoes, several Muslim women wearing Turkish trousers and with their faces veiled to the eyes came in and started a long discussion with one of the monks. With him they approached the tomb of one of the old Serbian kings, a large wooden chest covered with velvet on rather high carved supports. He seemed to invite them to crawl under it; then as they hesitated, he did it himself, sliding under the chest on the long side and emerging at the short end of it. Upon which the Muslim women one after the other followed his example. We tried to find out what it all meant from our guides, but they only shrugged their shoulders. B.B. felt sure that it was a health or fertility rite going back to the days before the Turkish conquest of 1350 and in which the Muslim population has gone on believing.

Novi Pazar   July 26th
    We have just been to the post office to send you a news telegram. It looked as if a telegram to England had never before been sent off from Novi Pazar and it took us a long time to find out what it would cost. They had to ring up Mitroviza, a biggish place we passed yesterday and where there are lead mines managed by English people, consequently with a little more telegraphic experience. Thanks to our official way of travelling we were invited to lunch by the Scottish head manager and after all our queer night quarters it seemed almost incredible to be in a perfectly comfortable and well-kept house surrounded by gardens and lawns. I forgot to tell you that at the convent I had an encounter with one bug and came out of it triumphantly as I managed to kill it. No others followed. The W.C.'s have been varied but not too horrible. One was built over a precipice and here it is in a garden over a rushing stream, a kind of primitive water closet and one has to ask for the key before going to it. This is still old Turkey with magnificently ragged figures grouped in the streets. There was a terrific thunderstorm yesterday and it has become much cooler. The hotel here is clean and quite *gemütlich* with lots of amusing rugs in the rooms.

Ilidje Banja   July 28th 1936
    Yesterday to Studeniza, a church of yellowish marble built by Dalmatian workmen. The site was lovely near a stream and all the slopes around wooded with northern pines like a Japanese sanctuary. It is worthwhile enduring primitive night-quarters in order to see such marvellously unspoilt country. B.B. has stood it all very well. No bugs except the one in the convent. Chicken and trout and boiled potatoes have been our fare. There are almost no fruit except watermelons and hard green pears and sometimes real melons. Coffee is being served continually just like in the East and very good it is.
    I have ventured into fields of real Serbian cooking to

249

B.B.'s horror. The stuffed green peppers are excellent and various other dishes done with pastry and cheese. All very rich but without mutton fat. The other day at Sieniza a whole roasted calf's head was offered to the table next to ours and it grinned amiably and looked very succulent.

Our two companions are very hearty feeders and their table manners leave much to be desired. They tend to make a dash for the food on the common dish with their own forks and Mitrovich occasionally wipes his forehead with the table-cloth. But we must be grateful that they know how to use knife and fork. Their fathers probably used their fingers and made agreeable noises to show that they were enjoying the food.

Ilidje Banja   July 29th 1936

We have been to Sarajevo and found the *New Statesman* but no letter from you. The Turkish quarter is absolutely charming. The modern one hideous. At the convent of Mile-ševo on our way from Novi Pazar the whole population had assembled to receive us and we were offered roast pork, cucumbers, fried fishes, cheese, black bread and jam at six o'clock in the afternoon. I ate everything except the roast pork. The head of the pork was placed in the middle of the dish and somehow put me off.

There followed brief stays in Spalato and Sebenico (Split and Sibenik). When our two journalist friends left us, we returned by boat to Spalato and spent our time looking at the palace of Diocletian and going by motorboat to Trau (Trogir). A gifted and congenial young art historian, Fiskov-ich, and also a delightful retired schoolteacher, Josip Barač, acted as guides for us. From the latter we heard a great deal about the political situation in Dalmatia before the war, when Italy had been the ideal of all young Dalmatians, whether of Italian or slave descent, who, when they went to study in Italian universities, would kiss the Italian soil after crossing the frontier. If only Italy had recognized the importance of preserving her cultural centers in Dalmatia instead of destroying them by adopting a policy of blind nationalism!

In Sebenico we were told that by looking out of the window we might catch a glimpse of Edward VIII, the new king of England. We looked but saw only a group of people walking towards the pier. Among the king's travelling companions was also Mrs. Simpson, and later the regent of Yugoslavia told us how difficult it had been to keep very indiscreet snapshots of the king and his ladylove out of the press.

At the end of our tour we stayed in Bled near the Austrian frontier and spent a day with Prince Paul and his family in their summer residence, Berdo, a château with four massive towers and a lovely park. Then went on to Salzburg, where Alda came to meet us and to enjoy some equisite performances with us. Also Addie Kahn [Mrs. Otto Kahn] was there and took us in her car to Sankt Florian and to Wilhering. Jean Rouvier, her young friend, the son of a French diplomat and a pasionate sight-seer, came with us on these expeditions and turned out to be a very congenial companion. He became one of the I Tatti habitués from then on. Then another visit to the Khuens in Moravia, a few days in Prague, and straight from there to Holland and London. I shall never forget B.B.'s despair when he realized that our train had stopped at the station of Dresden, that the town he loved so dearly was there before him without his being able to get out. When the guard who looked at our tickets greeted us with "Heil Hitler" he felt the horror of it all more keenly than ever.

WE MET MARY in Lady Horner's dear house with the Burne-Jones panels and the grand piano decorated by him and spent the whole of September there very comfortably although scared to see that most of our friends were far more interested in the doings of King Edward VIII and Mrs. Simpson than in the threatening situation in Central Europe.

It was during this stay in London—our last one—that a kind of *rapprochement* with Bertie Russell took place, engineered I believe by Trevy. He came to lunch and seemed to me utterly fascinating. B.B.—probably comparing him with former days—found him cold and contemptuous and did not expect any further developments, in which he was right. Lord Russell came repeatedly to Italy after the war but never near I Tatti.

From Paris where B.B. and I went without Mary I wrote her:

Paris   October 17th 1936
   . . . We are taking it on the whole much easier here than in London; at least I am as I have hardly any shopping to do and not anything like the number of friends I have there. Our rooms are very comfortable and certainly very quiet and the food delicious. Paris makes a very normal impression, the same crowd of cars racing each other and filling the hearts of the foot-passengers with alarm and the same light atmosphere. Not as many foreigners as usually at this season. The light and colours, the soft autumn sun, the trees in their reddish-brown dresses, the pink obelisk all too beautiful for words. Yesterday evening there was an air defence alarm practice with total darkness and sirens howling in a sinister way. We had Lionello Venturi to dinner and many of the subjects we talked about were well adapted to those gruesome noises and to the horror they symbolize. . . .

IN 1937 we again set out for a trip to the three islands—Cyprus, Rhodes, and Crete.

Nicky to Mary   Nicosia   May 3rd 1937
Dearest Mary,
   The great and important day of the mail that goes straight to Brindisi has come and I want to begin operations in good time and send you one of my post-card letters. Unfortunately these views do not give an adequate idea

either of the mosque near Larnaca placed on the banks of the salt lake with a charming atmosphere of contemplation and serenity nor of the fortifications of Famagusta and their magnificent profiles. We are having a very good and restful time here. The people we know are relatively few and except for the dinner at the governor's house we have spent our evenings reading together. Perhaps the greatest sight of all those we have seen is the palace of Vouni, one of the most beautiful Greek "holy places." Today we have been near the very heart of the island to see one of those small Byzantine cavern-churches but really to enjoy the landscape, the slopes covered with a blue-mauvish pea-blossom and with wild peonies, and the sound of the murmuring streams and the tinkling of bells from the grazing flocks of sheep and goats. The whole countryside is quite unspoilt and the villages keep a good deal of their Turkish character with wooden balconies and pergolas.

The people are not handsome at least not as a rule but the older people very picturesque. One sees a lot of the usual Eastern processions of families on donkeys with a tiny towsled donkey galloping alongside and we have also met camels carrying burdens. We are constantly reminded of one or the other Mediterranean site we love, sometimes the Roman Campagna, sometimes North Africa, the drive from Djidjelli to Philippeville for instance and most of all of Syria of which this island is in so many ways a continuation.

The boredom of the food is unbelievable. One has to concentrate on the oranges and the coffee as we did in Syria. I forgot the toast and the potatoes though which are really excellent.

Nicky to Mary   Paphos   May 14th 1937
   . . . No views to be had of the best things we have seen, Turkish villages and Byzantine convents nestling in the folds of the mountains. The view from Platres, the mountain *Sommerfrische* on top of Troodos, was superb with the clearest sunset sky and a thin elegant new moon to rejoice B.B.'s heart. . . .

Nicky to Mary   Rhodes   May 23rd 1937
         . . . One of our last impressions of Cyprus was the Neo-
phytus Convent with its stately and courteous monks. We
ended by being experts in the ceremonial required from
guests, the quiet and patient sitting on a divan in the reception room struggling through a difficult half Greek and half
English conversation until a novice appears with fresh water
and jam or a kind of preserved fruit.

         Here the poor Greeks are very much in the background
and the Turks more favoured. They are apparently pleas-
anter to deal with, more trustworthy and probably also more
stupid which is always an advantage for him who governs.
What remains of their civilization here as well as in Cyprus
is infinitely charming, marvellous trees spreading their huge
branches over quiet squares, lots of balconies and pergolas,
and small fountains, gardens full of pomegranate and hibis-
cus trees in full flower. Some of the old plane trees are supported by small columns to prevent their giving way to age.
Our Italian guide was shocked when I said that we wanted
to have tea in a Turkish café. He thought it was out of the
question because they were too dirty *e non possono servire
per i turisti.* A few steps more and we met a boy carrying
one of those charming brass trays with small glasses of tea
on it. I followed him and we found a charming café close
to the harbour with a small verandah, a lovely view, a
samovar and first-rate tea. . . .[7]

An episode for obvious reasons not mentioned in our
letters to Mary comes into my mind as I remember our
days in Rhodes. We had been given by Ojetti a note of introduction to the governor of Rhodes, De Vecchi, one of the
Quadrumviri—the first companions of Mussolini—and another one to a former naval officer who was at the head of
a tourist office. He took us personally on the tour around the

---

[7] When a year later we touched Rhodes on our way to Asia
Minor all the picturesque Turkish cafés along the harbour had
been ruthlessly destroyed on the Fascist governor's orders.

walls and as we were walking along I asked him whether the governor was in residence. He said yes, he was there. "We have sent him a note of introduction and have had no answer." "How can you expect one? Now that he represents the king and the emperor he cannot be bothered with receiving visitors to the island, be they ever so distinguished." "But we have just been to Cyprus where the governor also represents the king and the emperor and he had time to receive us most politely and asked us to tea and to dinner." Suddenly the man's defences broke down. "When Governor Lago was here he took the trouble to send down to the boats on their arrival to ask for the passenger list in case a person worthy of his special attention should be on it and now we are obliged to behave in this uncivilized way." We became very friendly after this and he told us a lot about his life and experiences in Rhodes. Hearing that he had been there for over five years B.B. asked him whether speaking Greek had become quite easy for him. "I would not dare to learn it," he said, "as it would set up a bad example to our people stationed here. As it is, regrettable things happen all the time, like members of our armed forces getting married to Greek girls." "Probably people from southern Italy?" "Why do you assume that?" "Because they are so close to the Greeks in their manners and customs if not of the same stock."

Of course not all the Italians were so indoctrinated by Fascist nationalist propaganda. For instance the head of the fine arts service for the whole Dodecanese at that time, Laurenzi, spoke Greek perfectly and both he and his wife felt at home among the Greek population.

It was a relief to touch undisputed Greek soil in Crete, free from nationalistic antagonisms and political undercurrents. On the boat that took us there from Athens B.B. created a sensation among the passengers. Everybody looked at him, pointed at him, laughed. Then a jovial man who could express himself tolerably in English came up to us, introduced himself as a former secretary of Venizelos, and explained that B.B.'s likeness to Venizelos was so striking that these compatriots of his—Venizelos was himself a Cretan —could not stop looking at him. Following this man's advice we left the boat at Cannea and drove from there to Heraklion, fulfilling B.B.'s wish to see the famous Suda bay with his own eyes. We had an excellent lunch in our new friend's home-town, Retimo, and found his company very entertaining. He was definitely what the Americans call a "colourful guy."

We stayed at Knossos in the British School and Hutchinson, then its director, devoted a great deal of his time to B.B., taking us all over the palace, to the museum of Heraklion, along the northern coast to Mallia where the French excavations were under way, and finally to the southern part of the island and the Italian house at Faistos. Professor Pernier, the head of the excavations, and his assistants received us most hospitably and one of the assistants, Luisa Banti, took us to Hagia Triada on the wild southern coast, she and I walking and B.B. riding. It was a sparkling June morning, the air intoxicating, the oleander bushes on the banks of the dried-up stream in full flower. A wonderful conclusion to our Aegean wanderings.

In Venice we met Katie Lewis and enjoyed the Tintoretto exhibition with her, that is to say, whenever her very exacting and jealous lady friends and travelling companions allowed her to do so. Morra too came to join us and left with us for Florence. There in the train looking at the morning paper we read the ghastly news of the Rosselli brothers having been assassinated in France—doubtless on Mussolini's orders.

Our last Mediterranean trip to Asia Minor was the most adventurous of all. B.B.'s old friend the British ex-diplomat Sir Robert Greg joined us and thanks to him and to the British consul general in Smyrna we got in touch with Albert Whittall, a member of one of the old English families established in Smyrna since the end of the eighteenth century. In his quiet leisurely way Whittall seemed curiously Turkified (perhaps the result of Turkish wet-nurses?), yet provided all we needed in an astonishingly short time, a car, a driver, a truck, a Greek cook, tents, field-beds, provisions, two Turkish boys for all the rough work. Only Sir Robert was not pleased, being probably used to very elaborate and carefully planned expeditions, and he found much to criticize in our leader's habit of doing everything according to mood and inspiration, in a haphazard way. What exasperated Sir Robert particularly was his suddenly stopping quite late in the afternoon in a destitute-looking village because "he had to buy something for our supper." B.B. with his nomadic instincts enjoyed none of his journeys as much as this one and adapted himself perfectly to our caravan leader's way of proceeding.

Nicky to Mary   Aydin   May 16th 1938

Dearest Mary,

I am sure B.B. has written you most poetical letters about the wind in the pine trees and shepherd boys piping and I have been longing to send you a more realistic account of our doings but as long as we were leading our "ambulant slum life" I simply could not manage it. Today we are having a restful afternoon, evening, and night with the same Scottish couple who received us so hospitably last week. It seems incredible to be in a real room again with a lot of space over one's head. My tent is so small that I have to do all my cooking sitting on the floor in Turkish fashion. As for attempts at washing myself they get more and more feeble as the days go on and I might end by adopting the standard of cleanliness of a real tramp. But apart from such small discomforts I love this life and am happy that B.B. stands it well and enjoys it thoroughly. I wish we had had the courage to take a "gamping"[8] expedition in former years,

---

[8] Our dragoman in Syria, Hayek, always spoke of "gamping."

for both you and Elizabeth would have loved it and Hayek's arrangements would have been more satisfactory than Whittall's. Everything is done in a most sketchy and haphazard way. The water is boiled in a tin can but there is nothing with which to carry it about. One precious basin must do for all of us. The sugar is kept in Quaker oats tin, the butter idem. But the important thing is to see such grand wild country in relative comfort and being sure of a clean bed and clean food. The old Greek cook is a pet, starts lighting the fire among the bushes at five in the morning and at five or at six-thirty at the latest we all begin to stir. First I go and look into B.B.'s little tent and find him generally awake with a white knitted cap on his head and ready for a cup of tea. Then we hear Greg beginning to bellow for his shaving water and generally he comes round to get some of B.B.'s tea. His intense disapproval of what he calls Whittall's *mollesse orientale* is too comical. In spite of his having lived so long in the East he has kept up an ideal of precision and efficiency which is far from being realized by Whittall and his vague charming ways. Greg would like to be sure when we will eat, what we will eat, when and where we shall camp, how many kilometres we have still got to drive and will not admit that in a country where the high-road suddenly changes from relative goodness into a narrow muddy lane kilometers mean very little. Ten kilometers may take over an hour or may take 20 minutes. Greg is altogether not the type of Englishman most attractive to me but we owe him a lot because it is thanks to him and to his pull in Smyrna that this arrangement could be made and he does procure a lot of amusement for us. You should see him when we reach our destination and the bus is beginning to be unloaded stalking about with a very important manner "because Whittall needs my moral support." This moral support consists in his seeing to it that his tent and his bed are put up first of all. I suppose most men remain like little boys only some show it in a more naif way. What exasperates him are the often quite incomprehensibly long stops when we reach a larger village or small town. Whittall and the cook start buying provisions in a very leisurely way, the chauffeur who does not know how to shave himself disappears into a barbershop, the bus driver and his help, two very capable boys, light a cigarette and order a coffee. Everybody seems happy and not in the least pressed for time, except Greg who was I think at first rather disgusted with B.B.'s and my placid acceptance of these unavoidable delays and with our settling down in a café under a tree or a pergola and having tea out of small glasses. Now he has learnt to adapt himself, orders tea or has his boots cleaned to pass the time. He is keen about the sights and does a lot of reading about them which I am grateful for as I have too much housework to do and am too sleepy in the evening to do it myself.

Now I shall have a real hot bath and use a real lavatory again. On the whole we have been lucky on that score, all our camping places having been surrounded by convenient bushes or rocks or ditches which made the necessary retirements quite easy. I wish you could have seen B.B. disappearing for a similar purpose among the pine trees in his white fur lining and his pointed night cap looking like one of the King Magi in an early relief or mosaic where they wear the Phrygian costume. We have seen enchanting wild flowers, masses of iris japonica in the marshy regions and lavender on the mountains and many others. The birds are fascinating too; turquoise-blue turtle doves, nightingales and those same many-coloured birds that we saw near Aleppo and storks everywhere rattling along with their long red beaks. Very often they build their nests on the classical ruins. . . .

One of B.B.'s most alarming outbursts took place at the beginning of our Asia Minor trip. On its way to Smyrna the Lloyd Triestino boat stopped at Rhodes and gave us the chance to revisit the museum and some of the palaces. On walking down towards the harbour in the late afternoon I noticed that shops were being closed and flags hung out and wondered what sort of a holiday it might be. As dessert for dinner the waiter presented us with a huge chocolate cake decorated with a swastika in spun sugar. Taken aback by this sight I unfortunately asked the waiter what its meaning was and he answered rather pompously, *"Perchè oggi il Fuehrer arriva in Italia"*—Because to-day the Fuehrer arrives in Italy. B.B. whose voice was generally low and soft answered in a shrill penetrating tone: *"Il giorno della vergogna"*—the day of shame. The table close to ours was occupied by the *commissario* (corresponding I suppose to the purser on an English boat) and I saw him blush crimson and put up both his hands to his ears as if to shut out what he had just heard, then jump up and leave the table obviously in a rage. Thoroughly alarmed I decided to speak to him at once. When I found him pacing up and down on one of the decks he would not listen to me at first and told me that he had the duty to denounce both B.B. and me at the *sede del Fascio* in Smyrna next morning. "Please let me ask you only one question," I said. "Is your father still alive?" "Yes, he is alive," he said. "But what has that to do with it?" "I would like to know whether your father is happy over what is going on in Italy?" His face fell. "As a matter of fact he hates it all." "You see," I said, "there it is. You cannot expect these older men grown up in a liberal tradition to approve of the Fascist regime. Only young people can be carried away by the force and the dynamics of the movement." Then I told him about B.B. and his having lived most of his life in Italy and what his contribution to Italian culture had been. It ended with B.B. and the *commissario* having a very friendly talk and later on we sent the *Italian Painters of the Renaissance* in Cecchi's translation to his address in Bari. What would have happened if his father had *not* been alive or had been a roaring Fascist I do not know but I know that several protecting saints must have been on my side on that occasion.

CHAPTER XIX

Pre-war Anxieties and the War Years [1935–45]

ALTHOUGH THE PRECEDING YEARS had been full of alarming political symptoms it was with 1935 that the real war scare began. When B.B. and I left early in January for Hyères we found ourselves stuck for over an hour at the station of Pisa and our questions as to the reason for this unusual delay were answered evasively. As the train at last moved out of Pisa we noticed that all along the line soldiers were posted at regular intervals. Obviously somebody very important was on the train. Finally we found out that it was Laval returning from a conference in Rome. "What has he been up to?" said B.B. "It is very ominous that he should have gone there at all." In Genoa I wanted to get out and have a look at Laval but B.B. would not allow it. "Why should you want to look at such a monster?"

Early in October that same year I see ourselves in Venice on a *vaporetto* going to the Titian exhibition at Palazzo Pesaro when suddenly all the bells of Venice began to peal, passengers left the boat precipitously at the next stop, people were seen running up and down the bridges and along the narrow *calli*. Everybody hurried to the *piazza* where during a melodramatically staged Fascist *adunata* (rally) the first hostilities on the Abyssinian frontier were announced. The next day we got a telegram from Mary, who was trying out a new treatment in a Viennese sanatorium, asking for help and advice. "What does it mean?" said B.B. "I can understand her worrying about her children in case war breaks out but why should she herself be alarmed?" The same evening I was able to ring up Elizabeth at the sanatorium and begged her to remind Mary that her passport was American and not British. "That's true, Miss. We did forget. Madame kept thinking of herself as still British and was afraid she might not be able to return to Italy."

Nicky to Mary   Venice   October 19th 1935
    . . . We are indeed behaving like the man in the Eastern tale who gave himself up to the enjoyment of the sweet berries on the bush he was hanging from while below a roaring dragon and above his enraged camel were threatening him. I daresay Roger takes the place of the berries for you. . . .

Nicky to Mary   October 20th 1935
    . . . to all outward appearances nothing is changed here. People sit in the cafés and walk in the *piazza*, the bands play, foreigners arrive and leave, gondoliers quarrel. The only noticeable difference is that a frantic reading of papers, local and foreign, goes on everywhere. Poor Morra is deeply sad, quite ill morally, I think, over what is going on. Johnny is taken up most of the time with leading his fellows about. He says that it is very difficult to make them see and enjoy anything. The painters are a little more responsive but the architects are hopeless, full of criticism and incapable of conceiving architecture that is not technically perfect and useful. . . .

In 1936 during one of our quiet after-dinner gatherings at Sainte-Claire the butler burst in to inform us that the occupation of the Saarland by the Nazis had just been announced over the wireless.

In May 1936 we were in Rome when the spectacular proclamation of the new Italo-Abyssinian empire took place. Only people with very firm convictions were able to withstand the appeal of such an undeniable success.

In July 1936 we got the first news of the Spanish conflict in Zara as we landed to start on our Yugoslav tour.

In the autumn of 1937 our stay in Vienna at the Neue Bristol became much longer than we had calculated and brought us very close to the feverish condition of Austria during its last months of relative freedom. Close to our hotel on the Kärntnerstrasse a German travel agency had been turned into a shrine of Nazidom, with huge photographs of Hitler, flags and proclamations in both windows, and invariably a crowd of adorers assembled before them. We saw Jewish friends like Franz Werfel and Bruno Walter in the deepest gloom and without the slightest illusion about the future. We saw Austrian friends filled on the contrary with the most naïve illusions, talking of Austria's deep-rooted civilization, of the lasting effect it would have on Nazism to the point of perhaps changing its fundamental character. We saw others, like for instance the philosopher Rudolf Kassner, who felt that the *Anschluss* would be prevented by Mussolini. Kassner got very angry when B.B. told him that Italy had exhausted her military resources in Abyssinia and in Spain. "Who gives him the right to express such opinions?" he asked me. "Simply his being well informed on the Italian situation."

Nicky to Mary   Vienna   November 12th 1937
    . . . We had the Werfels yesterday evening and they will probably come again with Bruno Walter if it is true that Bruno Walter's wife has left Vienna. When I told Werfel that she looked like a *böse Sieben*[1] he said, "*Sieben ist zu*

---

[1] A nasty seven—an idiomatic expression for an ill-tempered person. Werfel said that seven was not enough in this case and that it should be nine.

wenig; man muss schon neun sagen." If she is still on the map the Werfels prefer to come another night.

. . . It is astonishing how B.B. stands all the medical treatments. Of course he gets tired but he is not a bit nervous in fact seems to have thrown off all his desperate nervousness of the past summer. Partly because the Consuma air has a better effect on him afterwards than while he is there, partly because political worries weigh on him more heavily when inside than when outside my beloved country and perhaps chiefly because his whole connection with the Duveens is definitely coming to an end on January first. It will mean a considerable difference in income, I know, and yet I think it is a blessing, for he was using himself up over it and it had become a real complex. . . .

One of our last evenings in Vienna we spent in the house of Count Coudenhove Kalergi, the head of the pan-Europa movement. His wife was a famous actress of Jewish descent, a brilliantly eloquent and vital woman. She was that evening in a state of frenzy against the Nazis and kept denouncing Hitler as being a Jew himself. Her information on this point was based on rather unconvincing evidence. Finally her husband said very gently, "Do you really think, my love, that you do the Jewish cause a very great service by believing and propagating this legend?"

It was in 1938 during our first summer at Casa al Dono that the fruits of Mussolini's and Hitler's encounter began to ripen. Doro and Anna Levi were staying with us and on returning from a walk-drive we told Parry to stop at the post office and ask for our mail. A telegram for Doro was handed in. I saw him open it and change colour. It told him that he was no longer expected to take part in an archaeological expedition to Greece. The dismissal from his chair at the University of Cagliari followed a few days later. In shameful subservience Italy had adopted the racial laws.

Then warnings from friends began to reach B.B. himself. Had he not better leave Italy before it was too late? One of B.B.'s younger friends from New York, Alfred Frankfurter, the creator and editor of *Art News,* drove up from Florence to represent the seriousness of the situation to him. It was touching to see this generally gay and very entertaining young man so desperately in earnest and anxious about B.B.'s welfare.

On our return to I Tatti a wealthy Italian Jew whom we both knew only slightly announced himself. B.B. took him for a walk in the garden and told me later that according to this man he was no longer safe even in his own house and that any day regular pogroms could be expected. On the following day B.B. thought of asking the advice of his doctor, who assured him that this was a ridiculous invention but being a chatterbox of the first order spread the story all over the town. That same afternoon I was summoned to the *questura* and interrogated as to what had been said by our guest. I tried to save him by declaring a falsehood, namely, that I had heard every word of the conversation between him and B.B. and that although both were much concerned with the Jewish question neither of them had said a word against Mussolini. Nevertheless the man was arrested and later deported to the Tremiti Islands.

In September 1938 there was breathless anxiety over the Munich crisis and only momentary relief through its unsatisfactory solution.

In the spring of 1939 we happened to be in Rome when on Good Friday the Italian occupation of Albania was suddenly announced. I do not remember any genuine enthusiasm. Perhaps something sinister about the whole business was felt also by upholders of the regime.

Early in the summer of 1939 B.B. and I went to see the Prado exhibition in Geneva.

Nick to Mary Geneva August 1st 1939

Dearest Mary,

. . . Before leaving this dear and restful country I want to send you a line. I am thankful for any excuse that makes us stay on here for it has done us both no end of good to be in this atmosphere. It is like a cure.

The first days I thought that it would be impossible to get any enjoyment out of the exhibition with such crowds of people pushing each other about and standing in each other's way. As time goes on a sort of personal relation forms itself between the pictures one loves best and oneself, and one manages to look at them without minding the people all around. It is an interesting crowd, not at all *chic* and very *andächtig*, mostly Swiss and French. . . .

In Geneva I had the joy of meeting my friend since childhood who had taken such an active part in my vicissitudes, Byba Giuliani Coster, just before her departure for the United States, where Harry Coster, her husband, already awaited her. They generally spent half the year in the old house at the Costa Scarpuccia that Byba had inherited after her mother's death. Thus we had kept up the habit of seeing each other regularly. For the second time in our lives a world war was to separate us for a number of years.

We met Prince Paul at the exhibition and he urged B.B. not to return to Italy as a general conflict was in his opinion no longer avoidable. Nevertheless we returned to Vallombrosa and barely two weeks later the Hitler-Stalin pact was announced. Optimistic friends went on writing to B.B. that important negotiations were giving good results and that real war would not be declared. On September 3rd we had to leave Casa al Dono as the circulation of cars had been forbidden, and we went straight to Borgo San Jacopo. Alda opened the door and told us that war had been declared. Now came the burning question: what was Italy going to decide? The Duce happened to be on a round of visits to

North Italian towns and every few hours another threatening speech of his was transmitted by the wireless. Then, probably following superior orders, he calmed down and but for various restrictions life went on in a fairly normal way.

When in October Addie Kahn left for Egypt, where her son-in-law, General Marriott, was stationed, we went to Venice to see her off. Never have I seen Venice more enchanting in glorious autumn light and utterly free from tourists. It was on that occasion that we met Santayana at the Hotel Danieli, an encounter which both he and B.B. have described, each from his own point of view.[2]

From Venice we took an excursion to Prince Paul's castle in Slovenia. At first I was refused a visa to Yugoslavia. Then the police agreed to telephone to the frontier station giving orders to let me go out. At Berdo we found a warm welcome, delightful rooms, and delicious food but a depressing atmosphere. The official reports our host kept receiving all day long about Germany's military efficiency were frightening and while outside the park was hidden in mist and rain the general outlook seemed to be getting gloomier and gloomier.

On our return to Venice Guglielmo Alberti arranged our first visit to Marina Volpi[3] in her Palladian villa at Maser, near Treviso. We found her very congenial and sharing our fears and hopes wholeheartedly.

Late in the autumn of 1939, while we were again in Rome, Ambassador William Phillips gave B.B. an account of his expedition to King Victor Emmanuel's hunting lodge, Sant' Anna di Valdieri, in the Piedmontese Alps. He was to hand a letter from President Roosevelt personally to the

---

[2] See B.B.'s *Selected Letters*, ed. Arthur McComb (Boston: Houghton Mifflin; 1964).

[3] Countess Marina Volpi, daughter of the Italian financier Count Giuseppe Volpi; since 1945 married to Count Enrico Luling.

king. It contained an urgent appeal not to allow Mussolini to drag Italy into the war. It was a wet chilly day and Phillips, looked forward to some warmth and refreshment after his long motor drive. The king received him under an open porch, read the letter, said he would transmit it to his prime minister, and dismissed him then and there.

THE WINTER of 1939–40 brought plenty of rumours but very little positive news. B.B. was one of the few to keep up a firm belief that Mussolini could not be such a fool as to join the fray and run the risk of losing the advantages already won. At first events seemed to confirm this thesis but during the spring the climate changed, demonstrations against France and England were being staged, even the funeral of England, the hearse followed by screaming and jeering students and schoolboys. Harold Acton came back from China at that time and was supposed to give lectures in support of the Allied cause at the British Institute. Keenly aware of the hopeless belatedness of such enterprises he came to pour out his heart at I Tatti again and again and B.B.'s warm affection for him dates from that moment.

The famous American journalist Dorothy Thompson came to see B.B. straight from Germany and her information about the attacks on Norway and Holland turned out a little later to have been amazingly exact. Walter Lippmann, who also came to see B.B., was still a firm believer in the solidity of the Maginot Line.

About the middle of May B.B. and I left for Rome and were plunged at once into an atmosphere of tense anxiety over the invasion of Holland and France. From the Hotel de la Ville we used to walk across to the Kinkaids[4] and collect the latest news from them.

---

[4] Captain Kinkaid, later Admiral Kinkaid, was then naval attaché at the American embassy.

It was in those same days that the dramatic "Acta Diurna" crisis occurred, "Acta Diurna" being the name of a political rubric in the Vatican paper *L'Osservatore Romano* which had gone on giving Italian readers an objective account of the general situation. For thousands, probably millions of Italians it represented the only open window on the world outside Italy. Suddenly it was brought to an end not by sequestering the paper but by posting Fascist militiamen near the newspaper stalls to keep watch over the buyers of papers. Whoever asked for *L'Osservatore* was arrested and even beaten up. We went several times to get the paper at its source of production inside the Vatican.

Asked to lunch by the Volpis B.B. met Balbo there and heard him speak of his firm opposition to the war policy without the slightest reticence, also of his despair over the consequences of such folly in the North African colonies, of which he was then still the governor. He regarded them as already lost and said he had told Mussolini that his only duty would be to evacuate women and children as quickly as possible. Knowing this we were not surprised to hear that when Balbo's airplane was shot down a few weeks later his death was regarded by many not as an accident but as a well-calculated act of punishment.

Around the first of June we left for Naples with Olga Loeser and the archaeologist Bianchi Biandinelli and tried to drown our preoccupations in the study and enjoyment of classical remains. Croce was absent but returned in time to see us off at the station in a state of passionate grief. B.B.'s forlorn hope that Mussolini's folly could not go as far as declaring war did not convince him.

Back in Rome on June 10th, as we were ushered into the salon of the Iberts[5] at Villa Medici, we heard Mussolini's

[5] The French composer Jacques Ibert was for several years before and again after the war director of the French Academy at Villa Medici.

bellowing voice in double force from the wireless set of the Iberts and from a loudspeaker in the street declare war on France and England. A sadder, emptier, more subdued town than Rome was on that evening would be difficult to imagine. Noisy demonstrations had been expected and troops were massed up in expectation of them near the French and English embassies but nothing happened. In the night French airplanes threw down leaflets over the city and the noise of the Italian air defence was deafening. The people we met next morning looked green and haggard and seemed petrified with fear.

Nicky to Mary   Rome   June 12th 1940
> . . . We had an air alarm last night and I went out on my terrace and listened to the sinister howls of the sirens raging over the completely dark city. I thought it was an experiment or exercise but apparently it was a real alarm and French airplanes are supposed to have been chased back from Gaeta. I am told that one of the Roman ladies who is French by birth manages to get over her despair by knitting and am telling B.B. that his type of knitting is called sightseeing. So we spent the morning in the quiet and almost empty Sistine Chapel and wandered on to the *Stanze* of Raphael and there were at the utmost ten other visitors in all the Vatican galleries. . . .

We stayed on in Rome, as B.B.'s plan to return at once to I Tatti could not be carried out. A messenger sent by Countess Serristori came to warn us that nasty rumours were being circulated in Florence about B.B. He was represented as a dangerous foreign agent who kept receiving guests from abroad and carrying the information gathered from them to his embassy in Rome. The messenger also reported that these rumours were kept alive by Mary (without her being aware of it, of course), who wishing to forget her despair over being suddenly cut off from her nearest and dearest had filled the house with her new pets, Igor and Kyra Markevitch, their little boy, the Russian pianist Nikita Magaloff and his wife, and other guests. We heard that she was giving parties that lasted late into the night and that the police had been making enquiries about these festivities. We both wrote to her entreating her to be more careful and to remember how easy it was for foreigners to create suspicion once the war psychosis had got hold of a nation. While waiting to hear that I Tatti had been emptied of all foreign visitors I took steps to get a visa at least for Switzerland. One of B.B.'s friends, the famous surgeon Raffaele Bastianelli, provided me with an official declaration as to my being indispensable to Mary and B.B. in looking after their health. Armed with it I went to the home office and was received by an official to whom I had been recommended. He shook his head sadly. "No effort of yours will ever get you a visa," he said. "Put it out of your head." We returned to I Tatti and found it not only emptied of its visitors but deprived of its two English servants. Parry and Elizabeth had left on the evening of June 10th, on the last train guaranteed by the Swiss consulate. Later we heard that caught in the pandemonium of France they never reached England and were both arrested by the Germans.

The general atmosphere in Florence was very ominous and full of unpleasant reports. Most English people had left in time. Those who had not were arrested and then sent to live in small Italian towns, and only in exceptional cases— like the parents of Harold Acton—were they allowed to leave for Switzerland. Our watchdog, Naima Löfroth, having got into an argument with a militiaman, was also arrested and later expelled from Italy. Life at I Tatti went on very quietly. Although the United States was not yet at war, many Italians —and among them even friends like Carlo Placci and Ugo Ojetti—considered it more prudent not to frequent B.B.'s house any longer. The wireless set had been transported to what was called "Alda's library," where nobody could hear it from outside and where my sister regularly got news items from London and wrote them down for B.B. We all felt terribly sorry for Mary, completely cut off as she was from all her dear ones in England. To cheer her up B.B. persuaded her to go to the Tyrrhenian coast close to where her pets, Kyra Markevitch and her little boy, were spending the summer. Parry's wife—who had taken Elizabeth's place—and I accompanied her there. On my return B.B. met me with the news of Ray Strachey's death. The American consul had received a wire saying that she had died under an operation. I had to return to the seaside and break the news to Mary. Her fortitude in meeting the worst blow that could hit her was staggering, for nobody was closer and more precious to her than Ray. "I have had the most perfect daughter for fifty-two years and I must be grateful for it."

Then she joined us at Casa al Dono for the first time and we spent a quiet and uneventful summer there. News of events beyond the Italian frontier, in particular of the blitz over London, reached us through the wireless. Only one Fascist devilry happened in our nearest neighbourhood. Prince Filippo Doria, the only member of the Roman aristocracy, I believe, who dared to express his horror of the war very openly, was spending a few weeks in one of the Vallombrosa hotels and came to see us with his wife and daughter. A few days later he was arrested by Fascist militiamen in the church of the Abbey while he was following the mass, carried off to Rome, and later exiled to southern Italy.

From our two English servants we heard first through the Red Cross and then directly. Elizabeth Percival managed to escape from a camp near the Swiss frontier with two other women and after spending some time in a hostel in Neuchatel was able to return to England. Parry had no such luck, having been interned in the *Grande Caserne* at Saint Denis. When he returned to us six years later I asked him

*B.B., Nicky Mariano, and Count Vittorio Cini
leaving the Lotto Exhibition, Venice, 1953*

B.B. writing in bed

whether he ever got news of world events. "Oh yes," he said, "regularly." "But how?" "A woman in a house right opposite to the *Grande Caserne* had put up a blackboard on the wall facing the window and every day chalked down the most important news in large block letters. Sharpsighted persons could read them clearly and then the news went round the whole huge prison. Only the German guards never noticed anything."

IN A WORLD becoming ever gloomier new friends served as a consolation. The painter Giovanni Colacicchi and his friend—and later on his wife—Flavia Arlotta were brought up by Kyra Nijinsky and almost from the first moment became what B.B. called *unsereiner*—one of us. Giovanni had like Morra a special gift for drawing B.B. out and making him discuss artistic and aesthetic problems with him. His manner with B.B. was charmingly filial and respectful yet firm and straightforward in the defence of his own point of view. And that was just what B.B. wanted. Then there was the archaeologist Ranuccio Bianchi Biandinelli, with whom B.B. was continually in touch from 1939 and until B.B.'s exile separated them. After the war divergences in political opinon and subsequently Ranuccio's transfer to the University of Rome drew them away from each other.

It must have been in one of these last pre-war years that through Harry and Byba Coster we met Alice Dick-Lauder, the widow of Sir George Dick-Lauder and owner of a villa on the Via San Leonardo. Her gay playful temperament and her love of nature suited B.B. perfectly. Before as well as after the war she was a welcome guest at I Tatti and at Casa al Dono.

Luisina Milani and her attractive youngsters were brought up by Alda and B.B. enjoyed them all, but particularly *la zingaraccia*—as he used to call Luisina—because of her independent spirit and complete detachment from any social conventions.

For Mary there was her new doctor, Vittorio De Bosis.[6] He had taken the place of Giglioli, the family physician of many years who had suddenly died in 1939. De Bosis was not only very good-looking and full of charm but excellent and imaginative as a doctor. He took good care of Mary and she adored him and allowed him to exert more authority over her than Giglioli or any other doctor ever had. Unfortunately Mary's love for him was not only extended to his very dear American mother but to a South-American "vamp" he was in love with. When Mary invited this young woman for the first time both B.B. and I had a bad impression of her—and B.B. in spite of her really glamorous physique!—and begged Mary to keep her at a certain distance. She would not listen to us and without warning us gave her permission to work in the library. To my amazement and disgust I found this "painted crocodile" (Logan's name for "vamps") prowling about in the library in the late afternoon when my sister and her assistants had already left it. A few days later two *questurini* (plainclothes men) appeared and asked to be shown the library. I took them up and showed them where the catalogue was. They started fumbling about in it as if not quite knowing what to look for. "What is it you want?" "A book written by Bosis." "There is no such name. You must look under De Bosis." Of course it was Lauro De Bosis' poems they were after. "Has this been given to you by his brother the doctor?" "No, it was sent to us several years ago by Miss Ruth Draper." Fortunately her letter accompanying the book was still in it. My declaration was written down and they disappeared with the book. In the evening Vittorio De Bosis

---

6 Brother of the poet Lauro De Bosis, who had been killed in 1931 during his foolhardy attempt to scatter anti-Fascist leaflets over Rome from a private plane.

came in and entreated Mary never to receive that young woman again. Having quarrelled with him she had taken her revenge in that way and both he and his mother had suffered a police raid that same afternoon. All this was as usual the result of Mary's incapacity to admit any danger, any necessity to be cautious, any reason for not giving way to a momentary caprice. B.B. used to quote from, I believe, Custine's book on Russia: *"un désir russe peut détruire une ville"* as very appropriate for describing Mary's irrespressible wilfulness.

DURING THE WINTER of 1940 to 1941 my chief preoccupation was what to decide about B.B.'s and Mary's leaving or not leaving Italy. How was Mary to be moved without getting a visa for at least one of her nurses? How was B.B. to be moved without moving Mary? The Swiss consul, Carlo Steinhauslin, who became our friend and constant adviser in those days, managed to renew B.B.'s and Mary's visas for Switzerland every two or three months against all established rules. B.B. was of no help to me. His firm belief in Allied supremacy and in the ultimate outcome of the war seemed to make him indifferent to all minor questions. Behind his passive and uncooperative attitude was hidden the wish not to leave Italy and the curiosity to see how the Italians would behave to him if war with the United States became inevitable. No doubt the fact that I had no hope of getting a visa played its part in his reluctance to make any decision.

An unexpected encouragement to B.B.'s passive resistance came from two young friends, the architect and painter Gordon Morrill and his wife Elizabeth. After spending several years in Florence they had to go back to the United States in 1941 and sent a cable to B.B. containing only two words: STAY PUT. Nothing could have been more welcome to him.

275

In January 1941 William Phillips returned for the last time to Rome, travelling by car from Spain and stopping over at I Tatti for one night. I hoped that B.B. would discuss his plans with him but he avoided it carefully. As the ambassador had announced himself by telephone from Genoa the fact of his having paid a visit to I Tatti soon became public property and started up a campaign of calumnies against B.B., engineered of course by his local enemies. It was clear, they proclaimed, that B.B. was a dangerous political agent, if the American ambassador could not return to Rome without first getting his instructions from him! All very comical but at the same time alarming in view of possible future developments.

In May 1941 I went for a few days to Rome partly to say good-bye to Amey Aldrich (whose brother Chester had died in Rome in December 1940) and to Caroline Phillips as they were both leaving for the States, partly in the hope of having a private talk with the ambassador. He received me one morning in the garden of Villa Taverna and listened patiently to my appeal. Then he said: "My advice would be for B.B. to stay on in Florence and not to try to go away. His property is very valuable and his personal presence would be the best protection for it." Much relieved I went back to Florence and stopped altogether worrying about visas.

UNTIL THE DAY of Pearl Harbor and the Italian declaration of war against the U.S.A. we went on living quietly and fairly normally. Only once in the early summer of 1941 was there a threat for B.B. The rumour of Vincigliata—the pseudo-mediaeval castle above us belonging to a French woman and consequently under Italian sequestration—having been chosen as residence for English war prisoners had only just reached us when I was rung up by the *vice questore*

—the assistant chief of police—because of an urgent communication he had to make to me. I went down and was told that the order for B.B.'s expulsion from I Tatti had arrived from Rome. It was the result of the constant agitation kept up by B.B.'s local enemies, who had probably convinced some of the men in power that it was dangerous to let B.B. go on living so close to Vincigliata. Through the American vice-consul, Mr. Washburn, who was leaving by car for Rome, I was able to send an S.O.S. to the ambassador, still in residence at that time. His protests at the Foreign Office had the desired effect: the order of expulsion was cancelled while we were up at Casa al Dono and before B.B. had heard anything about it.

When Mary was told about the British officers being expected at Vincigliata her reaction was typical of her. "What fun it will be," she said, "to have them drop in to tea."

IT MAY HAVE BEEN as a consequence of the steps taken by William Phillips on that occasion that on December 10th the *questore* of Florence got a telegram signed Ciano giving orders to leave the Berenson couple unmolested and free to live their normal life. A few hours later—Mussolini's declaration of war having meanwhile been proclaimed—a group of fanatical Fascists burst into the *questore's* office and accused him of not having yet put an outspoken enemy of Italy like Bernard Berenson into custody. They were furious at the sight of Ciano's telegram. This scene was described to me by my friend the *vice questore,* who happened to represent his chief on that day.

The "normal life" as recommended by Ciano was of course not to be thought of. B.B.'s political enemies were too busy intriguing against him and we were advised by friends in Rome to live as quietly as possible. The library went on being frequented by scholar friends and one or

the other of them would occasionally sneak into the sitting-
room at tea-time to have a chat with B.B. For walks we had
the garden and the closed-in *Laghetto* wood for which our
neighbours at Maiano had given us the key. The small
Markevitch boy, the son of Igor Markevitch and of Kyra
Nijinsky, brought life and cheerfulness into the house. His
nickname was Funtyki, which in Russian means "a small
pound." Both his parents had been too busy struggling with
financial difficulties and marital complications to bother
much about him and therefore Mary offered to take him
and provide a nurse for him. He became deeply attached to
I Tatti and to all its inhabitants but chiefly to me. When
later on his father—after his separation from Kyra—settled
down at the Villino and began to take an interest in the
boy he must have felt jealous of his clinging to me. I daresay
I had grown into the habit of deciding things without asking
anybody's permission. In any case it became a rather exasper-
ating situation and only B.B.'s wisdom kept me from having
a real row with Igor. I had prepared an infuriated letter
and read it to B.B. before sending it to the Villino. He said,
"Now that you have had the satisfaction of writing it, put
it away and do not send it. The boy is enchanting and we
all love him, and Igor is a delightful neighbour and companion." This was perfectly true. As he lived on the same
estate, nobody objected to his coming and going, and many
were the evenings we spent together, enjoying Igor's stimulating conversation or listening to his reading aloud to us.
In 1943 the little boy went to live at the Villino, but remained very close to us. There were no further occasions for
clashes between his father and me.

Meanwhile the local Fascist campaign against B.B. never
let up but by good luck the police, the *carabinieri*, the prefec-
ture, all based on pre-Fascist traditions did not take it too seriously. In 1942 when some of the British officers managed to
escape from Vincigliata B.B. was believed to have helped

them. The police made a perfunctory perquisition in the house and our telephone was cut off. At the protests of our sequestrator its reinstallation was allowed although not in the villa but in Gioffredi's, our agent's house. I was advised to thank the prefect personally for this concession and was told that I would meet a charming and politically very open-minded man. Introduced into his sumptuous salon at the Palazzo Riccardi I found his reception anything but encouraging. Very loudly and officially he reminded me that under the circumstances Mr. Berenson could only be regarded as an enemy of Italy. But when I had expressed my thanks and got up to go he got up too, accompanied me to the door, and in a soft whisper assured me that he would do whatever was in his power to protect I Tatti. Of course I understood that he was afraid of a microphone near his table.

B.B. remained perfectly indifferent to such pinpricks. Nothing semed to upset or to depress him, neither the sequestration of his property nor his restricted walks nor the isolated life we had to lead. He never wavered in his firm belief that the Allies would end by winning the war, nor did my sister, who provided him with daily bulletins of Radio London news and together they interpreted all unfavourable and even catastrophic reports in an optimistic way. He read enormously or listened to Mary or me reading aloud. When his beloved *Züricher Zeitung* suddenly stopped coming (probably because of the detailed descriptions it had brought of Italian bombardments of Corfù, which no Italian paper had ever mentioned) he began reading the *Deutsche Allgemeine* and managed to get a lot of interesting information—chiefly between the lines—out of it.

In 1942 B.B. did get official permission to spend the summer in Vallombrosa but I was strongly advised not to make any use of it. Having been once expelled from I Tatti the danger of his not being allowed to return to it was too great.

As if it had happened yesterday I remember the Sunday morning in November 1942 when, happening to go through the library, I switched on the wireless and caught the description of the Allied landing in Algiers. From then on there was a change in temperature all over Italy, discipline seemed relaxed, pessimism and criticism began to be openly expressed, Italian friends who had kept carefully away reappeared and spoke freely about the possibility of the regime coming suddenly to an end. Rumours travelled with astonishing swiftness. The Allied landing in Sicily at dawn on July 10th was announced to my sister's housemaid by the milk boy on that same morning. And yet when Mussolini fell it came as a staggering surprise. Joy was great all over Italy but immediately damped by the disappointment over what followed, the ambiguous attitude of the Badoglio government and the steady increase of German troops on Italian soil.

Carlotta Orlando came down on foot from Campiglioni (about twenty-five kilometres) to find out how we were and to talk things over. She then began to warn me and went on doing so all summer long (and so did several others among our Italian guardian angels) that I should be ready to get B.B. out of I Tatti at any moment. "If the Germans should be in full control of Italy and this time not as allies but as enemies he cannot go on staying at I Tatti. As an American, as a well-known anti-Fascist, as a Jew he is in immediate danger of arrest." Two hours after the armistice had been announced over the wireless on September 8th a car was at our door, sent by Carlotta, with an urgent invitation to come up to Campiglioni at once. Unable to make up my mind so quickly I had to send it back empty. Orlando was too well known himself as an enemy of the regime to make his house a safe shelter.[7] Besides, my sister and brother-in-law

---

[7] Orlando ended by seeking refuge in the Vatican.

happened to be taking the cure in Montecatini and we could not have left Mary alone with the servants. Next morning I decided to ask for the advice of Marchese Filippo Serlupi, who was acting as our sequestrator. When I got out of the bus in Piazzo San Marco my heart sank, for there before the Italian military headquarters were several cars filled with German officers and it was clear from their gestures and from the scared faces of the Italian sentinels that they had come to take possession of the building. Marchese Serlupi agreed with me as to the doubtful safety of Campiglioni and urged me to take B.B. to his villa above Careggi. "My diplomatic rights as ambassador of San Marino to the Holy See seem very unimportant yet I expect them to be scrupulously respected. I know that the German army command is not partial to entanglements with the diplomatic service. We have plenty of room for you both and you had better make the change as quickly as possible."

That same afternoon I sent a car to fetch my people in Montecatini and begged them to transfer themselves to I Tatti. We left without telling Mary where we were going. Her natural optimism and her contempt for any kind of prudence or secrecy made her incapable of even imagining any real danger. In her eyes it was all nonsense and she would have blurted out the name of our refuge to the first comer. We told her that we would always find ways of letting her have news and that we hoped to return as soon as possible. A few days after our settling in at the Serlupis my nephew Cecil Anrep came to tell me that the German consul Gerhard Wolff had asked for me and wished to speak to me. I had never met the consul but had heard from friends we had in common how bitterly opposed he was to the Nazi regime and how anxious to help. At the consulate in Via dei Bardi I was received at once and found that the consul's face and expression corresponded to what I had heard about him. Both inspired me with the greatest confidence. He seemed at first a little embarrassed and talked about indifferent things but finally came out with an assurance that he would do all that was within his power to protect the collection and library of I Tatti and then added that it would be easier for him to carry out his good intentions if B.B. was no longer in the house. When I told him that he had already left he seemed greatly relieved. This eased my conscience as it proved that I had not been too alarmistic and that the decision to take B.B. away had been the right one.

Meanwhile at I Tatti, following the advice of the *Soprintendenza*[8] and of the German Institute,[9] all the more valuable pictures were packed up and sent to the Fontanelle, as the Serlupi villa was called, the less valuable ones distributed through the house so as to make it appear in perfect order. The books were partly walled up, partly sent to the Fontanelle, a great number to Quarto, Baroness Ritter's villa,[1] others to Giannino Marchig's studio. All this was achieved in an unbelievably short time by my sister and our agent Geremia Gioffredi with the help of Giannino Marchig. On top of that my sister had all the worry over Mary, who after our departure became so much worse that three nurses had

8 B.B.'s relations with the Florentine *Soprintendenza* had been for a long time rather difficult (as a result, I believe, of Mary's tactlessness) but became very cordial in these critical years, particularly with the *soprintendente* himself, Giovanni Poggi. He came repeatedly to see B.B. and took a personal interest in the safety of the I Tatti Collection.

9 The German art historians at the head of the German Institute of Fine Arts—first Friedrich Kriegbaum (killed during one of the few air raids that Florence endured) and his successor Ludwig Heydenreich—could not have been friendlier and more helpful. It was due to Heydenreich's calculated bureaucratic slowness that Goering's emissaries were never able to grab anything from I Tatti.

1 Baroness Kiki Ritter de Zahony, born Salignac Fénélon, mother of Marchesa Gilberta Serlupi, our hostess at the Villa Fontanelle.

to take turns in looking after her. Not to speak of the
Germans threatening again and again to occupy the whole
house. When my sister had already made all the necessary
preparations for transporting Mary and her nurses to her
own house in Borgo San Jacopo, the German officers suddenly changed their minds and decided that the neighbouring castle of Poggio Gherardo would suit them much better.
But they obliged I Tatti to make room for the very disagreeable and very Fascist tenants of Poggio. Our secluded
life was certainly much more peaceful.

OF COURSE neither the Serlupis nor we expected our stay
at the Fontanelle to last longer than a few months. Rumours
of Allied landings south of Spezia or north of Ravenna kept
us in a mist of pleasant illusions. The way in which both
Serlupis accepted our prolonged occupation of their guest-
rooms could not have been more heartwarming. The best
idea of the life we led there is given by two letters I wrote
to Mary. I also add one of hers to me.

December 10th 1943
    My darling Mary,
        When three months ago on the tenth of September we
were kind of snatched away from our peaceful daily life at
I Tatti I expected to return at the end of a week or ten
days or two weeks at the utmost. And here have thirteen
weeks of *confino* gone by and how many more are before
us? It is not a painful *confino* by any means and has allowed
us to keep nicely away from all the turmoil of packing up
pictures and books and in making room for others at I Tatti.
Like the girl who said "It makes me tired to see mother
work" I might say that it makes me tired to think of all
the work that has to be done. If B.B. manages to navigate
through this sea of troubles and dangers simply by staying
here quietly he can call himself unusually lucky. So far he

has kept in very good shape. He has had one tummy upset and got over it by keeping the grated-apple diet for 24 hours. Then he caught a cold and started in with his horrible old cough and said he would go on having it till spring came around. But inhalations with Salsomaggiore salts have been very effective and he has got rid of it almost completely. By good luck this happens to be a very dry and sheltered place, sheltered in a miraculous way from the north wind and the vegetation around us reminds us of Sainte-Claire. Our days go by in a very regular and peaceful way. B.B. says it is like being on a transatlantic liner (minus the storms) where you have got all your belongings inside your cabin and where you live always in the expectation of landing and lead a kind of provisional and suspended existence. When we started on our journey a port seemed to be in view but it was an illusion. No land showed itself anywhere on the horizon and in that way it is more like being on a windjammer than on an ocean liner.

Would you like to know how our days go by? When you know about one you know them all. I get up soon after eight and start making coffee and grating an apple for B.B. Then they bring me milk and toast and butter and I have got some honey or jam among my own provisions. Then I prepare his clothes and we discuss the weather and the temperature in connection with this important choice of heavier or lighter things to wear. Happily it has not been very cold yet and we are well off with an electric stove in B.B.'s room and wood stoves and open fires in the other rooms. Then I settle down to read aloud for about an hour and a quarter. We have finished Hodgkin's account of the barbarian invasions and I have realized, as I never did before, that the Lombards were a beastly lot, ever so much worse than the Goths. Now we read about Byzantine history, first Diehl's *Figures Byzantines*, very readable and amusing and this morning we have begun his *Justinien* which promises to be very good too. Follows the daily adventure of the bath which heated on an old-fashioned system in dependence from the kitchen is one day hot, one day warmish, one day tepid, and one day cold. I go first to experiment the temperature and B.B. follows if it is warm enough. When we are both ready and while our rooms are being cleaned we go out for a stroll. When we arrived everything was the colour of tobacco after the terrible drought and gradually it has all revived again. Now the white narcissus is beginning to come out and there are masses of small pink roses blooming. At one of the peasant houses we meet two magnificent geese and several black ducks and when it is fine we see an old man of eighty-six sitting in the sun and he tells us that but for his legs not being what they were he has nothing to complain of. He always ends up by saying *"bisogna contentarsi."* His son and daughter-in-law know nothing about the present whereabouts of their only son who was as a soldier down in Lecce when they last heard of him. Their impatience at the slow progress of things is greater than ours. When we get back to the house B.B. goes on with his writing until lunch time and I either do some typing, copying out the innumerable notes he has gradually assembled in connection with his work, or I have some mending or washing to do. At lunch we meet our fellow *confinati*. One of them is a very quiet charming man, an officer who does not want to serve under the present government. He has a wife and two small children and a third one on the way and worries a great deal about them and about his own future. The other is a very corpulent *Monsignore* whose reasons for keeping out of the way are not quite clear. He does not seem to be politically compromised but is probably mortally afraid of air raids. For us it is very nice that he should be such a coward, for he is a most entertaining person, very cultivated, especially in the field of Italian and French literature and has an excellent sense of humour. B.B. gets a lot of fun out of him. The food is very good, plentiful and hearty, and I see B.B. eating and enjoying things that he would never accept at home like thick *minestroni* or beans or *bruciate—* roasted chestnuts. After lunch we try to get some hopeful

news out of the wireless and generally fail to do so either
because the radio works badly or because the news is not
what we would like it to be. Then we return to our rooms
and before B.B. has his nap I read to him a book of which
he does not mind missing a good deal by falling asleep. Just
now it is a very amusing one by Crispolti about the popes
between 1870 and 1900. Between 4 and 4:30 we go out again
and while the days were long enough we used to take a
beautiful walk by a steep path through terraced olive groves
to the hill just behind us where there is a stretch of wooded
country and a wonderful view. In October the wood was
full of wild cyclamen. Now it gets dark too soon and we
must content ourselves with another stroll through the two
poderi. Then we get tea and some conversation with *Monsignore*. Then back to our rooms and our private occupations
until for about half an hour before supper I read aloud
again. After supper we sometimes have a very good time and
sometimes a pleasantly dull one according to how conversationally inclined B.B. and *Monsignore* are. *Monsignore*
does not seem to care either to read himself or to listen to
reading. But when we return to our rooms we have some
more reading. Just now it is very frivolous, Boni de Castellane's recollections full of gossip and surprising bits of
information. Yesterday for instance we were told that at the
time of the peace conference in Paris Berenson's whole
ambition was to become Polish ambassador in Washington
or American ambassador in Warsaw.

Now you know everything about our daily life. On
Sundays I go to hear *Monsignore* say Mass and have got to
feel quite at home in the liturgy. It is most beautiful and well
deserves being recited in a more dignified manner and not
in such a preposterous hurry.

Sometimes we see our neighbours, a Jewish family in
hiding composed of a widowed mother with a son and daughter-in-law and two grandchildren, one little girl of five and
a baby four weeks old. In these four weeks it has already
changed its residence three times and the grandmother says

of him *il vero piccolo ebreo errante.* I am not going to enlarge on this subject because it is too heartbreaking and we cannot do anything about it. I would like to enlarge on the subject of your health although about that too I cannot do anything except to tell you that we think of you a great deal always hoping for better news of you. You must do your best to get better again and be ready to celebrate your eightieth birthday with us.

Meanwhile it has got to be the 12th of December and day before yesterday it was two years that the war between Italy and the United States was declared and tomorrow is my birthday which for the first time since 1919 I am not celebrating between I Tatti and the Anrep house. There is more and more to remember as one gets older and for me such a lot of wonderful things connected with you and B.B. All our trips and journeys, all the fun we have had together, a whole vast world that has been opened out to me through my living with you both. And above all I owe it to you, dearest Mary, for had you not made up your mind that you wanted me as a secretary and librarian and had not insisted on having "the house painted pink" my life would have taken a very different and probably very uninteresting course.

In these recent years I have on top of everything else owed another thing to you and that has been the joy I have had through little Funtyki. How glad I am to hear that he has now at last what he should have had long ago, a really nice and capable governess who gives him a good discipline. Even if I had had more time to devote to him I would probably have been too weak to educate him really well. I do not allow myself to dwell on it but if I did I would feel it as a real privation not to hear his voice calling for me, not to read with him, not to be able to prepare anything for his little Christmas, not to watch his further development. The relation between a child and a grown-up is a very elusive thing and needs daily or at least very frequent watching over. After a separation of several months it may never be quite the same thing again. But as I said already

I don't dwell on it and my bearded baby keeps me busy enough.

In the hope of having an occasion for sending this off tomorrow I shall say good-bye to you for today and remain with ever so much love from both of us your deeply devoted
Nicky.

Mary to Nicky   February 5th 1944
Dearest Nicky,

I am very sorry not to write this with my own hand but neither hand nor eyes are working well. The truth is I am dying only I cannot die. The doctors will not give me receipts for medicines that might kill me and I am too ill to go out of my room to look for anything or to die in the garden. I suffer so much that the gate is already open on the long road we have to travel alone, but I cannot start. However all this is not important. What I want to express I never could express even if I had the use of my hand and eyes. It is the love and admiration and affection of many years. There is no cloud in the thought of you as there is in almost everything else. The end of life, if you remain conscious, is a sort of purgatory in which all your sins and mistakes come crowding upon you, but between you and me there is nothing of the kind—all is perfectly serene and I think of you with the deepest love.

If I die in time I hope you will marry B.B. You will have my deep sympathy, but all the worldly things are fading away. . . .

. . . I am almost glad that B.B. should not see me in my pain and weakness. I love to think how in spite of all our failings and so-called infidelities we have always stuck together and stuck to Italy and when I am able to think at all I think of him with tender affection.

Nicky to Mary   February 9th 1944
My darling Mary,

Your beautiful letter has moved me more than words can say and I am utterly miserable over this long and ever-

lengthening separation from you. I daresay it is a foolish
illusion of mine but I feel as if B.B., had he been near
you all this time, might have with his surprising vitality
kept you from getting into such a despondent state of mind
that you long for death and would like to help it on yourself.
He, by the way, does not really take it in that you might not
be there any more when the day of his return home finally
dawns. He has such a belief in your vitality, in your power
of recuperation, and I daresay he does not want to face it.

Thank you with all my heart for what you say to me
and for the trust you put in me regarding your family and
what you want to be done for them. I shall try to be worthy
of it. I don't think B.B. and I would get married if you
should die. Surely everybody would find my living near him
and for him perfectly natural. So why should we change?

My thoughts go back to the time when I first came to
join your and B.B.'s life at I Tatti. And you remained ever
the same loving understanding friend that I found you to be
in September 1919 at your return to I Tatti and when we had
our first trip together with Hamilton to Verona and Vicenza
and Padua and when we finally got to Pomposa and ate that
wonderful sole in Adria. Do you remember?

. . . *February 10th* The only change in our daily life
is one among our fellow refugees. *Monsignore* and the officer
have left and in their place we have now a youngish couple
with a 7 months old baby. They are people who would
under normal conditions enjoy very privileged positions but
in this topsy-turvy time they are not to be envied, have had
to hide in the mountains without the slightest comfort and
suffering bitterly from the cold, then had to run away from
there over steep stony paths for about 15 miles with the
baby in a sack on the father's back. Here they can rest and
recover. The baby is not beautiful, with ears standing off
its little completely bald head like the handles of a pot, but
is well-behaved and merry and intelligent-looking. Yesterday
I found the father with his shirtsleeves turned up washing
all its little dirty napkins and he adores giving it a bath and

feeding it. B.B. is quite touched by the spectacle of their devotion to each other and to the child.[2] . . .

It surprises me now while copying my letters to Mary not to find the three most important inmates of Le Fontanelle ever mentioned in them. But of course I could not have done so without letting Mary understand where our refuge was. These three inmates were Filippo Serlupi himself, his wife, Gilberta, and her mother, Baroness Ritter de Zahony, born Salignac de Fénélon. B.B.'s chief relaxation and entertainment were conversations with his landlord, who was inexhaustible in the subjects of his varied interests, in his passion for art and literature, his erudition in juridical matters, his information on all historical questions connected with the Vatican. And how B.B. enjoyed Filippo's masterly way of reading prose and poetry aloud! Admirable was his acceptance of heavy responsibilities in a period full of difficulties and dangers anyway. Not once did he make us feel that our prolonged stay in his house burdened him with an irksome task. Perhaps he could not have carried this weight without the support of his wife, an unusual woman on the material as well as on the mental and moral side. A *mulier fortis*, as B.B. used to call her. The remarkable collection of rare illustrated books in the Serlupi library had been brought together chiefly by her.

Baroness Ritter, having put her villa at Quarto at the disposal of refugees, joined her daughter's household, and to this we owed our close friendship with her. She belonged to the reserved, almost severe type of French aristocrat, and had we not been thrown on each other's company day by day for many months, we would have remained on terms of distant politeness with her. There were real treasures of humane un-

---

[2] The duke and duchess of Ancona of the House of Savoy went through great hardships until they found a refuge at the Fontanelle.

derstanding, sharp intelligence, and ready wit hidden in her. Complete harmony in our political hopes and fears also acted as a strong link between us. She used to accompany us on our walks almost every day and frequently took turns with me in reading to B.B.

In the height of summer that same year, 1944, we found ourselves from one day to the other and without any warning on the front line of the German retreat and remained for a month surrounded by parachutists and exposed to Allied shelling. At first threatened with expulsion from the house we were left in it thanks to Marchese Serlupi's diplomatic rights which were as he had foreseen respected by the Germans. German soldiers gave us instructions as to where in the house we could get the best shelter from the shelling. We were lucky in having the parachutists around us commanded by very decent officers and therefore relatively well behaved. It was a weird experience with some very tense moments to live through but we all came out of it unharmed.[3]

Two days after the first appearance of Allied and partisan troops at the Fontanelle an English major and head of the Displaced Persons Office and his assistant, a charming young Yugoslav, came to fetch us in an armoured car and took us on a brief visit to I Tatti. German shells were still whizzing through the air but nobody seemed to care. Everywhere we saw people walking about generally carrying buckets of water and all of them looking haggard and famished, *succhiati dalle streghe*—sucked dry by witches—and presenting a strange contrast to the well-fed and prosperous-looking Allied soldiers. For some reason we had to stop at an army command post in Piazza dei Giudici. We got out and walked as far as the parapet and suddenly the whole group

---

[3] For those who might like to know more about those days, the diary I kept during our month in the front line has been added as an appendix (pages 321–352).

of blown-up buildings was revealed to us in its weird spectral beauty. At I Tatti too everything seemed strange, gipsy camps of soldiers in the fields, trees mown down, the lemon-house occupied by English soldiers, windows and skylights blown out, the house pock-marked with shell holes. My sister and brother-in-law were amazingly cheerful and welcoming in spite of having just had the news that their house in Borgo San Jacopo on the Arno had been blown up by the Germans. Separately B.B. and I went to see Mary. Physically I found her better than I had expected but listless and apparently indifferent to political events and developments. When we drove away B.B. seemed sad and crushed and I thought it was over the condition of the house. "Oh no," he said. "That can be remedied. What I am in despair over is Mary. The moment I entered her room she said that now everything was so changed and the house so heavily damaged she hoped I too would change my mind and give up my foolish plan of leaving it to Harvard University." These emotional upsets, the sight of what he called the heart of Florence in ruins, and Mary's discouraging remarks may have contributed to his falling dangerously ill next day with an intestinal infection. Again the Serlupis helped in every way, called in their excellent family physician and slowly he recovered but felt weak and despondent. He told me afterwards that only from then on had he become aware, in his 79th year, of being old.

We stayed on for several weeks at the Serlupis because of B.B.'s illness and slow recovery. A number of his friends came to look him up there and found him in better condition than they had dared to expect, probably because the joy of seeing them and talking to them had a momentary vivifying effect on him. Also new friends came, English and American officers, some with letters of introduction, and began to provide him with foreign papers and to satisfy his burning curiosity about the aspect of things from the Allied point of view. Great was his scepticism as to fruitful contacts between Italians and the Allied occupying forces. "Only society people—and they are with few exceptions ex-Fascists —speak really good English. To them the Allied authorities will turn and not to the really worthwhile Italians who rarely can express themselves freely in a foreign language." He was also without any illusions about any possibility for him to intervene or to give advice. "American officials, be they military or civilian, do not as a rule believe in getting information from the man on the spot. He is supposed to be incapable of an objective opinion."

B.B. had already foreseen that after the liberation he would be asked for recommendations to the Allied authorities or for testimonials of impeccable behaviour. It was exactly what happened. "I am to serve as soap," he said. "And it would be no use telling these people that I have no political influence to speak of. So write whatever you think fits their case and I will sign it. Let them have the illusion of having an important document in their hands." Several times I went to the office of the field police and tried to put in a word for people arrested or in danger of being arrested when we knew that they did not deserve such punishment. Invariably I found these police officials, whether American or British, odious and almost rude. They were obviously eager to listen to denunciations but treated favourable reports with insolent contempt. Once it happened that on the day after one of these fruitless attempts of mine a man who had been arrested was set free and of course he and his family regarded this as the result of my words and vowed eternal friendship and gratitude to me. Both B.B. and I felt sure that the release was due to other reasons.

On our return to I Tatti at the end of September the worst damage in the house, the broken windows and skylights, had already been repaired, the pictures had been re-hung, the books returned from their various hiding places. It was again one of those unbelievable *tours de force* that only my sister with her undauntable energy and supported by Giannino Marchig and Gioffredi could carry through.

After our long seclusion it was bewildering to find ourselves in such a confusion of old and new faces and confronted by another confusion, that of political unrest and uncertainty. B.B. tried hard to catch up with all the arrears of publications outside Italy and more often than not felt exasperated over developments of thought and opinion completely alien to him.

No electric current, only candles and small petroleum lamps, no bells, the main gate and the house door kept open and at every hour of the day jeeps or army cars would drive up and Allied officers or men would walk in. Some had been written to from home to ask how B.B. was, others had heard vaguely that he was somebody worth looking at, others brought up Italian friends who had no transport to reach us with, others were friends from former days, like Fred Hartt of the Fine Arts Commission or Cecil Pinsent in the same employment or Bob Berenson, a distant cousin of B.B.'s who happened to be aide-de-camp to General Clark. All of them and particularly Bob helped us solve the problem of how to procure food for such a large household. The other problem of how to get fuel was solved mostly by our neighbours, the Derbyshire Yeomanry established at the Villa Strozzi, who again and again put trucks at our disposal for getting peat in the Val d'Arno. The officers of this same regiment went so far as to send one of their men every second day to I Tatti in order to recharge a small battery for a reading lamp near B.B.'s bed.

GREAT WAS THE JOY of taking up the broken threads with friends near and far, but great also the shock of hearing about the disappearance of others. Thus we learned that Riri Visconti had been blown up by a mine during the advance of the Eighth Army. In spite of his being beyond the age of military service he had felt it his duty to prove by a definite gesture the seriousness of his opposition to Fascism. When Forlì was occupied by the Eighth Army a rumour that had been circulated and then denied was definitely confirmed. Both Pellegrina Paulucci and her husband had been shot by the Germans, presumably as a consequence of their having given shelter in their country-house to a messenger sent from across the fighting-lines to the partisans in northern Italy. The Pauluccis must have been spied upon and denounced to the Germans. Bit by bit the whole grim story was revealed to us. Later on in 1945 we heard that Byba Khuen had died during her flight from the invading Russians.

FOR MARY the liberation had come too late. In days gone by she would have thoroughly enjoyed the coming and going of all these young Americans and Englishmen; but now even visits from one of her special pets, like Cecil Pinsent, left her almost indifferent. Only exceptionally did she seem disposed to talk and to listen. She had entrusted her last dispositions to me, foremost among them her wish to be cremated. A few weeks before her death, on a favourable day, I was able to explain to her what a shock and grief it would be to the women who had nursed her with such devotion if her body was carried away without any religious service. "The feelings of these humble people around you," I said to her, "the respect for what is sacred to them, are more important than your personal whims." She was silent for a moment and then said, "All right. I leave it to you. You can dispose of my body in the way you consider the right one, but perhaps later on, at night time, you could dig out my bones and burn them."

Late in March 1945 she died without suffering and was temporarily buried in the cemetery of Settignano. Years later after B.B.'s death her coffin was buried next to his in the small chapel at I Tatti.

CHAPTER XX

The Light Burns Down [1945–59]

URING THE SPRING and early summer general conditions improved slowly and imperceptibly. Mail service, electricity, telephones began to function normally; the greater part of the Allied occupying forces were transferred to northern Italy or Germany; the problem of how to procure food became less acute and then vanished altogether. Petrol remained severely rationed and only with the help of army cars lent to us for the occasion did we manage to return to Casa al Dono for the summer months. We had a small car run on *metano* gas at our disposal strong enough to bring us up provisions once a week but not to carry our own weight.

I remember it as an ideally quiet summer, as most people were unable to circulate if Allied officers did not give them a lift. We took up neighbourly relations with the Campiglioni group and with Don Patroni; my little Markevitch pet came up once more to stay with us (he was sent to a Swiss school later that year) and for the first time we enjoyed the company of Luisa Vertova, who until then had been only a name for us. Friends we had in common asked B.B. to invite her for a few weeks, as they were anxious about her being overworked and undernourished. She had been doing secretarial work for the first daily paper published under Allied control in Florence and while food conditions were still very precarious. We kept her with us all through the summer and ended by inviting her to help in the library. For ten years she went on spending the greater part of the week at I Tatti, looked after the photograph collection, translated four new essays and various shorter articles of B.B.'s into Italian, later on his book on Lotto, and finally the *Drawings of the Florentine Painters*. She helped him in his work on all of them, but particularly on the revised edition of the *Lorenzo Lotto*.[1] But even more than her invaluable help I remember the pleasure and comfort of being in constant touch with this unusually gifted and sensitive young woman.

ONE OF THE FIRST if not the first civilian friend who turned up from the U.S.A. in the late summer of 1945 was B.B.'s lawyer-cousin Lawrence Berenson, brought up from Florence by a member of the American consulate staff. Great was our surprise and joy to see Lawrence's powerful figure climb out of a jeep. He attended to the changes in B.B.'s will made necessary by Mary's death and promised to take care of all the debts incurred by us in B.B.'s name during the war years in Italy. Lawrence, being himself a graduate of the Harvard Law School, took the keenest interest in B.B.'s plans for the future of I Tatti and in the following years acted again and again as negotiator between him and the Harvard Corporation.

While we were still at Casa al Dono my sister and brother-in-law moved to the San Martino house near the parish church of San Martino a Mensola. As the house in Borgo San Jacopo in which they had rented an apartment had been blown up by the Germans, they had gone on living at I Tatti and waiting for the San Martino house, offered

---

[1] Several of B.B.'s scholar friends helped him during the revision of the *Lotto* and the *Drawings*, particularly Philip Pouncey, Agnes Mongan, Sidney Freedberg, and Bernard Degenhart.

to them by B.B., to be free from military occupation. It soon
became very attractive and inhabitable, the nicest kind of
neighbourhood for us and a great attraction for many of our
guests.

Another although less important addition to the neighbourhood—but several years later—was the house which B.B.
allowed his colleague and friend Roberto Papini and his wife,
the Hungarian sculptor Livia Kusmich,[2] to build above the
Villino on the understanding that at the termination of their
life it would become part of the Berenson Foundation. The
Papinis were wild with joy and excitement over the building
and furnishing of the house but especially over its position
and the superb view on the whole complex of I Tatti, house
and garden, on the surrounding vineyards and olive groves,
and farther on, over the Arno valley and the city of the distant range of the Apennines. Unfortunately they were not
allowed to enjoy their new home and their companionship
for long. Roberto began prematurely to suffer from circu-
latory troubles and in 1957 was suddenly snatched away.

OUR FIRST EXCURSION in the early summer of 1945 took
us to Siena to watch the Palio, which, strange to say, neither
of us had ever seen. A fascinating spectacle, traditionally
ceremonious and at the same time utterly wild. We were
taken there by one of our new "post-liberation" friends, Exer
Robinson, head of the American officers' club. A delightful
woman full of youthful energy and curiosity, a first-rate
organizer, ready to help her new civilian friends in all the
complex difficulties of daily life.

---

2 With the help of photographs and a number of sketches taken
while talking to him Livia Kusmich managed to do a bust of
B.B. in his last year when he was no longer able to pose for
her. Considering all the difficulties, she was successful in pro-
ducing a good likeness. The bust, cast in bronze, belongs now
to I Tatti.

It was on this occasion that Marilù Stucchi took us for the first time to Guido Chigi's palace. We had both been in it as tourists but never as guests of the owner. It was, like I Tatti, a sort of seaport with every kind of craft finding shelter in it and the most courteous reception from the founder of the Accademia Chigiana. In the following years we returned to it many times.

In the autumn of 1945 a trip to Venice was arranged for us—in spite of serious transport difficulties—by Carla Garabelli and young Count Cini, the son of the prominent industrialist Count Vittorio Cini. The latter had been minister of transport in 1943 and before retiring had expressed his adverse opinions so openly that he had been one of the first to be arrested when the Germans took over the control of everything after the armistice. His son Giorgio got him out of the concentration camp many months later. When we met Giorgio at Campiglioni in the summer of 1945 his father was still in Switzerland waiting for his position to be cleared by the Allied authorities. A Sicilian banker and member of the Orlando group drove us over emergency bridges and through heavy military traffic to Venice, where we stayed in the Cini house, all the hotels being still at the disposal of the occupying forces. At the end of our stay we found ourselves stuck in Venice without transportation until my nephew Cecil Anrep, who was at that time working for an industrialist in Prato, managed to borrow a car from his boss and came to fetch us. I remember B.B.'s consternation when we stopped for lunch at the famous Pappagallo restaurant in Bologna and he watched my nephew paying the bill. We were already used to the depreciation of our currency but for him who had not handled nor discussed money for years it was a bad shock!

Giorgio Cini was killed in an air crash four years later and it was in his memory that his father managed to get the old convent of San Giorgio Maggiore in Venice freed from its military occupation, thoroughly restored, and turned into a cultural institution, the Fondazione Giorgio Cini. B.B., who had become a close friend of Vittorio Cini, discussed the first plans for the Foundation again and again with him and with his chief adviser Nino Barbantini, the art critic and organizer of exhibitions. Most of the Biennale shows and the famous Titian and Tintoretto exhibitions were due to him. B.B. had the greatest regard for Barbantini's taste and sense of quality. During our subsequent stays in Venice but also in Rome, in Naples, and in Taormina, where the Cinis owned a villa, B.B. went on seeing a lot of Cini and found the charm of his "Faustian" personality irresistible.

In 1946 I had to go once more through pangs of anxiety over B.B.'s position. Walter Orebaugh, the first American consul in Florence after the war, rang me up one day and asked me to come to his office. When I got there he told me about a message he had received from the State Department according to which B.B. was in danger of losing his passport because of his being alien-born and his not having returned to the United States for over twenty years. Orebaugh, who was on very friendly terms with B.B., asked me whether I knew no important person to whom I could send an appeal. I wrote to several friends but first of all to William Phillips. He addressed himself at once to the State Department and got from it the assurance that an exception would be made for B.B.—"Although," the State Department's answer said, "Mr. Berenson could have given a better account of himself." This sentence confirmed my suspicion that the chargé d'affaires who took over the American Embassy when Mr. Phillips left had on his return to Washington represented B.B. as a black sheep. Years later a friend who claimed that B.B.'s dossier had been shown to her at the State Department assured us that it was quite elaborate and among other accusations contained the one of "premature anti-Fascism." A story to which the Italian proverb could be applied: *se non è vero, è ben trovato*—if not true, at any rate a clever invention.

MEANWHILE THE "TATTI BUS" had resumed its services for clients so steadily growing in numbers that it was often harassing for me to regulate their influx. Many of the old friends came again: Katie Lewis, Addie Kahn, Sibyl Colefax, Judge Learned and Frances Hand, Harold Acton, John Walker, Harry and Byba Coster, Kenneth and Jane Clark, W. G. Constable, Barbara Strachey Halpern, Agnes Mongan, William Milliken, Alice Dick-Lauder, Percy Lubbock (Lady Sybil had died in Switzerland in 1944), Salvemini, Morra, the Colacicchis, Alberti, Loria. Also Naima Löfroth reappeared, no longer as an alert watchdog but as a rather lame and slowed-up one, yet ready to bark and growl at the slightest provocation. The number of the new friends was so great that it would be impossible and tedious to enumerate them all. Some stand out more vividly than others, like for instance Count Carlo Sforza, our minister of foreign affairs from 1945 till 1952, a man with a political and historical horizon almost too wide to be appreciated by the average Italian. Of him one could say that a prophet counts little in his own country. I remember the conversations on the evenings he came to spend with B.B. in our hotel in Rome as among the most interesting I have ever heard. He let himself go completely on these occasions and spoke without any arrogance or self-adulation (the two faults he was constantly accused of by his enemies) and was always ready to listen to B.B.'s comments.

The young historian Hugh Trevor-Roper was sent to B.B. by Alys Russell and besides being always a welcome guest he became one of B.B.'s most cherished correspondents. The same was true of Hamish Hamilton. After their first

introduction to I Tatti through Sibyl Colefax he and his
wife, Yvonne Pallavicino, came almost every year to I Tatti
or to Casa al Dono and in the intervals Hamish's letters gave
B.B. the greatest pleasure. Another much appreciated correspondent was Diana Menuhin. She and Yehudi were sent to
I Tatti by Iris Origo (the daughter of Lady Sybil by her
first marriage with Bayard Cutting) and from then on Diana
sent him most entertaining accounts of her and Yehudi's
fast-moving life. For discussions on history and politics B.B.
found new partners, apart from Sforza and Trevor-Roper,
in Lewis Namier, Johannes Schwarzenberg,[3] Frank Giles,[4]
Alphy Clary,[5] and in several other more casual visitors. And
of course there were many new contacts with his younger
colleagues, like for instance John Pope-Hennessy of the Victoria and Albert Museum, Philip Pouncey of the British
Museum, Henry Francis of the Cleveland Museum, John
Coolidge and Sidney Freedberg of the Fogg Museum, Francis
Taylor of the Metropolitan, Christian Salm[6] of the Alte
Pinakothek, Fred Hartt,[7] Charles Seymour, Jr., from Yale
University.

B.B.'s hatred of abstract art did not prevent him from
being on excellent terms with contemporary painters who

[3] Prince Johannes Schwarzenberg was Austrian ambassador in
Rome from 1946, and subsequently in London.

[4] Frank Giles was *Times* Correspondent in Rome from 1946 to
1950.

[5] Prince Alphonse and Princess Lidi Clary Aldringen, the former
owners of Schloss Teplitz in Bohemia; since 1948 established in
Venice, where we met them in 1949.

[6] Altgraf Christian Salm we had already met in Moravia during
our visits to the Khuens and our stays in Vienna. He was then
a wealthy land-owner and at the same time art amateur and
student. Having lost everything he had the courage to go back
to the university, and to take his degree and is now a recognized
authority on North European Schools of painting.

[7] Professor of fine arts at Smith College at that time, later in
the same capacity at St. Louis, and now at the University of
Philadelphia.

followed traditional lines. I have already spoken of B.B.'s deep affection for Giovanni Colacicchi and of their frequent and animated discussions. In 1949 a young English painter, Derek Hill, was introduced to B.B. in Venice. B.B. took to him and offered to lend him the Villino to facilitate his studies of the Tuscan landscape. Derek occupied it for several years and became a congenial neighbor and real friend for us. Two Florentine painters—by election if not by birth —Hans Joachim Staude and Pietro Annigoni, were good friends of his and so was the Sicilian Renato Guttuso, who was introduced to him by Sylvia Sprigge. Also with Chagall, introduced by Roberto Papini, B.B. felt very much at home, perhaps partly because of their common Lithuanian origin. Oskar Kokoschka also came to see him after the war. When B.B. met him at the Khuens in Moravia, he had found him fascinating in his spontaneity and vigor of expression. But somehow they did not hit it off, and when Kokoschka insisted on B.B.'s looking at his painting of the Florentine Duomo, it was a disaster. B.B. remained stonily silent and said afterwards that Kokoschka had used raspberry jam to paint his picture with. Very different were B.B.'s relations with the German-Ischitano painter Edoardo Bargheer, whose life-enhancing presence he always enjoyed. We saw him in Florence and met him again in his beloved Ischia.

For talks on Far Eastern art and literature B.B. could always count on Harold Acton and on friends brought by him, and on Fosco Maraini, the son of the sculptor Antonio Maraini who had been a close friend of B.B. before the First World War. Then they had stopped seeing each other because of a clash between Mary and Fosco's Anglo-Hungarian mother. B.B. was delighted to discover a kindred spirit in Fosco, and took a great interest in his career as explorer and writer.

A young American historian-poet, Peter Viereck, turned up at I Tatti in 1945, sent by Mario Praz. He was working for the P.W.B. and delegated to lecture to groups of G.I.'s. B.B. took immediately to this absent-minded, impulsive young genius and went on seeing him through the years either alone or with his Russian wife, Anya. They came for the last time in 1955 after B.B.'s ninetieth birthday and brought their nine-year-old son Alexis. B.B. said to him: "I am ninety and you are nine; what is the difference?" "Just a difference of zero," said the boy.

Another of the new friends whom B.B. loved seeing and with whom he could discuss theological and ethical problems freely was Sturgis Riddle,[8] minister of the American Church in Florence. He and his very attractive wife were introduced to B.B. by Fred Hartt. Both were very popular in Florence among the Italians, too, and the rectory became a delightful center of social life.

Almost every autumn the crown prince, later the king, of Sweden came to stay, first alone and then with his wife. Only once did this visit become rather troublesome for a private household: when he came the first time as king and we were pursued by photographers and journalists. All the queen's angry protests about their travelling under an assumed name and having the right to be treated like ordinary tourists were of no avail. She had to submit but showed her intense displeasure very clearly. During all the other visits we were left in peace to enjoy the easy informal atmosphere created by the royal couple. One day I remember the queen telling us about her early years as the daughter of a British admiral in Malta and of her having been brought up like an ordinary human being. Upon which the king said very gently: "But I too would like to be considered as an ordinary human being." Each time the Swedish archaeologist Axel Boethius came up from Rome to meet the crown prince and later king at I Tatti. B.B. had met Boethius in the early

---

[8] Since 1950 dean of the American Procathedral in Paris.

thirties in Steinmann's salon at the Hertziana Library and had found him very congenial but then had lost sight of him. Now on meeting him again he discovered in him a friend after his own heart, gay and lovable and at the same time intellectually stimulating like few others. Besides meeting frequently in Rome and at I Tatti they exchanged a great many letters throughout the post-war years.

B.B.'s curiosity for people and events did not diminish at the same tempo as his bodily strength. Invariably he undertook too much and had to pay for it. Not only at home but wherever we went he was sought after as he had never been before. When travelling conditions became normal again he spoke repeatedly of his wish to return with me to the United States, to look up old friends there, and to show me the art treasures. But after our first stay in Rome in 1947, where he was ceaselessly invited and courted, he came back exhausted and said to me: "All right, I will take you to America but I will never come back. It will kill me." Of course I begged him not to think of it again.

B.B.'s health was looked after, also Mary's during her last year—De Bosis having died of an infection in 1943— by Alberto Capecchi, the district doctor from Fiesole, with great skill and complete devotion till the very end. Both he and Camillo Ramorino, B.B.'s dentist, were family friends as well as medical helps.

B.B. USED TO TELL THE STORY of the man who, when asked what he wanted for breakfast, said he liked tea but liked also to see coffee on the table. That was what B.B.'s attitude to me became during this last period of his life. It was the result of our having been inseparable during a whole year at the Fontanelle. He got used to having me constantly at his beck and call and clung to the habit as old people tend to do. He would not hear of my leaving the house for more than a few hours. Only two, at the utmost three, times did I spend a night away from I Tatti or from Casa al Dono. If I said to him: "But you have so and so to keep you company," his answer was: "I like to have you there as well." Often he went so far as to say that all he wanted was an uninterrupted tête-à-tête with me. But I knew that what he needed like daily bread was somebody to stimulate him, to draw him out, to make him feel fully alive. From me, who lived with him all the time, he could get complete devotion, tenderness, sympathy, but no intellectual stimulus. He suffered from fatigue but would perhaps have suffered more from feeling solitary, wistful, forgotten by his friends. Clotilde Marghieri tells me that she remembers him comparing himself and me to a nomad and his camel. "She carries me through the worst deserts and allows me to enjoy the enchanting mirages on their horizons."

Again and again we discussed the possibility of handing over I Tatti to Harvard during B.B.'s lifetme and of retiring to one of the smaller houses where life could have been organized in a simpler and less expensive way. He felt half attracted and half reluctant and the reluctance or perhaps the apathy of old age won out. Perhaps the thought of living within easy distance of I Tatti, of being an embarrassing presence to the new regime there, of watching the changes that he knew would be necessary frightened him. Or he dreaded becoming a monument where he had been the live centre of things for so many years and thought that he would have been more exposed to this danger if he had left I Tatti.

The rhythm of his daily life was resumed very much on the old lines, only unavoidably the hours devoted to reading and study became shorter, the range of his walks more restricted, the enjoyment of sights, of nature, of old and new friends concentrated like a precious liqueur in a small glass.

A new daily habit that we both loved dearly was listening to recorded music. Exceptionally to live music. When Nikita Magaloff happened to have a concert engagement in Florence and stayed at I Tatti, he never failed to play for B.B., who found this gesture of unaffected generosity very lovable. Later on when the Menuhins were established at the Villino, Yehudi played for B.B. sometimes alone and sometimes with others. I remember a small concert of Yehudi's accompanied by his brother-in-law, Louis Kentner, and another with Yehudi, Gaspar Cassadò, and two friends of theirs playing quartettes in the library.

TWO THINGS remained unaltered. One was B.B.'s interest in the growth of the library and its improvements. Under my sister's direction a new wing was added to the library and the small *settecento* room on the ground floor—a rather unfortunate experiment made by Geoffrey and Cecil when their enthusiasm for the stucco decorations in Venetian villas was at its highest—was turned from its former stiffness into a very cosy library dedicated to French literature. In the two last years, when B.B. was no longer able to sit at the dining-room table, he used this French library constantly for having his meals in a comfortable chair at a low table and for receiving his guests.

The other habit to which B.B. clung stubbornly was doing a certain amount of work each day. On our return from the Fontanelle he had still very ambitious plans and wanted to bring his *Decline and Recovery in the Visual Arts* to a conclusion. A long introduction and the first three chapters had been written before and during the war. But somehow the interruption had been too long and too harassing or new events and people absorbed him too much. He suffered acutely from not being able to pick up the broken threads.

A revision of the introduction and of an autobiographical sketch was all he managed to do at first. Later on he composed and published various essays and shorter articles and worked on the revision of one of his earliest books, the one on Lorenzo Lotto, but never felt any of this to be an equivalent to what he had failed to achieve. And even less importance did he attach to the diary he had started keeping in 1941,[9] probably because it cost him no effort to write it. Only what he had struggled hard to drag out of himself seemed to him really worthy to be published.

B.B.'s RENEWED ACTIVITY as an author brought also renewed and new contacts with publishers. Renewed as in the case of Kurt Wolff, who had published B.B.'s four early essays, *The Painters of the Italian Renaissance* in German translation twenty years earlier. Established in New York as the manager of Pantheon Books he brought out *Aesthetics and History* and *Sketch for a Self Portrait*.[1]

Among the new links first and foremost was the one with Electa Editrice and with its founder the Sienese painter Dario Neri and his partner, Paola Moroni Fumagalli. We used to call Neri the man of the five professions—painter, publisher, factory manager, landowner, and captain of the *Onda* (one of the *contrade*—sections of the town—taking part in the *Palio*). Our various visits to Siena after the war all took place under Neri's protection. It was he who arranged B.B.'s first visit to the *Palio* (in B.B.'s *Seeing and Knowing* there is a charming description of it) and who took him to Campriano, his country seat, where B.B. met the woodcutter Alberto Sani, whose natural talent for sculpture fascinated him so

---

9 All through 1942 B.B. kept a special diary about whatever he happened to be reading. It has appeared as *A Year's Reading for Fun* (New York: Alfred A. Knopf; 1960).
1 Both appeared a little later in England and Germany.

much that he wrote about him in "An Artist Out of His Time."[2]

In the spring of 1951 Max and Ray Schuster, introduced by John Walker, came to lunch, and in the course of conversation Max asked B.B. whether he had not something to give him. "Only my war diary," said B.B., "and nobody wants that." "Let me read it," said Max and took the manuscript to his hotel. Next day he rang me up and said he had hardly slept all night for being carried along from one diary entry to the next. "I will not only publish it, I will make a best seller of it." It appeared under the title *Rumour and Reflection* and brought B.B. more praise and recognition than any of his preceding publications with the exception only of the *Sketch for a Self Portrait*. The clamorous success of both these books surprised and grieved B.B. His purely art-historical publications seemed to him far more valuable although only a restricted group of readers had appreciated them. Max Schuster and his wife remained close friends of B.B.'s and came to see him whenever they happened to be in Europe.

Another publisher who became a friend and frequent visitor at I Tatti was Bela Horowitz, the creator of the Phaidon Press, introduced to B.B. by Kenneth Clark. With the help of the Samuel H. Kress Foundation he began by publishing B.B.'s four early essays in a richly illustrated edition. There followed the revised edition of the *Lotto* and finally an illustrated and revised edition of the lists. Horowitz was a dynamic man with a rare gift of persuasion and B.B., who felt at first doubtful about carrying out such an ambitious scheme—he was at the time almost eighty-eight—

---

2 With the exception of the war diary, published in Italian by Mondadori, Electa Editrice took care of all the new books and of several earlier ones, like the *Sassetta*, the *Lorenzo Lotto* and the *Drawings*. All the new essays appeared first in Italian and then in the original text.

ended by giving in. I would have liked to interfere because I foresaw what would happen. B.B.'s fast diminishing energy was sucked up to the last drop by this partly very interesting but partly also very tedious revision. But my opposition might have hurt B.B. by showing clearly that I doubted his capacity to do the job. A young Englishman, introduced to us by Rosamond Lehmann, had started frequenting the library and made so good an impression on B.B. that he invited him to be his assistant. Willy Mostyn Owen not only helped B.B. with the two first volumes, *The Venetian School*, but was a gay and vital presence in the house, also touchingly tender and solicitous with B.B. during the last difficult years.

Out of the publications grew satisfactory contacts with various translators, with Luisa Vertova and Arturo Loria, with Mario Praz, who did the Italian translation of *Aesthetics and History*, with Guglielmo Alberti, who translated the "war diary," and with Hanna Kiel. The latter, a gifted German writer established in Florence, became a friend and frequent visitor at I Tatti after the war. Her excellent mind and cultural preparation were highly appreciated by B.B. but above all he was grateful for her having turned several of his books into a language as fascinating to him as German was. He went so far as to say that he liked his own writing better in Hanna's German translations than in English.[3]

Every summer we spent at least two months at Casa al Dono and many of the old friends came to stay with us there. Some of them, like Addie Kahn, were a little put off by the rusticity of the appointments but most of them felt happy

---

[3] There was also Zezette Du Bos, the widow of Charlie Du Bos, who translated the *Sketch*, the *Sicilian Diary* and the *Caravaggio* into French but B.B. had no direct contacts with her in connection with her work nor with his colleague Jean Alazard (1886–1960), professor of fine arts at the University of Algiers, who translated the *Sassetta* and *Aesthetics and History*. The correspondence with both of them over difficult points in B.B.'s text was carried on by me.

in the old house. For longer stays came the Serlupis, Baroness Ritter, and of course Ralph Perry (Rachel, his wife, had died in 1933), as well as B.B.'s sisters Senda Abbott and Bessie Berenson. After Senda's death in 1953 Bessie spent every summer with us. She too loved the views, the woodland walks, the quiet evenings by the open fire.

Among visits from old friends I remember one from the Italo-American composer Mario Castelnuovo-Tedesco and his wife, accompanied by Arturo Loria, as particularly harmonious. They stayed on till late in the afternoon and Castelnuovo was inspired by the atmosphere of the old house to write down then and there the themes for the four tempi of a quartette. Years later he took them up again and completed the quartette whose first performance in Italy will take place in the great library at I Tatti.

And many new friends came, each in his way bringing B.B. the stimulation and the warm affection he needed. Having no very pronounced family feeling, B.B. was surprised and a little incredulous on discovering that several of the newcomers claimed relationship with him. Three women among them, each distinguished in her profession, became nevertheless real friends of his and instruments in his "orchestra." One was the journalist Judith Friedberg from Pittsburgh, another the psychoanalyst Francis Arkin from New York, the third the lawyer Freda Maltz from Johannesburg, South Africa. But in his last years B.B. invited and welcomed also younger members of his widespread cousinage of whose existence he was fully aware. Such was the case with Elizabeth Gates—sister of Bob Berenson—an unusually attractive and intelligent woman, married to a lawyer in Cleveland; with Joe Newmark, a relation of B.B.'s mother, established in Salem, Mass.; and with Richard Berenson, Lawrence Berenson's nephew, a Harvard graduate and classmate of President Nathan Pusey. The same Richard Berenson told me how in 1955 he had thought of presenting to B.B. for his ninetieth birthday a copy of *Rumour and Reflection* bearing the signatures of various distinguished personalities to which he had hoped to add also President Eisenhower's signature. A friend of his at the State Department had, however, told him that it would be impossible to get it in time for the birthday as it would take "several months to screen your cousin fully."

ONE OF THE CHARMING and clarifying symptoms of B.B.'s old age was his readiness to get rid of old "feuds." After a long period of coldness between him and the American art critic Frederick Mason Perkins they became again quite devoted to each other and met regularly during our frequent stays in Assisi. When B.B. spent his ninetieth birthday in Lady Berkeley's house, Perkins and Nesta De Robeck were the only guests invited for lunch.[4]

The same happened with Richard Offner when he returned to Florence after the war. B.B. forgot his old grudges and enjoyed his talks with Offner thoroughly. Offner was one of the last friends who saw B.B. (when B.B. could only show his agreement through nods and smiles but was unable to speak) a few weeks before his death.

It was Samuel Kress who persuaded B.B. to meet Count Contini Bonacossi, the famous art dealer and collector, again. As a consequence of some disagreeable experience he had not seen him for many years. From then on B.B. was on friendly terms with the whole Contini family but particularly with Contini's daughter Vittorina and her husband, the writer Roberto Papi.

Yet another "feud" with a happy end was the one with

---

[4] Nesta, a highly cultivated Englishwoman and an old friend of B.B. and Mary, had settled down in Assisi after her mother's death and divided her time between writing good books and doing good works.

the Cliffords, Henry and Esther, the owners of the Villa Capponi in Arcetri. The feud was based on some silly gossip, taken too seriously and all the more incomprehensible as there were family ties between Mary and Esther Clifford. By good luck one of the Clifford boys married one of the daughters of Hester Pickman, for whom B.B. had the greatest affection, and out of this event grew a complete clarification of the trouble.

Finally there was the reunion with Roberto Longhi, of whom B.B. had seen a lot before the First World War. Then something went wrong. Perhaps Mary's heavy-handed criticism of Longhi's translation of B.B.'s early essays enraged the proud and sensitive young man. B.B. went on considering him the most gifted among Italian art critics and historians but did not see him again until in 1956, when Longhi wrote the very fine oration for the honorary degree offered to B.B. by the University of Florence. With the rector and other colleagues Longhi came up to present it to B.B. and they met very naturally and cordially like old friends.

BETWEEN 1946 AND 1957 we took a number of trips, most of them inside Italy and only a few beyond its frontiers. At first we travelled alone, then Emma Melani—who since 1940 when she had been a housemaid at I Tatti had become B.B.'s valet-maid—began to accompany us. A formidable woman, very intelligent and capable, proud and self-righteous in an almost Calvinistic and somehow un-Italian way. She made a full career out of her taking care of B.B. and looked after every detail of his toilet and bodily well-being with jealous and meticulous efficiency. B.B. made a special study of her character and got great fun out of his discussions with her and out of her sharp and forthright way of measuring and summing up his friends and acquaintances. It would need the genius of a Proust to paint her portrait.

Objects of Emma's disapproval were those of our intimates who dared to burst into B.B.'s bedroom early in the morning to have a chat with him. Particularly Derek Hill, the English painter who occupied the Villino for several years and became like a member of the household, had this, for her, deplorable habit. Being an early riser he enjoyed these morning chats and so did B.B., but Emma, interrupted in her complicated ministrations, took a dim view of them.

When we began to take Emma along on our trips she was full of contempt for our sight-seeing and refused categorically to take any interest in it. "My work," she said haughtily, "is all I care for." Gently and persistently B.B. got her to change her mind and to become keen not only on looking at works of art or buildings but at nature itself, sunsets, storms, cloud formations, effects of light.

FREQUENTLY OUR TRIPS were combined with visits to friends. We returned to the Gazzada, Don Guido's villa near Varese, and were taken by him to see the newly discovered seventh-century frescoes at Castel Seprio. Several years older than B.B. he too was astonishingly active and when he saw B.B. climb up a shaky ladder to look closer at the frescoes nothing would keep him from achieving the same stunt. Several times on our way to and from Genoa and Turin we stayed with Percy Lubbock, who after Lady Sybil's death in 1944 had returned to the house built for them by Cecil Pinsent on an olive-grown promontory near Lerici. In 1949 on our way to Naples we spent two delightful days with Laurance and Isabel Roberts (the new director of the American Acamedy in Rome) at the Villa Aurelia. Clotilde Marghieri received us in 1949 in her white terraced house at the foot of Vesuvius, where B.B. felt as if he was inside a Pompeiian landscape. Again and again we stayed with Lady Berkeley—born Lowell, from Boston—in the pilgrim's hostel of San Lorenzo at the top of Assisi; it had been transformed by Cecil Pinsent into a very original house. Incomparable was the view from it on the south side over the roofs and bell towers of Assisi to the valley of the Tiber and on the north side to the Gentile da Fabriano-like foothills of the Apennines.

In Tuscany there was Marilù Stucchi, the owner of the former Vallombrosan Convent of Coltibuono, on the heights of the Chianti, with whom we spent enchanting summer days. On one side of it a wide view over the upper valley of the Arno to the bold profile of the Prato Magno, on the other a sunken rose-garden surrounded by *pergolate* of vines against the dark background of the forest.

Finally there was the Veneto and in it Freya Stark's house at Asolo and Marina Volpi's Palladian villa of Maser. B.B. loved both them and their owners dearly.

His last trip abroad he took in his ninetieth year to stay with the other Volpi sister, Anna Maria Cicogna, in her Turkish villa on the outskirts of Tripoli. She made it possible for him to spend a couple of days in the superintendent's house at Leptis Magna and to visit the excavations in the most leisurely way.

Inside Italy our last journey took us in 1957 to Naples, where B.B. was anxious to see the new museum in the palace of Capodimonte. It began rather inauspiciously, for B.B. reacted badly to the air conditioning in our hotel and spent several days in bed with a bad chill. Then he recovered but felt too tired to attempt the endless walk through all those rooms. Bruno Molaioli, whom we had first met as young *ispettore* in Fabriano in 1927 and who is now our director general of fine arts, was then superintendent of fine arts in Naples and responsible for the installation of the new museum. He arranged to have a wheelchair at B.B.'s disposal and in that way he was able to see everything comfortably.

When we were stopping over in Rome, an unusual

visitor came to lunch with us at the Hotel Eden, the Russian Byzantinist Victor Lazareff. We had met him more than thirty years earlier in Munich as an eager young scholar rapturously enjoying his first glimpse of Western art treasures. He was now professor at the University of Moscow and an important member of the Russian arts council. We found him just as spontaneous and easy to talk to as before. He promised B.B. to get his *Italian Painters of the Renaissance* translated into Russian and has kept his word. It appeared in a richly illustrated edition, translated under Lazareff's supervision by one of his pupils.

On our way home we spent B.B.'s ninety-second birthday at Assisi in Molly Berkeley's house, and driving from Assisi to Florence we stopped at Monterchi to see Piero's *Madonna del Parto* again. It was a glorious day in June and B.B. seemed so much his own self, so ecstatic in his enjoyment of the landscape, of the monumental Madonna in the small cemetery chapel, of the sturdy curtain-pulling angels that I began making plans for other excursions. The only one we took was to the Belvedere Fortress on the Costa San Giorgio to see the exhibition of detached frescoes. Ugo Procacci and other friends from the *Soprintendenza* were there to receive us and were amazed at the agility with which B.B. climbed up and down stairs, so keen was his interest in the frescoes. Perhaps most of all he enjoyed the light of a radiant October day and the view of Florence against the long extended profile of the hills. It was to be his last sight-seeing expedition.

THE EXTRACTS from B.B.'s diaries[5] show clearly how much he suffered from the fear of getting too tired, from sadness over his loss of memory, over his failing eyesight and hearing and other infirmities. His almost uncanny awareness

[5] *Sunset and Twilight* (New York: Harcourt, Brace & World; 1963).

of his diminishing strength and capacities made his old age more difficult than it perhaps appeared to those who saw him only in animated conversation with his visitors and, as it were, "cranked up." Again and again I entreated him to let himself go, to give up any kind of concentrated work, to just enjoy his gift for looking at art and nature, for getting the best out of his contacts with other human beings. It was of no avail. Something stronger than any dictates of reason or prudence seemed to drive him on, not only to work but to worry desperately over world events. Often his prophetic vision of future political and social developments was astonishing but who would have heeded it? B.B. had no political influence and tended anyway to look so far ahead that many of his utterances would have seemed absurd and utopian to practical politicians.

What also threw a shadow on his last years was the uncertain future of I Tatti. Before the war he was convinced that the first fellowships could be created out of his endowment of the property. After the war he had to realize that between the depreciation of the dollar and the rise of prices in Italy the income from the endowment would cover only the expense of running house, library, and garden. Although he had this problem constantly on his mind he was quite unprepared for the blow which struck him in 1952 when he heard from Lawrence Berenson that Harvard was not going to accept his gift. As usual he reacted also physically to the moral shock and had a serious upset. Many of his friends[5] came to the rescue and defended his cause so well that finally the acceptance was confirmed on the understanding that funds for scholarships would eventually be raised from other

---

[5] Particularly Lawrence Berenson himself, but also the Fogg Museum group, John Coolidge, Sidney Freedberg, and Agnes Mongan, Philip Hofer from the Houghton Library, Mason Hammond, the professor of classics at Harvard, and Francis Taylor, then director of the Metropolitan Museum.

sources. From then on relations with Harvard became very friendly. One of the chief legal advisers of the corporation, Keith Kane, and also the dean of the Faculty of Arts and Sciences, McGeorge Bundy, came to see B.B. who had very satisfactory talks with both of them. Nevertheless he did not share the optimism of those who assured him that "money would just flow in." The difficulty encountered by the Harvard Corporation ever since B.B.'s death in trying to raise funds for I Tatti has proved how right he was in his scepticism. Sometimes while discussing his programme for I Tatti with friends who took a lively interest in the whole problem —like for instance Ned Bayne of the Field University Service—he would stop and say: "Why do I go on making plans for the future? One cannot project one's own personality beyond the grave as Isabella Gardner and others have tried to do. Everything changes, currents of taste, interests, methods of study. One must trust those who follow us to make the best possible decisions or at any rate the least bad ones."

B.B. WAS CONSTANTLY AWARE of death and its threat. In his diary he speaks of his never saying good-bye to a friend without fearing that it might be for the last time. Most of his contemporaries or near-contemporaries died before him and he felt their loss particularly in the case of faithful correspondents like Lady Colefax, Addie Kahn, or Daisy Chanler, but not as keenly as the disappearance of younger friends. Perhaps because it was a question not only of a personal loss but of despair over the blindness of fate, the wastefulness of nature, in tearing them away too early from their active lives. Thus he was deeply grieved by the death of Pietro Pancrazi, of Delfino Cinelli, of Dario Neri, of Bela Horowitz, but particularly of Arturo Loria. Arturo understood B.B.'s temperament to perfection and never took his paradoxical utterances too seriously. When an interesting guest appeared Arturo was invariably summoned to meet him. And when he began translating B.B.'s *Sketch* and a number of articles they met constantly to discuss fine points of interpretation. Another more recent friend whose sudden disappearance B.B. felt as a great loss was Francis Taylor.[6] Half a year before his death he had spent a week at I Tatti, having long conversations with B.B. to be used for an article in *The Atlantic*.

But B.B. was not a bit morbid or apprehensive about his own death. Twice he came very near dying during the last years, when he was precipitated down a steep ravine in 1954 and when he fell desperately ill from some sort of food poisoning in 1955. He speaks of both these warnings in his diary. He kept absolutely serene and detached, just as when in April 1958 his relatively normal and active life was changed from one day to the other into an invalid's existence. Occasionally the pains in his back made him yell but he never complained and accepted his lot very quietly.

At first I was unable to realize that this meant the end and went on counting firmly on one of his miraculous recoveries. But slowly the light flickered down even if the flame was now and then steadier. There were days when his memory functioned perfectly, when his interest in books and events and people was revived. On other days, aware of a certain confusion in his mind, he showed this awareness by his complete silence and by an expression of deep sadness in his eyes. He still wanted to enjoy the garden either by taking a few steps himself or by just sitting out of doors on sunny days. And above all he liked to walk or to be carried through the libraries.

During his two last summers at Casa al Dono he was

---

[6] Francis Henry Taylor (1903–57), director of the Fine Arts Museum, Worcester, 1931–40; director of the Metropolitan Museum, New York, 1940–55. From 1955 until his death he was again director of the Fine Arts Museum, Worcester.

able to sit outside almost every day for a few hours, generally in the small hut with the view he loved so much down to the valley of the Arno and to the hills beyond Florence. In the last summer, 1959, he felt a little spurt of energy for work and looked each day for as long as his strength allowed it at reproductions of the principal Florentine Renaissance paintings. Aware of his growing incapacity to make himself understood because of bad swellings in his mouth he expressed his delight and admiration more with gestures than with words. He still enjoyed the early morning light, the swish of the wind in the pine trees, the glorious spectacle of the sunset. Early in September 1959, a month before his death, we discovered the new moon in an apple-green sky and his nurse carried him in her arms like a small child to his bedroom window. With a wistful smile he greeted the silvery shape for the last time.

Casa al Dono and San Martino a Mensola
August 1960–November 1964

APPENDIX

A Month with the Paratroopers
in the Front Line

THIS IS AN ACCOUNT of what happened during the month of August 1944 at the Villa delle Fontanelle in Careggi, about three miles from the centre of Florence.

After the armistice of 1943, B.B. was advised to leave his home, Villa I Tatti, and accepted the invitation of the Marchese Filippo Serlupi Crescenzi to his villa in Careggi. Serlupi, being minister to the Holy See from the Republic of San Marino, counted on his diplomatic rights being respected by both Republican Fascists and Nazis.

Saturday, July 29th 1944
A fairly normal day so far, except for the nuisance of being left without water in the pipes, and that means having to fetch every drop from a well in the garden. Opposite to us the woods above Scandicci have been set on fire, probably through air bombardments, and we can see the flames leaping from one pine to the other. From beyond the hills, in the Val di Pesa an almost incessant rumble of artillery fire can be heard.

In the afternoon my nephew turns up and gives us a detailed account of the latest happenings at I Tatti. The officers of the armoured car commando who have occupied the house last week are behaving fairly decently and have left the top floor to Mary, her nurses, and my people. Whether they mean to build up defensive positions on the hills above the house is not yet known. All the best things, also the pictures that were still left in the house, have been taken to my sister's apartment in Borgo San

Jacopo, between the Ponte Vecchio and the Santa Trinità bridges, and walled up there. It is an old tower with walls two meters thick and should be a good shelter even if the Germans decide to defend the bridges. The new town commandant, a colonel of the paratroopers, is apparently a particularly rough customer. He is reported to have said that there was no reason for respecting Florence any more than Smolensk, that it would be ridiculous to have any scruples on account of its art treasures and monuments, and that the Italians will have to produce another Michelangelo or something of that sort to build up their town again.

Just as we are discussing all this, the B.B.C. announces General Alexander's proclamation to the Florentines, urging them to defend their bridges and to prevent the destruction of all vitally important installations. As the waterworks and almost all the steam mills have already been destroyed, these recommendations sound a little comical. With what should this peaceful, unarmed, and not particularly courageous people prevent such military measures? Our host assures us that the proclamation will have very evil consequences and furnish the *Wehrmacht* with a good excuse for declaring Florence no longer an "open city." I should like to know in what exactly their respect for the "open city" has consisted? In letting their army transports cross the city following the broad boulevards instead of the narrow streets of the inner city and in placing important commandos in the suburbs instead of in the centre of the town? A grim comedy.

No sooner has my nephew left than we hear that an army order has been plastered up all over the town commanding the complete evacuation of the quarters along the river. The order says that this measure must be taken because the enemy has not made his intention of respecting the "open city" clear enough. Was his careful limiting of himself to a few air raids on the periphery not a sufficiently clear declaration?

The evening passes in the usual way. We sit on the terrace and watch the lightning flashes of the shell fire beyond San Casciano and discuss the possibility of the Allies preferring an encircling movement to a frontal attack on the town. It makes me think of the first act of Goethe's *Egmont*, where the bewilderment of peaceful burghers is described. While listening to accounts of the incomprehensible forward and backward moves of the approaching war, they can think of only one thing: "Will it be our turn next?"

At 11 P.M. the electric current fails and does not return. Henceforth only rumours and gossip will reach us.

Sunday, July 30th

Very sad accounts from town of the processions of wretched people pushing their few belongings and their old and sick people in little handcarts, of the endless queues of others carrying *fiaschi* and bottles to wherever the fountains are still running. The chauffeur, who has been to town, has also had a look at my sister's apartment and has found my nephew securing the main entrance as hermetically as possible.

Here everybody is busy preparing candlesticks and small oil lamps for the evening. Our hostess, who is an expert electrician and does all her repairs herself, thinks that it may take at least six months to repair such a radical destruction as this one is likely to be.

In the evening the spectacle is magnificent. The profile of the whole range of hills to the south of the town lit up by dazzling flashes of light.

Monday, July 31st

A strangely quiet day. Nothing but the shrill voice of the cicadas to be heard, and all around us the peaceful activities of the *contadini* among the ripening figs and tomatoes and grapes.

Tuesday, August 1st

Optimistic rumours about an Allied change of strategy which would mean crossing the river to the north and south of Florence. I hope the rumours are not merely wishful thinking.

In the evening huge fires have broken out in the plain to our right and the discussions as to which buildings are burning become very heated. In any case it is a fascinating spectacle and the tall columns of smoke lit up from below remind B.B. of

certain late and very dramatic Altdorfers, particularly in the
St. Florian series.

In the night we hear for the first time sharp detonations
which must come from a new German defense line somewhere
behind us.

Wednesday, August 2d

A messenger from Quarto (the villa on the slopes of the Monte
Morello belonging to Baroness Ritter, our host's mother-in-law)
brings the news that German officers have inspected the house
early this morning and have announced their intention of occupying it in full force tonight when the whole German front is going
to move to this side of Florence. So far at Quarto only the out-
houses had been occupied off and on, the villa itself being under
the protection of the German fine arts commission. Various
families of refugees live in it while the Baroness herself has preferred joining her daughter's household. A considerable part of
the I Tatti library and the whole photograph collection are
stored away in it, also works of art belonging to other people.
The baroness and I decide to walk over to Quarto at once and
find out what has really happened. All along our way people seem
alarmed and anxious, although nobody has had any definite
orders to quit their houses. The bridge over the Terzolle is being
guarded by two young soldiers. "Have you heard anything of the
front being moved to this side?" "No, we have heard nothing, but
if the Tommy has decided to move his front artillery, preparation
may start any minute." That does not sound very reassuring. We
overtake a fat man pushing a handcart loaded with fruit and
vegetables up the hill. He recognizes the baroness and greets her
most cordially. "As a boy I started earning my living by pushing
handcarts, and here I am at it again." Then he tells us about
all the cattle and provisions carried away in his neighbourhood
by the Germans and about his wife's despair over their losses.
"But I tell her, never mind, let them take whatever they want
if only our lives are safe (*che prendano quello che vogliono
purchè sia salva la pelle*)."

At the main entrance the roomy porter's lodge is occupied
by a German supply unit. A group of soldiers is sitting under the

ilexes, one of them busy at a sewing machine, the others smoking, chatting, eating. All are in shorts with naked sunburnt torsos. An accordion is being played in the house. We ask for the N.C.O. and are led into the house, where we find him busy spreading an astonishing amount of butter on a huge slice of bread. On the wall behind him I see Hitler's proclamation to the *Wehrmacht* after the recent attempt on his life. It speaks of the abominable and criminal "inner" enemy and of the unshakable *Treue* of the German soldier. We ask the N.C.O. whether he knows anything about the moving-over of the front. No, he does not. "A paratrooper officer drove past this morning, but he does not belong to our division and we did not bother about him." We walk on through the park and as we draw nearer to the large three-storied building we seem to hear a humming in it as in a beehive. All the refugees are in a state of alarm, run about, pack their things, ask for advice and help. Jewish friends of the baroness who have been in hiding here ever since last autumn and who understand German, seem more confident and assure us that no order for integral occupation has been given yet. Nevertheless the baroness decides to have some of the most valuable things moved down to the cellar. Just as she starts operations, a camouflaged German car drives up and four men get out of it, an officer with sharp bony features, a young ensign, and two stout N.C.O.'s with huge red faces. They are all of them very sunburnt, and in their camouflaged outfits and round helmets have something of colossal caterpillars about them. The officer tells me in a rather sharp but not discourteous voice that this very night the front will be moved back to this line, that big guns will be placed on the terrace, that he forces nobody to go away, but that it would be highly advisable for all civilians to clear out, as there is no telling where and whom the enemy guns may hit. All property will be scrupulously respected. He makes out a list of the rooms they require, and we start showing them all those available, but notice very soon that they do not pay the slightest attention to us. They go wherever it pleases them, rattle the handles of locked doors, and finally land in the apartment of the Jewish family, which, being the baroness's own and very attractive, meets with their fullest approval. One of the stout N.C.O.'s hangs his camouflaged coat over one of the charming eighteenth-century easy chairs as if to establish his right of residence. Meanwhile the young ensign falls in love with the Jewish baby, catches it up in his arms, makes it dance about, and his companions watch him benevolently and say: "Such a fine baby of your own would suit you, wouldn't it, Jochen?" Not a shadow of suspicion as to the baby's race.

The stout one is very ready to talk and tells me that in their last night quarters, at Monte Gufoni, on the road from Volterra, there were the most marvellous pictures by Rubens and by other great masters and that it broke his heart not to be able to take them along and to save them. "Now they are lost to Italy," he says, "for the Americans will of course sell them abroad." From this he goes on to complain about the abominable betrayal of the Italians. They are responsible for everything, the defeat in North Africa, the loss of Stalingrad. He also complains bitterly about the civilian population and their hostile attitude to the *Wehrmacht*. "Even in Russia the people have been friendlier to us than here. Would you believe it, last summer in Apulia they even resented our habit of going about clad only in shorts and protested against it." He is very much puzzled when I explain to him that in southern Italy men are very strict about their womenfolk and consider half-naked males a highly improper spectacle for them. The young ensign with the baby on his arm chimes in with contemptuous remarks about the Italian youth. "Think of the fighting spirit of our youngsters, while these are only good for walking about the streets and smoking." "Let us see who will be better off in the end," I say and, looking into his handsome young face, I think of the criminal way in which the German youth is being sacrificed. There are many other things I would like to say, but what is the use of starting up a discussion with these men, stuffed with propaganda like Strassburger geese. The only thing for me is to keep them in a good mood. The stout one gets very eloquent on the question of the partisans. "Even last night while crossing the city two fine German soldiers have been shot by these bandits. Who can blame us for taking the severest retaliatory measures?" Finally he mentions the Allied troops approaching Florence and says that we need not be afraid of them. According to him they are mostly New Zealanders and very decent people.

Meanwhile our Jewish friends have finished loading a little handcart with their belongings, and I watch them as they leave the house—these wealthy and until recently highly privileged people, the father pushing the handcart, the mother the perambulator with the baby, and the grandmother holding the little girl by the hand, not knowing yet where they are going to spend the night. Likewise the other refugees are leaving and dragging their belongings with them. One old woman from the south of Italy gives me an account of all she has been through already and insists on pulling the photo of a son fallen at the front out of her bag.

There is nothing more we can do here, and we also start on our walk home, leaving the house to its new occupants. How stately it looks in the late afternoon light with the statues on the balustrade of the terrace and all the oleander bushes in flower. Shall we see it again unchanged?

Thursday, August 3d
Earsplitting noises during the night from the German guns placed somewhere behind us. The greater part of the day is spent in assembling all the art treasures in the house—among them B.B.'s finest pictures—and placing them, protected by pillows and blankets, in the safest corner of the library. In the afternoon we hear that a state of emergency has been imposed on the town of Florence, which means that civilians are not allowed to leave their houses.

Friday, August 4th
Much excitement during the last twenty-four hours. Yesterday at 11 P.M. the inhabitants of Careggi, a little group of houses directly below us, were ordered out of their homes at a moment's notice by a German mine-laying unit. As many as possible were taken into the porter's lodge and the peasant's and gardener's houses inside this property. To admit them the gate had been opened, and presently German soldiers began to troop in by twos and

threes at a time. They seemed to be completely worn out, searching for their units and begging for a night's shelter. "If you can show us where to stretch out, do it quickly, for soon the morning will dawn and we'll have to move on." I try to explain to one of them that this is papal property (which seems to me easier for them to understand than the rigmarole about diplomatic rights), and he gets perfectly furious and uses one of the coarsest swearwords to express his contempt for the Holy Father. "He has betrayed us, has let the Allies enter the city while we had loyally and honestly respected the terms agreed upon." How deeply rooted this belief in their own traditional honesty and fidelity seems to be in most Germans, like a persistent *Wunschbild* of themselves.

At 2 A.M. I am waked up because it appears that paratroopers want to occupy the Belvedere villa (also the property of our hosts) and mean to place their machine guns there.

In the bright moonlight our host and I hurry through the olive groves to the Belvedere, where we find on the terrace two sleepy and exhausted-looking soldiers with childlike features and an anxious group of peasants trying to make out what it is they want. Again I try to explain why this property cannot be occupied, but with small success. They say that they have their orders but that they will report what I say to their superiors. As we walk back, terrific detonations in the direction of Florence. Could they already be blowing up the bridges?

At 6.30, second alarm. The peasants from the Belvedere report that a unit of paratroopers has appeared and evidently means to prepare machine gun positions. On getting there I have to contend with a very disagreeable and Slavic-looking N.C.O. He scorns the idea of respecting an important and exposed piece of ground for some civilian reason and thus allowing the "Tommy" to crash into it with his armoured cars. But finally he gives in to the point of taking me to his immediate superior, a lieutenant who has occupied the Villa Montanina on the height above us. As we walk up towards it, I look down on the city of Florence with its towers and cupolas framed by the hills of San Miniato, Poggio Imperiale, and Bellosguardo. Florence looks unchanged. Unusual and sinister are the immense columns of greyish black smoke rising up from various parts of the town into the clear morning sky.

The N.C.O. walking beside me rages against the Italian population and their unbelievably hostile attitude to the German troops. In the garden of the Villa Montanina, utter confusion and squalor. Everywhere paratroopers eating, sleeping, shaving, machine guns, soldiers' kits, heaps of refuse. Same disorder inside the house. The owner and his womenfolk huddling together in one corner. The C.O. is inspecting the new positions and we are told to wait. The N.C.O. keeps up the conversation and, cursing the Allies, insists on their having been the first to use air bombardments. "What about your air raids in Poland?" "Curse the Poles! They deserve a far worse treatment than they got." At last we get hold of the lieutenant, a tall, youngish man with a pleasant face, grey wistful eyes, and a soft voice. He listens very politely to what I have to say and promises to report it to his superiors. On our way home through the *podere*, one of our peasant women comes running to meet us with her arms lifted up to heaven like an antique mourner. "What has happened?" "They have come to the villa and they mean to set up their machine guns on the terrace." Yes, there they are, in a group around the chapel, waiting for further orders, unpleasant and sullen-looking fellows. My first impulse is to run into the house and to entreat our hostess to have whatever she can manage prepared for them— coffee, milk, bread and jam. She is willing and understands how important it is to get them into the best possible mood. On hearing the sound of their own language and an invitation to breakfast, the change is immediate. The sullen faces break into smiles and they follow me readily to the kitchen steps. But, alas, I see a second group crossing the terrace at the further end and turning into the *pergolata* armed with spades and shovels. Running after them, I ask where their C.O. is. "He is here, just ahead of us." A small man stops and turns around. I look into a tired, kindly face. He listens to me with a sad smile and shakes his head. "We are here on the foremost front line; rights and privileges have no longer any meaning. This is a most important position for us and we need the house for ourselves." On my insisting, he shrugs his shoulders and says that he has to follow his orders, but that nothing prevents my going to speak to his superiors, and that an N.C.O. who has anyway to take a message there could accompany me.

After seeing ourselves in my mind's eye chased out of the house and trudging along the highroad in search of another shelter, I gather new hope and run upstairs to get ready and to see how B.B. is getting along. I find him fully dressed, aware of what is going on, and prepared for the worst. In spite of my middle-aged appearance I feel that it is important when negotiating with men to make the best possible impression, and so decide to put on my freshest summer dress and my best high-heeled white sandals. A young N.C.O. is already waiting for me, and we walk down to the lower gate. "Where is the car?" He grins. "No car. We have to foot it." "How far?" "About three kilometers." Cursing my elegant sandals and wishing I had solid shoes on my feet, I follow him first along the highroad and then up into the hills. The N.C.O. seems a nice boy, and I try to coax world news out of him by telling him how completely cut off we are since we lost our electricity. He lets out a stream of propaganda: no Russian will ever put his foot on German ground; the south of England is being wiped out by the new weapons; the losses of the Allies in France are beyond all description; the collapse of the "Tommy" is near at hand; new secret weapons will soon come into use.

The path along the dried up Terzolle is enchanting: banks of brownish rock in layers and small cypresses growing out of them, the real Benozzo Gozzoli landscape. We meet a few scared civilians dragging along their household goods. On reaching the village a group of women stops me to ask whether it is safe for them to stay or whether they had better run away. The red wire of the field telephone which has been accompanying us all the way now turns off into the houses. It makes me shudder to look at it and to think of all those shot in the occupied countries as reprisal for the cutting of it. Paratroopers everywhere in various occupations. The N.C.O. leads me through a rustic wineshop into a horribly dirty kitchen filled with soldiers, and from there into a scantily furnished room where two officers are busy writing, a young captain and an elderly lieutenant. They do not look very promising. The captain especially has a nasty wolfish expression, the ideal *Boche*. My appeal meets with a very curt and sneering reception. "We are not lawyers and know nothing of such diplomatic rights. When a defensive line has been agreed upon, there is no further change possible." They spread out a map, a marvellously detailed one, on which I can recognize the Fontanelle and the outline of the terrace perfectly, and they point out to me the machine gun positions running all along it. "The utmost concession we could make would be to leave the house unoccupied, but the machine gun emplacements have to stay where they are." I go on arguing my point, tell them that the German consul himself has told our host how correct the *Wehrmacht* invariably is about all diplomatic privileges, remind them that even the "Reds" have respected them. I describe the hopeless situation of the refugees at the Fontanelle, to whom our host, the minister, has offered a shelter exactly because he knew he could count on his privileges. "Let me appeal to your sense of humanity," I say to the captain. He lets out a shrill laugh. "That is asking too much after five years of war!" Yet they gradually seem to get a little milder, ask me how I happen to speak such faultless German, advise me not to tell the "Tommy" that my mother was Baltic-German. Finally they give in to my entreaties and call up their *Divisionskommando*. The connection established, I hear the lieutenant asking: "*Herr Oberstleutnant,* have you ever heard anything about extraterritorial rights?" Evidently the *Oberstleutnant* does know something about it, and a long conversation follows. The captain decides that he will inspect the positions himself in the afternoon and orders a car to drive me back.

At the Fontanelle I find the paratroopers spread out over the whole length of the terrace and the C.O. seated under the loggia with the field telephone beside him. All the entrances to the house except the kitchen door are hermetically closed, the window shutters equally, and on the ground floor I find B.B., our hosts, and our fellow refugees by the light of oil lamps anxiously waiting for my return. We spend the next hours in great uncertainty, listening to the telephone conversations of the C.O. from behind the closed blinds, trying to keep him well disposed towards us by having his and the N.C.O.'s lunch prepared in the kitchen and by sending him coffee and cigarettes. At last the captain appears, and I am requested to show him the extent of this property by walking around with him. He interrupts the inspection to walk up to one of his men who, leaning against the parapet, looks over with his fieldglass to the other side of the Arno where a bit of the Via Senese running down from San Gaggio to the Porta Romana can be made out even with the naked eye. "How many have you counted?" "*Zu Befehl,* fourteen vehicles in ten minutes." The Allies driving into Florence! I must hold myself in not to show how thrilled I am.

There follows another long conversation with the *Divisionskommando*. I hear him insisting again on the advisability of keeping the important position along the terrace while allowing us to stay on in the house. But luckily the superior officer seems to be of a different opinion, for shortly afterwards the captain has me called out again, says that they will take up their positions on the hill above us and outside this property, and orders both flags, the San Marino and the papal one, to be run up on the tower. Unspeakably relieved, we see them roll up their telephone wires and pack their kits just as the sultry afternoon unloads itself in a storm. As the rain lets up, they go, and we see them climb up the path to the wooded heights above us in their caterpillar outfit. Only one of them, a very nice-looking Bavarian N.C.O., has made friends with the servants and prefers spending the evening in the kitchen.

Like moles we crawl out of the dark house to enjoy our freedom and the air, so deliciously cool after the storm. Besides empty tins and other refuse the terrace is strewn with type-written leaflets, which turn out to be the Army news sheets. Their content corresponds exactly with the information gathered by me from the young N.C.O. Added to it is the news that the Allies have already heavily bombarded the centre of the open city of Florence and that the leaning tower of Pisa has been wantonly destroyed by them.

In spite of the rain dense columns of smoke are still rising up from the town.

A messenger from Quarto brings good news. No heavy artillery has been placed there after all, and the officers we saw there are leaving. They seem to have behaved fairly decently inside the house, but they have amused themselves with pushing statues and lemon pots from their pedestals in the garden.

In the evening we hear for the first time the half whining, half whistling sound of Allied shells passing overhead and the burst of the explosions in the hills behind us.

Saturday, August 5th
Last night the shelling became so continuous and alarmingly near that our hosts called us and made us lie down on improvised couches in the big library on the ground floor. In the morning the ominous noises, redoubled by the echo from all the hills around, stopped, and we were able to return to our rooms.

The peasant woman from the Belvedere reports that the paratroopers not only make no sign of going away but are threatening to occupy the whole house. I decide to walk back with her, and we find them all assembled in the kitchen. The Slavic-looking N.C.O. is in the worst possible disposition towards me in particular and towards the Italian population in general. In search of the tall lieutenant I have the good luck to find him. He is full of excuses and says that they should already have moved and will do so shortly. They depart in the afternoon, and a few minutes later an Allied shell bursts in the courtyard of the Belvedere, fortunately killing only a few rabbits. Evidently the incessant coming and going of German soldiers has not escaped the vigilant eye of the "Tommy."

Two friends of our hosts, husband and wife, have turned up to ask for shelter after spending the night in a ditch. Their fine villa on the Via Bolognese was occupied until a few days ago by a perfectly well-behaved German unit. Yesterday paratroopers appeared who looked so nasty and took up such a threatening attitude that they decided to clear out, all the more so as the husband is young enough to be carried away by the Germans in one of their round-ups.

Sunday, August 6th
Another night spent partly in our rooms and partly in the library. In the morning the Bavarian N.C.O. appears hoping for some

breakfast and for a friendly chat. He gets both and I find him very reasonable, even inclined to speak with sympathy for and understanding of the Italians and the evil plight they are in. "It is the consequence of their stupid politics last year." "But after the fall of Tunis, with or without the armistice Italy was bound to get into a very difficult position." He keeps quiet for a bit and then says, "Badoglio's plan was not so stupid after all, only he had no power to carry it out." He admits that the worst sufferings are imposed on the Italians by their so-called "ally," who systematically destroys all their most necessary installations. "We have learned that from the Russians. Nothing must be left to the enemy that might be useful to him in carrying on the war." He recommends the dark windowless corridors and a small stack room at the back of the house as good shelters, not the library, which has too many windows and might be hit by splinters from the side. A new secret weapon, he says, in in use since yesterday on the Eastern front.

Monday, August 7th

A relatively quiet after a noisy night. A young police official who is at our host's disposition manages to get a pass for the town from the officer commanding the mine-laying unit at Careggi. He comes back with a rather confused report of the destruction, which he himself has not seen. All the bridges except the Ponte Vecchio are blown up, as well as many houses on both sides of the Ponte Vecchio so as to prevent any passage of troops. He also brings a letter from the secretary of the cardinal archbishop to our host in which he tells of a conference between himself, the Swiss consul, representatives of the *Prefettura* and *Questura,* and the colonel commanding the town, in consequence of which the desperate situation of the civilian population has become a little easier. At least the women are allowed to go out at certain hours to fetch water and buy a little food, some essential shops can be kept open, and one truck for the transport of the dead is allowed to circulate. A deputation sent over to the south side of the river is asking the Allied command to mend the water pipes as quickly as possible.

334

A bad report from Quarto. One group of soldiers after the other are forcing their way into the house, rummaging about, and creating such infernal disorder that it is difficult to make out what has and what has not been carried away by them. Our host prepares a letter to the *Divisionskommandant* in which, while thanking him for having respected the extraterritorial rights of this property, he begs him to have the looting of Quarto stopped, especially in consideration of the fact that it should be under the protection of the *Denkmal Schutz*. After translating this perfection of diplomatic wording, I take it to the end of the *pergola* to where the path goes up to the first German position, and give a call. A young soldier comes running down and promises to have it delivered.

Tuesday, August 8th
A ghastly night spent by B.B. and me in two small rooms in the servants' quarter looking out to the back and therefore safer than our own front rooms. The crashes seem so close that again and again I get up to look out, wondering whether the Carmelite convent near us has already been hit. But no, there it is quite undamaged in the bright moonlight, with the beautiful spreading umbrella pine before it, the image of peace. In the early morning I go down to see how the others have fared and find them very much alarmed and not unreasonably so, for the children's little wooden dollhouse in the garden at perhaps fifty metres distance from us has been shot into smithereens. Garden and terrace are full of splinters from it. Our hosts decide to send us all away to Quarto, where there are vast cellars to take shelter in, while they will remain here to guard the house. B.B., however, when I take this message to him, refuses categorically to move and says that he feels perfectly fatalistic about whatever may happen. I am delighted, for at least by staying here I may be of some service owing to my knowledge of German and may repay in a small measure some of our debt of gratitude. More than eleven months have gone by since we took refuge here, and had B.B. been their own close relation, our hosts could not have looked after him in a more considerate and affectionate way.

335

In less than half an hour everything is ready and the little procession starts out. The dear old Irish nanny, Baroness Ritter, the countess with her baby, and the two daughters of the house. The elder one with the baby on her arm seems delighted: any novelty brings new life into her beautiful face. The younger one's eyes are red from weeping over the separation from parents and home.

A little later our hostess and I decide to walk up to the Salvini villa just above us by a private path through the wood. Suddenly we find ourselves confronted by the barrel of a machine gun posted behind the hedge surrounding this property. The paratrooper serving it recognizes us and allows us to pass. Along the path many trees have already been hit and damaged by shelling. The surroundings of the house look dismally dirty and neglected. It was already occupied by Germans some time ago, but as the owner speaks German, he has been allowed to stay. We find him, his wife, his invalid mother, and a nursing sister huddled together in a corridor on the north side of the house. But the hope that brought us here—that he might possibly know something about German troop movements—is not fulfilled. Two of the officers staying in the house, he says, are Austrians and decent people, the others very rough and disagreeable. We hear the same song as from the peasants: "If they stay on a long time, we shall be ruined. Nothing will be left for the winter. Where are the Allies? Why must they advance at such a snail's pace?" Etc., etc.

A messenger from Via Bolognese brings bad news for our new guests. The paratroopers have plundered the house extensively, saying that it belongs to *Kapitalisten* and the servants have managed to save some personal things only by declaring them to be their own property.

In the afternoon an urgent appeal for help from the houses down by the gate. On getting there I find a yelling, cursing, half-drunk paratrooper loaded up with a bicycle and various other things. My endeavours to stop him have the result that he gets madder than ever and, swearing at me, tells me that Italians who speak German as well as I do are the really dangerous spies. He is almost comical in his spluttering rage. All I can do is preach patience to the victims and remind them of the need to build golden bridges for the enemy who leaves. They agree *purchè non duri troppo*—provided it does not last too long.

No sooner have I got back to my room than another appeal for help comes from the Belvedere, where the unit that left yesterday has returned in full force. Again the N.C.O. with the Slavic face and the nasty temper receives me very badly, sneers at my protests, and tells me that the villa has been hit twice already, which proves that the "Tommy" has not the slightest intention of respecting it and that it would be simply ridiculous to give in to all this diplomatic-rights eyewash. The lieutenant, he says, is off on an inspection tour but will be back in an hour. I find him installed in the porter's lodge of the Carmelite convent, as usual very quiet and polite, but he says that he cannot help having the Belvedere used as an observation post, but will do his best to protect other points inside the property from being occupied. Then we talk about his homeland, Schleswig-Holstein, its lovely beechwoods, about *rote Gruetze,* and the light of the summer nights. Also the N.C.O. is getting more human and speaks of the beauties of his Sudeten country. They show me the little boxes containing cigarettes and candy, of which they get up to two per day. A very different story from the miserable way the German soldiers were fed in 1918 when they occupied the Baltic region. No doubt the stubborn resistance of the Germans is helped by the faultless organization of supplies for the army.

In the lieutenant from Schleswig-Holstein with the wistful expression I recognize a type well known to me: a man who sees what is going on and suffers and yet does his military duty most scrupulously. I am sure the efficiency of the *Wehrmacht* is based much more on the likes of him than on fanatical party members. How tragic that the best qualities of a gifted people should have to contribute to its destruction.

Wednesday, August 9th
Satisfactory report from Quarto, where all further plundering has been stopped by the *Divisionskommandant,* clearly after receipt of our host's written protest. From Florence sinister rumours about burning houses, lack of water and food.

Thursday, August 10th

Both groups of paratroopers, those to our left and those to the right, keep sending down for this, that, and the other: wine, flour, oil, cigarettes. So far they are very polite in asking. Maybe the exceptional treatment of this house has filled them with a certain respect for it, or possibly the fact of being able to talk their own language has a softening influence.

Friday, August 11th

It is rumoured that the Allies are advancing rapidly in France and that the Russians have surrounded Warsaw, but we learn nothing definite about the Allied advance in our nearest neighbourhood. The German soldiers speak openly about the "Tommy" having crossed the river and say that some patrols have heard a tremendous noise of rejoicing in the eastern suburbs around Piazza Beccaria. New minor noises, apparently coming from the region between us and the Mugnone, have been added to the predominant ones: the rat-tat-tat of machine guns, the hum of heavy motors, and sharp detonations, perhaps of hand grenades.

There is nothing else to report. B.B. and I try to keep up our usual schedule, reading a great deal together and walking up and down on the terrace, as our hosts do not think it any longer advisable to go farther away from the house. The evenings are a bit trying, for just as it gets cooler and we would like to enjoy the terrace, the whining overhead begins and we have to take refuge indoors and sit together by the light of an oil lamp with all windows and blinds closed. Never before have I looked forward to the returning daylight or enjoyed the first flush of the dawn so intensely.

Saturday, August 12th

It has suddenly turned very hot, and everybody in the house is affected by digestive troubles. Today it is B.B.'s turn and I am worried about him.

Sunday, August 13th

B.B. is feeling better, and as the "Tommy" very kindly keeps quiet, we can get out on the terrace and get a breath of fresh air. Fighting between partisans and Germans is said to be going on at the beginning of Via Bolognese.

Monday, August 14th

Early in the day two paratroopers appear and violently insist on being let in, as they have orders to establish an observation post on the tower. It takes me a long time to convince them that this is out of the question. Reluctantly they depart and we see them climbing over the wall that separates us from the convent's *podere*. A few minutes later the peasant who looks after it comes running over to ask for help. Two Germans, he says, have forced their way into the papal *clausura* and mean to establish an observation post on one of the terraces. Walking along the convent wall, I notice that several of the fruit trees on our *podere* have been hit and that there is a large gaping hole in the wall, also that the vines have been stripped of their unripe grapes. I thought only Cossacks could enjoy and digest such sour stuff, but evidently all soldiers are alike. On reaching the convent I ring and knock and call at three different doors. At last I hear an enchanting voice behind one of the doors: *"Lodato sia Gesù Cristo."* "I am the one who is to talk to the Germans." Then the door is unlocked and I find myself in the presence of three nuns, a very old one, a middle-aged one with the face of a death's head, and a youngish one with noble features, apparently the prioress. It is she who has the lovely voice. The Germans, they say, after frightening them so dreadfully, have disappeared and may or may not return. I try to cheer them up by telling them that our host in his letter to the secretary of the cardinal archbishop has begged him to call the attention of the Allied command to the exposed position of the convent. And they cheer me up even more by telling me that the cathedral bells are ringing again since yesterday. So the Allies must have occupied the centre of the town.

Tuesday, August 15th

The Assumption of the Virgin and the greatest popular holy day of the year. Our hostess decides to walk over to Quarto in the early morning hours and see how they are getting on there. She returns safely and tells us that neither looting nor destruction have been as bad as we feared. Garden and park have suffered most, the one through the smashing up of statues and lemon pots and the other through an air raid which hit German trucks loaded with ammunition, causing fires and the blasting of several groups of trees. B.B.'s books and photos apparently have not been touched at all.

A curious thing happened yesterday at Quarto. Two Germans called first at the priest's house and then at the villa and, after putting a lot of questions, pretended that they were Englishmen disguised as Germans and were most anxious to find out where mines had been laid. Baroness Ritter did not like their looks or their English pronunciation and said she had no information to give. The parish priest, a very learned and unworldly man, was taken in by them and not only showed them where he knew mines had been laid but expressed his opinion on the behaviour of the *Wehrmacht* very forcibly. Now his house has been plundered and all his meteorological and astronomical instruments smashed up. He himself escaped just in time.

Our admirable hostess has managed to get a real holy day lunch ready and just as we are enjoying it, a terrific bang quite close to the house is followed by the noise of broken glass around us and the thud of something striking against the dining-room wall. A shell has burst near the convent wall and a good-sized splinter has crashed through the dining-room window and, passing between the heads of B.B. and our hostess, has hit the wall behind them. Then another terrific bang and this time a shell has burst on the other side of the house near the chapel.

The procession of paratroopers coming to ask for things never ends. Most regular are two youngsters with round children's faces under their helmets. They look as if they were playing at being soldiers, and very appropriately they come to ask for milk.

Wednesday, August 16th

The Germans are supposed to have definitely retired to this side of the Mugnone. An Allied landing is rumoured to have taken place between Marseilles and Nice. A distinguished radiologist and friend of this house who has watched the shellbursts and clouds of smoke all around us yesterday has walked over from his villa in Montughi to inquire how we are faring. A few days ago he was at the Montalto villa in our neighbourhood and heard from our friends there that the armoured-car division is still occupying I Tatti but that both officers and men are behaving decently. I daresay the knowledge of German is just as useful to my people there as it is to me here. Also, our Montalto friends have been helped through a very disagreeable encounter with German troopers by my nephew, who happened to be there and was able to pacify them.

In the early afternoon all our hens and rabbits have been stolen. Judging by the footprints it must have been done by the paratroopers to our left. Our host insists on my writing a letter of protest to the C.O. I wonder if after five years of war it is any use to expect delicate distinctions between mine and thine from any soldier.

Thursday, August 17th
Unbelievably noisy night, and such a rolling echo from the hills surrounding us that it is difficult to make out from where the detonations come. Anyway as long as the whining and singing are not directly over our heads, we do not bother much. B.B. and I have even stopped sleeping in the corridor on the ground floor and have returned to our rooms.

The young N.C.O. who accompanied me two weeks ago into the hills appears with a sack over his shoulder out of which he pulls seven cackling and ruffled-up hens, the rest of the twenty-two stolen ones. He excuses himself and promises to do his best about hunting up a few more. I never expected this, and it makes me appreciate our host's principle never to let yourself be sat upon.

We hear the cathedral bells quite regularly, but a general festive *scampanata* as they had it in Rome and in Siena was not to be expected from the poor hungry Florentines. A satisfaction for the O.K.W., whose motive in dealing so harshly with Florence must have been the wish to revenge themselves for the triumphal receptions in Rome and Siena and to make a repetition of them impossible.

Friday, August 18th

Earsplitting noises all through the night and particularly towards morning, when the blowing up of the bridges in our neighbourhood and of the houses just below us starts in. It looks like a *Götterdämmerung,* all these huge grey-black columns of smoke rising up as if they wanted to touch the pale early morning sky. I imagine the *Wehrmacht* getting into a sort of paroxysm of blowing-up, one destruction following logically upon the other. In the Belvedere villa, which is much nearer than we are to the Careggi houses, many windows have been smashed. Does it mean that they are going? Or will they hold the line directly behind the destructions? We are now practically cut off from the town.

In the afternoon I have to deal with an extremely nasty paratrooper. He asks for food, refuses what we give him as not good enough, lurks around the house, tries to force locked doors, bullies the gardener because he wants his watch. When he finally leaves, the cook discovers that his best shoes are gone. Following our host's instructions I write a letter of protest to the C.O., but as I am carrying it to the end of the *pergolata* for delivery to a soldier, such an infernal shelling sets in that I get frightened and run back to the house. This time they are German shells bursting in the space between us and Rifredi. It does not last long, but it leaves one a bit shaken up.

Saturday, August 19th

The Bavarian N.C.O. asks for me early in the morning and wants me to translate a fierce order for the local population. Prohibition to leave their houses except between 8 and 9 in the morning and 8 and 9 at night. Whoever dares to go out at other hours will be shot. On my reluctance to translate such an inhuman order, he explains that its object is mostly to frighten people and to teach them not to expose themselves to the shelling. Nobody, he says, would actually be shot. It seems to me that these poor people could not be more frightened than they already are, but possibly they fear the Germans more than they do the shellfire and are therefore foolhardy in leaving their houses. All the Germans want is to hem in partisan activity by confining people to their houses.

It is not likely that they care twopence about the lives of these wretched civilians.

Sunday, August 20th

No change except much more German shelling passing over our heads directed to the suburbs but now and then also the centre of the town. The hospital buildings have been hit. One gets more and more used to the incessant noise. B.B. is completely fatalistic as to the possibility of this house getting direct hits. He would only be afraid, he says, of having to deal with a convinced Nazi or a malignant Fascist. Our new friends from the Via Bolognese have now transferred themselves here. They are a very agreeable addition to our small circle and do not make any fuss about the distressing accounts they get from their home. The cache where their most valuable property was walled up has been discovered by the paratroopers, and everything has been carried away or smashed up. Again our host has prepared a beautifully worded protest addressed to the general commanding the paratrooper division, and I have translated it and asked the lieutenant from Schleswig-Holstein to transmit it, but I feel more than doubtful about the results.

From time to time the familiar alarm echoes through the house: *"Signorina, ci sono due tedeschi"*—Here are two Germans —either something they ask for or something they want to take forcibly. It does not look as if they mean to move on. Every day when the shelling quiets down, we listen to the sounds from the German positions above and they never change: voices talking or giving gruff orders, some singing, an accordion being played. The new moon was too enchanting today: in a citron-coloured sky over little pink clouds. It is the twelfth we see from this terrace. Will it bring us a little bit of luck? Shall we be free when it becomes full?

Monday, August 21st

The lieutenant from Schleswig-Holstein accompanied by an N.C.O. comes to tell us that the general has received the letter and is very much annoyed by the vandalism committed in the villa on the Via Bolognese. He sends his excuses and hopes that at least some of the unbreakable things will be recovered. If our friends wish to go on and inspect their home, the N.C.O. will be very pleased to accompany them. Our hostess invites them into the house and offers them a cool drink, which they seem to enjoy enormously. The lieutenant tries to explain the mentality of the front soldier to us: "He has only three dominating thoughts: (1) Shall I get through unhurt? (2) Shall I be wounded and how? (3) Shall I have to die?" Of course we understand very well that after five years of war these men should be desperately keen on shoes, linen, suits, on all things that have become almost unobtainable in their own country, and our friends here would not have dreamt of handing in a protest over the carrying away of such articles. What they resent is the senseless smashing up of objects of art, *bibelots,* porcelain, dinner sets, etc.

In the evening while we are sitting around our oil lamp, he appears again accompanied by two other officers, a captain and a lieutenant. They look around admiringly and tell me that since January they have not seen such a comfortable house nor sat on such soft chairs. The outfits of the two new guests seem more like those of sportsmen than of officers: khaki shirts with sleeves crumpled up, shorts, and sandals. They assure me that on the Eastern front every advance of the Russians has been stopped. "It is only a question of time for us. We must hold up the enemy until we are again ready to strike, and that will be quite soon." I ask them if they have noticed the lovely sunset. They laugh a little scornfully. "That is not the kind of thing we notice." "But why? Germans have always been lovers of nature." "For us any landscape becomes a *Gelände,* exists only in so far as it gives possibilities of defense or attack." He speaks of the Italian army and says that it should have been able to defend its own country. "Yes, numerically it should have, but it lacked sufficient equipment and the officers who knew how to lead the soldiers were the exception and not the rule." He agrees and tells about his experiences in Russia, where he found the Italian men first-rate but the officers with rare exceptions distinctly inferior. I try to explain to him the absolutely negative attitude of 90 per cent of the Italians toward a war fought at the side of their hereditary enemy, and he seems to understand. He speaks with contempt of the Allied army and all the different peoples and races represented in it, also of the astonishing resistance of the *Wehrmacht* against such a crushing numerical superiority. On the whole these officers make the impression of soldiers of fortune, enjoying a nomadic fighting life, but not of political fanatics.

Tuesday, August 22d

Early in the morning the usual call—*due tedeschi*. Very disgruntled *tedeschi* they are, fed up with the war, cursing the partisans and the horrible nights they have to spend going out to meet them on patrolling expeditions. Later a boy paratrooper with the face of a weepy child comes to ask for some candles for his lieutenant, who has so much work to do at night. He too describes the horrible night patrolling in the industrial suburb of Rifredi. "They know everything, the front doors and the back doors of the houses, and we know nothing." I cannot help feeling dreadfully sorry for him. He is not made for such a rough life.

In the afternoon the N.C.O. who was to accompany our friends to their villa comes to say that the situation is somewhat changed and that he cannot advise them to run the risk. He seems embarrassed and offers no further explanation, but we gather that either partisan or Allied forces must have advanced on the Via Bolognese. He describes to us the outfit of the "bandits," as he calls them, from which it would seem that many of them wear regular Italian uniforms. His cautious warnings give the impression that a major Allied attack is expected any day. He is a Silesian with an excellent trustworthy face and goes so far as to tell me that it seems to him folly to defend the Gothic Line when their homes are threatened by the Russians. "From Ratibor, where my parents live, it is only 170 kilometers to the Russian front. That is where we should be." Then he stops short and adds: "I must not go on, or I might end by telling you what I think of the whole bloody business."

In the evening both "Tommy" and "Gerry" keeping quiet for once, and we hope to enjoy the terrace for a bit when the well-known heavy-booted steps are heard on the lower terrace, and looking over the parapet we see three soldiers forcing their way into the lemon-house, in which not only the cows and oxen of our own *contadini* have found shelter but also several beasts from the neighboring peasant houses. "What is it you want?" No answer, only the sound of the heavy boots tramping off and some coarse swearwords. It seems obvious that in the night they will return and steal at least the calves. Our energetic hostess decides that the cattle must be brought up and tethered under the loggia before the house. By the starry light of a clear August night and following whispered orders the reluctant beasts are dragged up the garden steps while the two white calves caper about and the maids bring armfuls of straw for the improvised litters. The old peasant who sleeps in the lemon-house is stone deaf, and in spite of all the injunctions of *silenzio* and *sottovoce* one has to shout into his ears to make him understand what all the fuss is about.

Wednesday, August 23

The door of the priest's house in Careggi was smashed in last night with a hand grenade in order to carry away the provisions. It looks as if we are already in a sort of no-man's-land and the field police do not seem to frequent the foremost line. It is an extraordinary piece of luck that the two units of paratroopers near us are relatively disciplined people with decent officers.

One of them, the small *Oberleutnant* who meant to occupy this house, comes down in the afternoon and offers us a sack of bread and some tinned stuff in exchange for the stolen hens and rabbits. He says that he can guarantee the good behaviour of his own men but that troopers from other units have been added to his group of late and he cannot take any responsibility for them. I ask him whether the food supply becomes very irregular on the front line. "Not at all. It is surprisingly good and abundant, and there is no earthly reason why our men should exploit the local population. But they just love to snatch something extra, and particularly chicken and fresh meat they generally cannot resist." As the Abbé Coignard said: *"Quoi qu'en disent les gazettes, la guerre consiste uniquement a voler des poules aux vilains. Les soldats ne son occupés que de ce soin."* I would give a lot to know what goes on in the head of this quiet, gentle little man. He cannot be a Nazi. About the war he only says with a sad smile that it is a tremendous struggle for power and that nobody wants to be the first to give in. He comes from Bremen and seems completely worn out by the heat.

Thursday, August 24th

Just as we are going in to lunch, several *tedeschi* who ask for me are announced. This time it is the captain with the wolflike features and the sharp voice with whom I had to negotiate the first day, accompanied by a stout elderly officer and a young ensign, all armed to the teeth, even with hand grenades. They want to transmit an important message to our host. What is it? Well, the situation in the hospital is too ghastly. On top of the two thousand regular inhabitants and patients, there are about fifteen hundred refugees and hardly any provisions and no water. The minister must immediately let the Vatican know about this and have some measures taken. "But how is he to communicate with the Vatican?" "As a diplomat he has of course his private wire connecting him with it." "No, he never had one, and if he had, it would not function now after the cutting of the electric current." "You don't mean it! I thought diplomats always had a way of getting messages through." There follows an endless negotiation about the possibility of sending a deputation from the hospital with letters from our host to the cardinal archbishop and to the Swiss consul to ask for Allied lorries guaranteed by the Red Cross to fetch the patients and refugees. Our host thinks it a crazy plan, the hospitals in town being already overcrowded. "Would it not be better to come to an agreement that both parties should respect the hospital zone as neutral ground?" A contemptuous burst of shrill laughter from the captain. "The enemy would not dream of respecting such an agreement. Have you not seen the shells hitting the hospital?" "Yes, we have, but we are too ignorant in such matters to say for certain from which side they came." He seems intensely annoyed. "Of course it was the Allies who did it, and it would be important that the representative of a neutral state should have witnessed such an act of barbarism." His insistence confirms us in the impression that it was German shells that hit the hospital, perhaps not intentionally but because several shots fell short of the real object, the industrial suburb. More imprecations against the partisans. "Do you realize that they represent the very dregs of humanity? Of course the Allies protect them and help them because they systematically work only with the worst elements in each country and they want to reduce Italy to a state of complete anarchy." The stout officer turns out to be a doctor and seems really to care about the sufferings of the people in the hospital zone. "You should come down and see what it is like there. The water should be laid on again." "But was it not you who destroyed the waterworks?" "Yes, we did, but the state of things is absolutely unbearable and something must be done." His tone and manner are convincing but not the captain's, whose horrid sneering laughter and bird-of-prey snout fill me with suspicion and apprehension. He asks me how we have been getting on under the protection of our flags. "Fairly well so far." Another of these horrid bursts of laughter. "Just wait and see, the best is still to come." At last they go, having come to an agreement with our host about sending the Italian head surgeon from the hospital to talk over the situation with him. I watch them walking along the terrace and wonder what the "Tommy's" observers may think of so much coming and going of heavily armed Germans.

Monday, August 28th
I have not been able to write a line during the last days, as we have been spending most of our time behind closed shutters, lit up by oil lamps and candles in the little stack room or in the corridor at the back of the house. On Friday a shell smashed in a wall and one of the servants rooms in the kitchen wing. The whole night from Friday to Saturday, intensive shelling. After lunch it seemed to get quieter, and B.B. and I ventured out of the shelter and were on the way to the library in the front drawing-room when a deafening crash close to the house made us run back. We had barely reached shelter when the next salvo followed, crashing into the sitting-room where we had just been, and so on along the whole length of the house. Most of the shells burst on the terrace, sending a volley of splinters against windows and walls and killing one of the cows and her calf. The havoc wrought in the sitting-room is appalling, furniture, picture frames,

348

lampshades, chaircovers, everything pierced by splinters and covered with a layer of thick white dust. And on the terrace all is confusion and desolation. One can hardly believe that this is the same place where two days ago we were enjoying the coolness of the evening. Why did the Allied artillery aim so pointedly at this house in spite of the flags? Probably the ceaseless coming and going of armed Germans along the terraces and sometimes in and out of the house had been noticed by the observers and interpreted as definite occupation. So far there has been no repetition.

Needless to say that the absurd plan of getting Allied help for the hospital has come to nothing. Our host did write the requested letter to the archbishop and to the Swiss consul, and the deputation from the hospital did go into Florence, but the proposal was turned down. They brought back at least one encouraging piece of news: they were told not to worry, as it would be only a matter of days until we would be freed.

This morning an old peasant was killed either by a mine or by an unexploded shell while he was picking vegetables in the *podere*.

Our hostess has started making order in the sitting-room, also in the upper front rooms, all full of broken glass and white dust.

Rumours reach us about the New Zealanders, Moroccans, and partisans being already quite close to us. But the German positions above have not been moved, and consequently our troglodyte existence goes on unchanged. Happily B.B. keeps in excellent form, quite fearless and going back to his usual occupations, reading or writing as soon as there is a quiet spell. His nerves are evidently a great deal stronger than mine, for I do feel a bit shaken up these last days. The excellent behaviour of the servants fills me with astonishment. No fuss, no hysterics. The cook goes on providing for us and to the great glee of the others runs for shelter after the explosion. A young *carabiniere* who is in hiding here serves us our meals; the two housemaids go on with their work and even run out to pick figs or tomatoes. They hastened to help the old peasant who was hit, without a moment's thought of the danger they were running.

In large measure this is due to the example given them by our hostess, who goes on thinking of everybody's welfare, both of human beings and animals, always gay and active. Naturally the servants sleep, as we now do, in one of the dark corridors at the back of the house.

German soldiers have been allowed by the cook to broil a chicken in the kitchen, probably a stolen one and to the amazement of the Italians, they have stuffed it with plums and with hard unripe grapes.

Tuesday, August 29th

Yesterday afternoon we were all assembled as usual in the little stack room waiting for the shelling to let up when the sound of something hitting the house and then rolling about on the upper floor alarmed us. The young *carabiniere,* having gone up to explore the premises, returned to say that a shell, after crashing through two walls, has remained lying unexploded on the floor of our host's bedroom. A note asking the lieutenant from Schleswig-Holstein for help should have been taken to him yesterday, but no occasion was found for sending it until this morning, when the two "children" appeared to get their milk and promised to deliver it at once.

Later. The specialist for the unexploded shell has just come accompanied by an ambulance orderly. A huge fellow with the face of a child and a soft musical voice. He kneels down before the ominous object and says: "It is still sharp." Then he looks at his chum and asks: "Must I do it?" "Yes, you must." "Then show me the nearest door into the garden and all of you go as far away as possible." We wait in considerable anxiety until he returns beaming. He has carried it to the back of the garden. I cannot forget the childlike and trustful expression of his face, his gay smile. Why should such excellent human material become the victim of this devilish system? These last weeks have made me understand the tragedy of what has happened in Germany better than all I had read or heard before. The really good German qualities have something particularly endearing about them, at least for those who know the language as intimately as I do.

In the evening the women from the porter's lodge come up to assure us that they are already fighting on this side of the hospital and that tomorrow it will be the turn of Careggi.

Wednesday, August 30th

Asphyxiating heat enters through all the broken windows, accompanied by a plague of mosquitoes. In our corridor at night they hum like an organ.

The paratroopers on our right are said to have gone. Those on our left are still there, and we see some of them running over our lower terrace carrying heavy boxes. Do they contain mines, I wonder? The "children," when they come for the milk, are armed to the teeth and appear to be in marching outfit.

Thursday, August 31st

Early in the morning shouts of joy in the house: *Sono andati via* —They are gone. Five minutes later the usual cry of alarm: "*C'è un tedesco.* Yes, there he is on the terrace, a wild-looking boy with a mop of shaggy hair hanging down into a face blackened by smoke. He tells me that he and nine of his comrades, among whom are two wounded, forced their way into the convent last night. "All the others are already seven kilometers from here," he says. His little group has nothing to eat, and could we give him something to prepare a soup with in our kitchen? He gets what he wants. Soon another turns up, and they begin rummaging about, discover the gardener's rabbits, kill two of them, and add them to their menu. They seem very annoyed and defiant when I tell them that they had better hurry up and disappear, for now the access to the house is free and anybody can get in. Presently one of them disappears towards the convent; the other goes on cooking. Then an uproar of voices on the terrace and a group of partisans, mostly boys with a very decent-looking officer, having heard of the presence of the Germans, rush to the kitchen, arrest the paratrooper cook, and lead him off. Then they hide near the kitchen door and wait. Soon another paratrooper is seen climbing over the convent wall and coming quite unconcernedly to see if the food is ready. Him also they disarm, asking me to act as interpreter. He seems much relieved when I transmit to him the assurance of the officer that he will be handed over to the English and treated well. His sullen face lights up, and he asks for a cigarette. Meanwhile the game of catching them at the kitchen door goes on. Two more paratroopers come to ask whether the food is ready, and one of them tries to run away and is shot dead at the kitchen steps. The servants at the sight of the dead German suddenly lose their nerve completely and seem half crazy with horror and fear. The partisans, after enjoying a good meal in the kitchen, decide to take their prisoners to the next Allied post. They make a jolly impression, these famous "bandits," delighted with their exploits during the last weeks and proud of the few English words they have learned. With "O.K." they say one gets on beautifully.

While the partisans have been busy liberating us, we have had our first visitor from town, a cousin of our host's, who after getting out of a German concentration camp spent several weeks here in the spring and who is very dear to all of us. We can hardly believe our eyes when he suddenly knocks at our door. He has got through on his bicycle. He tells us about the destruction round the Ponte Vecchio, and I realize that the dear old house in Borgo San Jacopo, in which for more than fifteen years my sister and brother-in-law have had their home, no longer exists. At I Tatti it seems they are alive and well, and we must be grateful for that.

Our first messenger from the other side also tells us that the liberation of Careggi is already officially announced. He describes to us the anguish and alarm of all our friends in Florence last Saturday when the shells were hitting this house and it appeared to be wrapped in clouds of smoke. He tried to get in touch with the Allied command so as to prevent further shelling but met with utter incomprehension. For the first time we hear about the great Allied advance and the taking of Paris.

In the afternoon the first British "Tommies" come up in Indian file to inspect the German positions to the right and left of us. The dead paratrooper is carried away. The house has opened its eyes to the light; in the road below the people are coming and going as of old.

And now that life will have to return to a kind of normalcy, there is no sense in my going on with these notes. Their only object has been to describe our existence in the front line while cut off from the world, yet safe under the protection of our courageous, truly Christian hosts, Filippo and Gilberta Serlupi.

INDEX

i

Index

Index

Index

Index

A NOTE ON THE TYPE

The text of this book has been set on the Linotype in a type-face called Baskerville. The face is a facsimile reproduction of type cast from molds made for John Baskerville (1706–75) from his designs. The punches for the revived Linotype Baskerville were cut under the supervision of the English printer George W. Jones.

John Baskerville's original face was one of the forerunners of the type-style known as "modern face" to printers: a "modern" of the period A.D. 1800.

The book was composed, printed, and bound by The Haddon Craftsmen, Inc., Scranton, Pennsylvania. The illustrations were printed by Halliday Lithograph Corp., West Hannover, Mass.

Typography and binding design by

WARREN CHAPPELL